To Mark the Beginning

A Social History of
College Student Affairs

ACPA Media Board

To Mark the Beginning

A Social History of
College Student Affairs

Richard B. Caple

American College Personnel Association

Copyright © 1998 by
University Press of America,® Inc.
4720 Boston Way
Lanham, Maryland 20706

12 Hid's Copse Rd.
Cummor Hill, Oxford OX2 9JJ

Library of Congress Cataloging-in-Publication Data

Caple, Richard B.
To mark the beginning : a social history of college student affairs /
Richard B. Caple.
p.   cm.
Includes bibliographical references and index.
1. Student affairs services —Social aspects—United States—History.
I. Title.
LB2342.9.C36   1998   378.1'98 —DC21   97-43939 CIP

ISBN 1-883485-11-8 (cloth: alk. ppr.)
ISBN 1-883485-12-6 (pbk: alk. ppr.)

⊖™ The paper used in this publication meets the minimum
requirements of American National Standard for information
Sciences—Permanence of Paper for Printed Library Materials,
ANSI Z39.48—1984

Contents

Introduction

Coleridge wrote "If men could learn from history, what lessons it might teach us! But passion and party blind our eyes, and the light which experience gives is a lantern on the stern, which shines only on the waves behind us!" (*The Oxford Dictionary of Quotations*, 1979, p. 157). If this were true, it might mean that history is for old people only looking back as a recreational activity. I much prefer Bacon's adage, however, that "histories make men wise" (*The Oxford Dictionary of Quotations*, 1979, p. 27). Although this may be too much to expect of any written treatise, history can, if approached seriously, explain how we have gotten to where we are, give meaning to present behavior, and stimulate debate over where we are going next. It will not allow us to predict the future, to be sure, but it can help us choose the direction in which we move. Without some historical perspective, it is difficult to reap the most from philosophical, social, psychological, and scientific efforts. We often stumble over the same hurdle or flee the same harmless shadows in the dark because we have not learned from our own experience and the experience of others as well. No history is perfect, and certainly not this one, but I have learned much from chronicling the beginning and development of college student affairs in the United States and hope that I can share some of what I have learned with the reader.

History is always provisional because no one can be certain that his or her perceptions and explanations are correct, but there is every reason to look at what has occurred so that creating the future is a more thoughtful process. "What historians do best is to make connections with the past to illuminate the problems of the present and the potential of the future" (Appleby, Hunt, & Jacob, 1994, p. 10). History seems firmly rooted in a desire for self-discovery and self-knowledge. What does it mean to exist and what has that existence meant? Part of the answer comes from recreating social structures to interpret human activity described by the records.

Although there have been several good efforts aimed at tracing the history of education and the history of higher education, only a very limited amount has been written about the history of college student personnel or college student affairs. Most histories of higher education seldom, if ever, mention it. Outside of several doctoral dissertations, a chapter offered in a few edited books about college student affairs, or a page or two written in some of the early textbooks for the field, not much has been set down about the history of this profession. The purpose of this writing is to provide a more complete history of college student affairs and place it in a social, political, and economic context. Although influenced by European precedent, particularly the British system, higher education in the United States developed its own unique mode and has become a model for much of the present world. Perhaps no part of American higher education is more unique than the piece that is called college student affairs.

Americans have always believed that their country was the land of opportunity and, whenever this idea has been threatened, unrest was stirred among those who believed it most in danger. In fact, opportunity has been something of an expectation as Charles O'Connor's statement reflects. "In worn out, king-ridden Europe men must stay where they are born. But in America a man is accounted a failure, and certainly ought to be, who has not risen above his father's station in life" (Goldman, 1955, p. 80). From the beginning education has been viewed by most Americans as the major pathway to success and prosperity. Without it few people could hope to rise above their present status. In addition, early intellectuals like Jefferson injected into American thought the belief that to be free as a nation ignorance must be removed (Malone, 1970), and later Alfred North Whitehead (1933) concluded that "In conditions of modern life the rule is absolute, the race which does not value trained intelligence is doomed" (p. 282).

As strong as the belief in the need for education has been, education as a formal system has never been without its critics and reformers. It is not easy to distinguish between the role of critic and reformer. A critic is usually seen as a reasoned and knowledgeable evaluator of a product or event based on that person's understanding of accepted standards that exist. The true critic tends to remain somewhat apart from the object to be evaluated in order to comment about it with a detached objectivity not thought possible by those involved in the practice or creative endeavor of producing it. But, it is not so of the reformer; reformers are bent on changing things, and always, they believe, for the better. A reformer will believe, justifiably or not, that he or she is a capable and fair critic. But, criticism is not enough. The reformer is dedicated to change.

Although the act of criticism may flourish and rise to a high art in the hands of some or plunge to mediocrity and even meanness in the hands of others, it remains rather constant, only influenced by the popularity of its object. Reform movements, however, are conscious efforts to change existing conditions, to improve conditions by introducing new knowledge and methods, and to remove harmful elements and practices. The need to purposefully reform and change existing conditions and elements seems to vary with the needs of those most affected by them.

The American educational system has largely mirrored American society and has, therefore, been affected by the same conservative and progressive influences, the same reform movements as the larger social order. Student personnel work, or student affairs work as it is more often referred to today, was born during a period of reform and of accelerated change in the United States; and it was and remains today a unique American invention. To understand this peculiar phenomena, it is helpful to consider the historical and cultural climate in which it was born and developed, because, as I will describe here, student personnel was a child of the reform movement and fortunately, perhaps, has retained much of this early characteristic in its continued development.

Student affairs has its roots in the late years of the nineteenth century, a time influenced by social Darwinism and the same era in which a new psychology was born dedicated to the scientific study of human behavior. William James applied evolutionary theory to understanding the mind (Dennett, 1995), and John Dewey began to enunciate a philosophy that saw a democratic society as committed to change and organized as intelligently and as scientifically as possible. In his own words, it is "intentionally progressive" (Dewey, 1916). Social reform was underway and, in this same spirit and structure, college student personnel work was born. From very meager beginnings, probably first at Harvard and later at other institutions, it would develop into a major division in higher education administration.

The Progressive Era in the United States was characterized by Hofstadter (1965) as the Age of Reform, and it was an era in which change and reform were taking place on a broad scale across the total landscape of America. But, soon a reaction against progressivism and the evolutionary and scientific movement would set in. Knowledge was developing so rapidly, however, in fields as separate as physics and psychology that there was no stemming the tide of change and reform that was sweeping through science and education.

The Progressive period was the early years of student personnel work, and student personnel would not receive a clearly stated philosophy until later (1937), when a group of educational leaders who had been educated and matured during the height of the Progressive Era came together under the auspices of the American Council on Education and wrote *The Student Personnel Point of View* (American Council on Education, 1937). A little more than a decade later the document was revised by a committee of 12 college student personnel professionals, several of whom were members of the original group and all who had been influenced by the progressive era and Experimentalist philosophy. Experimentalism as an explicit and systematic theory of education is attributable primarily to the work of Charles Peirce and John Dewey (Phenix, 1961), which emphasized the importance of experience, experimentation, and learning by doing. The result was a statement that, like many other elements of the progressive movement, remains surprisingly contemporary in the present day.

In the years that would follow, college student personnel, or college student affairs, would struggle to achieve an identity and a legitimacy of its own in a mutualistic relationship with the rest of higher education. Despite predictions of its demise during the second half of the twentieth century, college student affairs survived one of the most violent periods on campuses in the history of higher education in the United States and then faced the effects of a declining economy. Throughout its history student affairs has maintained a position of advocacy for students, although it has not always been very effective in articulating its positions. What is clear from recent history, however, is the continuation of an Experimentalist philosophy as is evidenced in the student affairs literature of the 1970s. When idealism faded for other educational leaders, many student affairs professionals seemed able to continue the struggle for change and reform in the educational process to achieve a better learning environment and educational outcome.

The book is divided into five chapters with a short epilogue as the final section. Chapter I takes a summary look at the first years of the nation, indicating how it grew from a strictly agrarian society to become a major industrial power. It outlines the growth of knowledge during this period, the development of institutions of higher learning, and leads the reader to the beginning of college student personnel work. Chapter II describes the impact of the reform movement on American society and higher education during the first half of the twentieth century. It will take the reader from the beginning of college student personnel work to the point at which it established a guiding philosophy that reflected the Progressive Era. Chapter III describes events occurring after World War II that shaped American culture and higher education. It provides evidence to show that college student personnel or college student affairs would continue to develop within an Experimentalist philosophy and maintain a progressive approach to its work. Chapter IV considers the decade of the 1960s and the civil rights struggle in the United States. It looks at the impact of student political activism during this period and the student demand for relevance. It considers the significant influence this had on college student affairs for that moment and for the future. It was a defining period in higher education as colleges and universities moved from being elite institutions to popular ones. Chapter V outlines the changing status of the United States within the world economy and some of the affects on political and social attitudes. It considers the relationship between higher education and the Vietnam War and concludes by commenting on the new stage developing in the symbiotic relationship student affairs has with higher education. The Epilogue touches on the 1980s and 1990s but in no way substitutes for an in depth look at this period, which is left for a future time. Time as distance may then offer more objectivity. The primary goal of the book is not only to mark the beginning of college student affairs but to describe the social forces that would shape its development.

Ideas and purposes do much to influence the course of events. Social and political history is designed to look at the byplay of groups and individuals. The idea of individualism and progress were highly important to the historical story of the United States and to its institutions of education. Perhaps no two events in higher education illustrate this better than the Morrill Act of 1862 or the G. I. Bill at the end of World War II that resulted in giving the offspring of working class families the opportunity to climb into the middle-class educational mainstream of America. Student personnel was not present at the first event but was a major player in the second one.

Chapter I

In the Beginning: Before There was Student Personnel

The United States began as an agricultural and mercantile society and existed as such for almost 100 years. For more than a century prior to the Civil War in the United States, land represented the great issue around which political and economic struggles revolved. America had been developed and populated by an agricultural people operating family farms. It was a nation of many small rural villages and towns where farmers shopped, banked, obtained skilled craft services, and often retired. The urban worker was likely to be a skilled craftsman and the urban businessman a merchant (Hacker & Zahler, 1952).

The population of the United States established by the Census of 1860 was approximately 31,443,000 people. By this time the area bordering the west bank of the Mississippi River had been admitted to statehood (Louisiana, 1812; Missouri, 1821; Arkansas, 1836; Iowa, 1846; Minnesota, 1858). Further west only three areas had sufficient population to be admitted as states (Texas, 602,000 in 1860; Oregon, 52,000 in 1859; and California, 380,000 in 1850). By the 1860s two frontiers were established. One was eastward, moving along the Pacific coast; and the second was westward, extending unevenly along the 97th meridian. In the region between these two frontiers lay approximately one half of the territory of the United

States. In 1860, however, this area contained only one percent of its population. This portion of the nation was occupied largely in the three decades 1860 to 1890. It was settled by miners, ranchers, and farmers who were drawn by the discoveries of rich deposits of minerals and by the opportunities to exploit free grass and open fertile land. The process was hastened by favorable land laws, by rapidly increasing immigration, and particularly by the building of the transcontinental railroads, the invention of barbed wire, and the quantity production of windmills (Faulkner, 1954).

The pressure for free land was released when Lincoln signed the Homestead Act on May 20, 1862, that granted a quarter section (160 acres) of free land to the head of a family or to a person over 21 years of age who was a citizen of the United States or who had filed his intention of becoming one and who had not borne arms against the United States (Commager, 1949). The influence of the Homestead Act began slowly, but followed by other acts that were designed to liberalize the Homestead Act or make other land available, the frontier would soon vanish. For example, in 1887 the Hatch Act provided federal funds for the creation of agricultural experiment stations and the Dawes Act opened for purchase nearly 100 million acres of land from Indian territories. The frontier (technically a region with more than two and less than six people per square mile) by 1890 had disappeared. After 1890 westward settlement was largely a filling in process, although there were islands of good land unclaimed until the beginning of World War I (Robertson, 1955).

Americans in this time maintained a strong isolation policy from the world beyond, although the United States was not totally insulated from outside influence. There was no political interference and little foreign management of the American business enterprise. Foreign capital did play an important part in both long- and short-term capital investments that helped finance European imports into America. Ideas, too, crossed the Atlantic to subtly influence the attitudes and institutions of the new country. The tradition of English local government and English common law affected the development of American institutions. The theories of Locke and Montesquieu, who had laid down the great principles of the separation of powers; the coupling of social welfare and individual achievement by Bentham and Ricardo; the revolutionary thinking of John Stuart Mill and Charles Darwin were received by Americans and in rather unique ways internalized into their own beliefs.

Development as a Nation After
the Civil War

Although close economic relations existed and intellectual life depended heavily upon Europe, in international affairs the United States remained apart. The United States played no role in the system the British maintained to keep peace throughout the world and was only remotely in contact with the elaborate structure by which the British navy dominated the seven seas and in so doing maintained a "balance of power" system that kept Europe from major war. The United States sought no colonies, it set up no protectorates or spheres of influence, and although Perry had opened Japan to the West, it played no part in Japan's industrialization. The United States' policy of "manifest destiny" was totally confined to the Western Hemisphere, and although the Monroe Doctrine was directed against Europe, it was not a program for action to be taken by this country. The belief in two separate worlds was strongly influenced by the large European settlement of people in America who had been rejected in the land of their origin and wanted to promote equalitarianism traditions and a better standard of living. This chasm was broad, and a person need only read Henry James' *The American* (1907) to understand how fully different the two worlds were.

Railroads

The desire to link the continent together by rail existed almost as soon as the railroad itself. Asa Whitney of New York, a merchant in China trade, is credited with the first concrete proposal to do so (Robertson, 1955). In 1845 he recommended to Congress the construction of a railroad from Lake Michigan to the mouth of the Columbia River, but it was not until after the Civil War in 1862 that Congress granted a charter to the Union Pacific Railroad authorizing it to build a rail line from Omaha to the western boundary of Nevada. The Central Pacific Railroad, incorporated under the laws of California in 1861, was given authority to construct the western portion of the railroad from Sacramento to the Nevada border. With considerable celebration and pageantry, the two railways were joined together on May 10, 1869.

From 1864 to 1900, the greatest percentage of track was laid in the Great Plain states. Chicago became the chief terminal for railroads extending to the north, west, and south. Thirty-three thousand miles were built between 1867 and 1873 (Faulkner, 1954). Although the rate of growth of the railway varied in different regions, financial investment in it was large and continuous. It is estimated that the capital invested in railroads before World War I constituted approximately one tenth of the nation's total wealth and provided employment for 4.4 percent of the work force (Robertson, 1955). Railroads were built under charters granted by state legislatures, and the right of eminent domain was seldom denied. The attitude of the public and its legislatures was that railroads were to be encouraged by every possible means with the result that 242,000 square miles or almost 200 million acres, a region larger than Germany or France, was given to the railroads during this period.

Industry

Steel was first made successfully in quantity in about 1864 and between 1860 and 1900 there was a rapid transition from reliance on the power of wind, water, and animal to other sources of energy. The United States, like England and Germany, achieved industrial greatness as result of abundant deposits of coal. By 1890 coal had become the source of 90 percent of the energy for industry. In addition to coal and a rich agriculture (e.g., livestock, cotton), the United States was also blessed with large quantities of iron, oil, copper, and other minerals. The forces of technology and industrialization began asserting such influence that by 1876 the United States was a power to be reckoned with in the competition for industrial supremacy. The development of an industrial revolution was the most important element in the economic life of the United States during the half-century after 1860 (Faulkner, 1954). Until the 1880s agriculture was the primary source of wealth; but by 1890 manufacturing had by-passed it and 10 years later had more than doubled the income produced by agriculture.

Labor

In addition to abundant natural resources, the necessary labor force was available to support an expanding industry. The population of the United States doubled every 20 years until 1860. The percentage of the population living in cities of 8,000 people or more in 1860 was 16.1 percent. By 1880 it had increased to 28.6 percent. (This trend would continue until by 1930 the population living in urban areas was 49.1%, and it would reach 54 percent in 1950.) Millions of immigrants arrived in the U.S., many of whom were unfit for employment other than factory work because of lack of training and opportunity. Women were beginning to enter work in industry and the professions. This influenced more and more tasks that had been performed in individual households (e.g., slaughter of animals, preserving food, grinding grain) to be moved to industry. The population growth, the cheapness of manufactured products, and the growth of cities springing up around factories were major factors shaping the development of the labor force and helping create a new urban culture.

Business

With one notable exception, *Laissez faire* (complete governmental non-interference with business) dominated economic policy in the United States during the last half of the nineteenth century (Faulkner, 1954). Influenced by a young and developing industry, the United States committed itself in 1861 to a system of high protective tariffs that in general have been maintained until the present. In 13 of the leading industries of the United States from 1850 to 1910, the average manufacturing plant multiplied its capital 39 times, its number of wage earners seven times, and the value of its output by more than 19 times (Faulkner, 1954). The size of business units increased and competition became fierce. As a result industrial ownership by individuals or partners grew inadequate to supply needed funds and accept the necessary risk. The corporate form of business grew steadily after the Civil War until by the twentieth century, much if not most of the great products of the country were in the control of monopolies. The rapid development of monopolies and the abuse of power that accompanied it were viewed with growing concern by a number of thoughtful writers. Three widely read books stand out: Henry George in 1879 published *Progress and Poverty*, in which he advocated a single tax on land values as a solution to the problem of monopoly; Edward Bellamy in 1887 published *Looking Backward* that prescribed a socialist state; and Henry Demarest Lloyd published in 1894 *Wealth Against Commonwealth*, considered by most scholars the ablest and most effective attack ever delivered against trusts.

The Sherman Antitrust Act of 1890 was passed by Congress but provided little affect upon business consolidation. It was used effectively, however, by the government against labor unions (e.g., the Pullman strike of 1894 broken by the government through the courts).

Political Climate

This period was dominated politically with problems created by the aftermath of the Civil War. Although the Civil War had determined an end to slavery and established the ultimate supremacy of the federal government, it had created a good many other problems with social, political, and economic ramifications. In the North the stimulation given to economic processes was, perhaps, its greatest influence (Faulkner, 1948). In the South the problems of reconstruction were both social and economic.

"Black Codes" that severely restricted the social and economic rights of Blacks had been established in much of the South after the Civil War. In response to these codes, Congress passed the Civil Rights Act of 1866 (Commager, 1949) that "conferred citizenship upon the negroes, legislation necessitated by the Dred Scott decision" (p. 252). But, widespread concern about its constitutionality led to the formation and passage of the Fourteenth Amendment on June 13, 1866, and its ratification was made a condition of restoration to the Union. Undoubtedly, it has become one of the most important parts of the Constitution. In the second Civil Rights Act of 1875, Congress attempted to protect the civil equality of Blacks by making it a punishable offense to deprive them of accommodations and advantages in inns, public conveyances, and theaters; but the Supreme Court made it impossible to enforce this law. The Court held that this law had no Constitutional basis in either the Fourteenth or Fifteenth Amendment (Hofstadter & Hofstadter, 1982).

The Fifteenth Amendment to the Constitution had been passed by Congress in 1867 and ratified in 1868 to ensure Blacks the right to vote. When reconstruction ended in 1877, efforts were successfully made to enact laws that reduced or eliminated the Black vote without mention of race in order not to conflict with the Fifteenth Amendment. From 1871 through 1889, all former Confederate states passed statutes restricting suffrage. Although during this period significant numbers of Blacks continued going to the polls, pressure was increasing to reduce or eliminate their political involvement. In *Plessy v. Ferguson*, the Supreme Court in 1896 approved segregation of the races as being consistent with the Fourteenth Amendment and formulated the doctrine of "separate but equal" facilities. It served as a legal basis for segregation in education.

Growth of Knowledge and Expansion of Higher Education

The rapid expansion of knowledge in nearly all fields of study had a strong effect upon culture and the educational system. The influence of science, the scientific method, and evolutionary theory played a large part in this process. From within and from without, scientists in colleges and universities were pressed to investigate an expanded range of natural and physical phenomena. One sign of the time was the acceleration of professional associations of scholars and scientists. Before the Civil War these groups were primarily small and local with the notable exceptions of the American Academy of Arts and Sciences, The American Medical Association, and the American Association for the Advancement of Science. From 1870 to 1900, however, there was a rapid expansion in the number of such associations, only a few of which can be mentioned here: American Philological Association, American Library Association, American Bar Association, Modern Language Association, American Chemical Society, American Mathematics Society, American Historical Association, American Economics Association, American Psychological Association, and the American Philosophical Association (Butts, 1955, pp. 483-484). Illustrating the process of specialization already at work during this period, mining engineers, mechanical engineers, and electrical engineers all formed separate societies within a period about 15 years (Butts, 1955, p. 484).

Truth and Knowledge: The Scientific Method

Auguste Comte, writing between 1839 and 1853, proposed that the study of humans conform with the methods used in the natural sciences. John Stuart Mill's *System of Logic* (1852) constructed a philosophical and logical foundation for empiricism as the ground of knowledge and proposed the use of natural sciences in the study of human affairs. The work of Comte and of Mill was central to a general movement, that with other elements, produced an approach to the study of human behavior patterned after the natural sciences. It entailed a loose combination of naturalism, empiricism, and positivism for investigating the natural world. Naturalism held that all phenomena can be explained by natural causes and laws without attributing moral, spiritual, or supernatural significance to them. Empiricism directed that the experience of the senses is the only source of knowledge. Positivism held that propositions command belief only when they can be tested and confirmed by observation. Knowledge is confined to what has been experienced or can be experienced.

This combination of naturalism, empiricism, and positivism dominated science at the birth of student affairs about 1870 and would prove preeminent in the intellectual world for the next 100 years. It was only quite recently that other methods of knowing were developed, sometimes called the phenomenological and hermeneutic systems (Polkinghorne, 1983). The empirical-positivistic approach achieves knowledge by removing the observer from involvement with the world for the period of the observation. It separates parts from the whole for study and relies on mathematical relationships. The newer phenomenological method focuses on the structure of the observer's experience and the way form and meaning, communicable but personal, are given to what is experienced; whereas the hermeneutic or interpretive method concentrates on the historical meaning of experience, its developmental and cumulative implications at both the individual and social levels.

Nineteenth century opinions differed about how knowledge should be employed. One major view valued knowledge for its own sake. Following the lead of German universities, academic American scientists and social scientists began to propose that "pure" truth and "pure" knowledge were the aim of all research and study; and literature, language, science, history, art, and music were presented as the hallmarks of culture and scholarship. Truth for its own sake, undefiled by practical applications, became their slogan; and one major goal was to build an acknowledged intellectual elite as the guardians of truth and beauty, an enterprise in which the masses are incapable of participating (Butts, 1955).

In reaction to this position was the belief that knowledge had a social function to perform and must not hide away in the ivory tower. Scientists held varying views about the social role of knowledge. Many either resisted the idea of evolution or tried to show that no essential contradiction between evolution and religion existed. Gradually the weight of scientific research prevailed and scientific studies were accepted in the college curriculum alongside of literature. "The scientific movement was one of the most important factors in breaking down barriers between intellectuals and common people" (Butts, 1955, p. 487).

Borrowing from the scientific influence, social science made progress, too. Economics, political economy, political science, sociology, and anthropology became defined areas of study. Some scholars looked upon social evolution in Darwinian theory as almost automatic and natural change; others emphasized the possibility of controlling and directing social change as a means of promoting the general welfare through social reform. Schools were often perceived as great instruments of social improvement.

This same era that was influenced by social Darwinism "also witnessed the birth of a new psychology dedicated to the scientific study of human behavior in general and the phenomena of mind in particular" (Cremin, 1961, p. 100). During the year 1890, William James' *Principles of Psychology* appeared, followed by Francis W. Parker's *Talks on Pedagogic* (1894), Edward L. Thorndike's *Animal Intelligence* (1898), James' *Talks to Teachers on Psychology* (1899), and John Dewey's *The School and Society* (1899).

The most immediate effect of Darwinism on American psychology was probably to erect comprehensive systems of human behavior that were evolutionary in character. An example of this can be seen in the work of G. Stanley Hall, who earned Harvard's first doctorate in psychology in 1878, went to study in Germany, returned to Johns Hopkins, and then accepted the presidency of Clark University, from which he continued to write prolifically. Borrowing from Herbert Spencer (1864, 1876-97) and others, Hall's basic thesis was the "general psychonomic law" that ontogeny, the development of the human organism, recapitulates phylogeny, the evolution of the race (Ross, 1972). This thesis held that physical life and individual behavior develop through a series of stages that correspond generally to the stages through which the human being is supposed to have passed from presavagery to civilization; and, normal growth of the mind requires living through each of the stages because the development of any one stage is the normal stimulus for the emergence of the next one (Cremin, 1961). Working along the same line as Hall, William James proposed in the *Principles of Psychology* to apply evolutionary theory to understanding the mind, something that Spencer had done earlier. But, there was an important difference. Spencer believed that the life of the mind was a continuing process of adaptation to the environment, the principle of adjustment to circumstances applied to social organisms. Hall took one aspect of Spencer's work, the recapitulation theory, and developed it into a more general theory of human development. James insisted that although the mind is molded by the environment, it also acts upon the environment in an actively creative way. The knower is more than a mirror passively reflecting his or her world. The knower helps transform that world. Intelligence, therefore, is not merely to adapt to circumstances, but to change them as well (Cremin, 1961).

Thorndike, who studied under James, began his first work in animal learning while at Harvard. Out of his work with animals came a new theory of learning that maintained learning involves a specific response connected to a specific stimulus through a physiological bond in the neural system so that the stimulus regularly produces the response—what Thorndike called the "law of effect" (Thorndike, 1898). In later work he rejected the Biblical view that human nature is essentially sinful and untrustworthy, the Roussearian view that human nature is essentially good and always right, and Locke's view that human nature is plastic and modifiable. Thorndike believed that human nature is simply made up of "original tendencies" that can be exploited for good or bad and is dependent upon what learning takes place. John Dewey, too, had read James' *Principles of Psychology* and took from it the idea of an objective psychology that was firmly rooted in evolutionary biology. The key to what was new in Dewey's work was the concept of social reformism (Cremin, 1961). Dewey believed that a democratic society is committed to change and organized as intelligently and as scientifically as possible; it is "intentionally progressive" (Dewey, 1916). In short, American culture had become an interplay of several major factors: democracy, nationalism, capitalism, science, industrialism, religious traditionalism, Humanism, and a new psychology. Higher education reflected this culture and its changing nature, which would play a large part in creating the need for services in higher education that would become the field of college student personnel.

Colleges and Universities (1636-1783)

American higher education began in the Colonial period with a small number of isolated colleges, each administered by one person, a president. This individual sometimes would have the help of one or two others. Together they did nearly everything required to maintain the institution's existence. Strongly patterned in the British tradition, early American colleges began as residential institutions, and these institutions acted fully *in loco parentis*. This term means acting in place of the parent and specifically referred to the role of the college acting for the parent. Their stated purpose was to train young men for the ministry. Literate people were required to read the Bible and support the church, and this was believed true in particular for the ministry. In time the needs for educated people would develop to serve commerce and government; but learning in early Colonial times was unmistakably first and foremost, as stated by Samuel Johnson, the first president of Columbia University, "to know God in Jesus Christ, and to love and serve him, in all sobriety, Godliness, and righteousness of life, with a perfect heart, and a willing mind" (Leonard, 1956, p. 23). The life of the early college student was tightly regimented to achieve this outcome.

College attendance ordinarily required a difficult and somewhat lengthy journey from home. College life was usually an intense and all encompassing experience lived as one of a group of young men or women in an isolated community that served as a surrogate family and church and fulfilled many of their functions during this crucial stage of life-development (Cremin, 1988). Prior to the Civil War, colleges were generally administered by strong men, who almost always were clergy, assisted by one or two colleagues who were also clergymen. A professor was responsible for the instruction of 40 or 50 students in the entire range of the curriculum from the classics to moral philosophy. In the larger institutions, he was assisted by tutors who were recent graduates. With the few exceptions of those trained in the natural sciences, a professor had normally been educated in the classics and divinity. Terms such as personnel services, personnel officers, or guidance services were not part of the thinking or vocabulary of Colonial educators. Spiritual and moral guidance were provided by the family and the church in this period, and no formal attempts at psychological understanding were made (Beck, 1963). Edicts based upon religious doctrine provided guidelines for human behavior and, to the extent that people conformed to this image of the "good life" presented by the church and supported by the family and community, they were considered "good." Nowhere was this more visible than in the schools and colleges. Although far from universal, a slow movement in some of the larger institutions would begin toward presidents and faculty who were laymen and trained as scholars.

The Colonies were first established largely as commercial enterprises, but they soon were populated by a people escaping religious and political persecution in Europe. In turn they would attempt to lock out all influences other than their own beliefs. But, as a result of increased immigration that brought a mixture of religious beliefs and of an expanding social order that required more specialized skills in business, government, and the professions, education would gradually become more generalized in definition to serve good citizenship and the broader needs of society. This migration from Europe would bring with it, somewhat belatedly perhaps, the fruits of the great awakening that had bloomed during the late Renaissance period (Cremin, 1970).

The work of Mill (1852) and Comte (1853) constructed a philosophical and logical foundation for empiricism that was central to a general movement and, with other elements, produced an approach to the study of human behavior patterned after the natural sciences. This thought entailed a loose combination of naturalism, empiricism, and positivism for investigating human events, as well as for investigating the natural world. Naturalism held that all phenomena can be explained by natural causes and laws without attributing moral, spiritual, or supernatural significance to them. Empiricism directed that the experience of the senses is the only source of knowledge. Positivism held that propositions command belief only when they can be tested and confirmed by observation. Knowledge is confined to what has been experienced or can be experienced.

On the eve of the Civil War, college attendance could be numbered in the thousands and newspaper readers in the millions. Although the desire of the American people to give their children a better education was there, until this time colleges had built their programs primarily to serve one class of people. Little they were doing seemed important to the majority of people and their enrollments were declining. After the Civil War, higher education in the United States was confronted with issues that forced it to choose new directions. The influence of science was increasing rapidly and would become a major influence in reform of the college curriculum (Rudolph, 1962). Although no one person or institution could create the changes needed, the combined effort of a number of men and institutions directed reforms that destroyed the old structure and replaced it with a new one (e.g., John Howard Raymond of Vassar, William Bartram Rogers of Massachusetts Institute of Technology, Andrew D. White of Cornell, and Charles William Eliot of Harvard)(see Cremin, 1988; Rudolph, 1962).

The Morrill Federal Land Grant Act of 1862 unquestionably did the most to alter the attitude of the American people toward attending college. The act provided for the support in every state of at least one college "where the leading object shall be, without excluding other scientific or classical studies, and including military tactics, to teach such branches of learning as are related to agriculture and the mechanic arts . . ." (Commager, 1949, p. 413). Each state was given public lands or land script equal to 30,000 acres for each senator and representative under the apportionment of 1860. Every state would in time achieve its land-grant institution. The second Morrill Act, passed in 1890, provided regular annual appropriations for the land-grant institutions and stipulated that no appropriations would be given to states that denied admission on the basis of race unless they established separate but equal facilities. Seventeen states did establish separate facilities, thereby creating two such institutions within their boundaries.

It took some time to forge a clear direction for these new land-grant colleges and to convince farmers that an agricultural education for themselves and their children made sense. By 1890, as a result of a growing body of applied agricultural science, the development of agricultural experiment stations, federal and state financial assistance, and a program that literally took the college to the farmers (the extension service), a new attitude was achieved. Evidence of larger crops, higher income, and a better standard of living had its effect. The National Grange organization clearly stated in 1874 its attitude toward education:

> We shall advance the cause of education among ourselves and for our children, by all just means within our power. We especially advocate for our agricultural and industrial colleges that practical agriculture, domestic science, and all other arts which adorn the home, be taught in their course of study. (Commager, 1949, p. 80)

In a statement of principles that Andrew D. White read at the opening exercises when Cornell University opened its doors in 1869 (the year of Grant's inaugural as President), he recognized the oldest purpose of all for higher education, to develop the individual in the fullest sense and to prepare the individual for a useful role in society. He declared that all courses would be equal (Rudolph, 1965). The decline of the classics and the free election of courses were clearly a result of the vocationalism of the land-grant concept and pushed institutions of higher learning toward a spirit of free and universal inquiry. Truth sought in religious study was giving way to truth sought through science.

Universities were strongest in the South before the Civil War. A dozen universities had been created in this region by the government practice of giving federal lands to support seminary learning. The development of state universities was cultivated by western migration. It was not until after the Civil War, however, that state universities with the leadership of particularly the Universities of Michigan, Minnesota, and Wisconsin, achieved an identity of their own. As a result of the rapid expansion of the population in the western states and the emergence of new leadership in these areas, state universities were largely defined in the midwest and west. Their rise to eminence was difficult due to dependence upon legislative support and the inherent political strategies. They were often attacked for offering both classical and scientific courses of study and for being Godless, but eventually were able to combine in one institution something of the

Chapter I

Jeffersonian spirit of excellence with the practical characteristic of the land-grant institution.

By 1872 the state universities in Michigan, Minnesota, Iowa, and Wisconsin, followed by Indiana and Illinois, were developing certificate systems with the high schools that created a feeder system to the state universities and land-grant colleges, and more than 150 private institutions had adopted some method of accrediting that established high schools as college preparatory schools. By 1895 only 17 percent of the students admitted to American institutions of higher learning were graduates of college preparatory schools, whereas 41 percent were graduates of the public high school, a major factor in making the American college and university a democratic institution (Rudolph, 1965). Changes in American education after 1876 were rapid, prodigious, and on occasion even revolutionary in nature.

Although Reconstruction in the South officially ended in 1877, the practice of social injustice continued during the Progressive Era, and real efforts to change this demon would only come much later. From the Reconstruction Era through the Great Depression, black higher education in the South existed essentially through a system of private liberal arts colleges. An elaborate system of denominational colleges for blacks was created and sustained by a large missionary effort, and many of these institutions were essentially mission schools with white sponsors and teachers seen as the means for redemption of the South through the regeneration of former slaves (Cremin, 1988). Many whites came south to evangelize African-Americans, not unlike what had been attempted on foreign soil. It is not surprising, therefore, that many of these schools resembled the missionary schools in China, India, and Africa. They included a combination of moral and academic instruction, and the lives of their students in and out of the classroom were closely regulated with this in mind. Social codes such as temperance and monogamy were strongly enforced; and personal values of thrift, industry, and responsibility promoted (Cremin, 1988).

During this same period, the federal government gave little aid to black land-grant schools, and the southern states provided minimal funding for black normal schools and colleges. Between 1870 and 1890, nine federal black land-grant colleges were established in the South, and this number increased to 16 by 1915 (Anderson, 1989). A 1917 survey of black higher education conducted by Thomas Jesse Jones (1917) indicated the Florida Agricultural and Mechanical College enrolled 12 black college students; 7

black state colleges or normal schools had no black students enrolled in collegiate grades; and of 7,513 students enrolled in the combined 23 black land-grant and state schools, 4,061 were classified as elementary level students, 3,400 were considered secondary level, and only the 12 previously mentioned at Florida A&M were enrolled in a college level curriculum. As late as World War I, almost all black college students in the southern states were enrolled in privately owned colleges. Although somewhat improved, this structure of black higher education would persist through the 1920s. During this period the history of black higher education was the primary result of the interrelationship between philanthropy and the black community (Anderson, 1989).

The Beginning of College Student Personnel Work

At Harvard in 1870, Ephraim Gurney was appointed as what might be called the first college dean. Although he was primarily an academic dean, he did take the burden of discipline from President Elliot's office. In 1890 a Board of Freshman Advisers was set up at Harvard, and the deanship was divided into appointments that essentially created a division of labor between an academic dean and a dean of student affairs (Brubacher & Rudy, 1976). The vision of William Rainey Harper, president of the University of Chicago, was also of significance. He predicted in an address given at Brown University in 1899 that what he called the scientific study of the student would eventually be made a part of the work of the American university (Goodspeed, 1916).

In the 50 years following the passage of the Morrill Act in 1862, more than 600 colleges and universities were founded, and enrollments in institutions of higher learning shot up from approximately 40,000 to over 400,000 students. Early universities were being transformed into modern and complex research institutions that offered an expanding array of liberal arts and professional courses of study (Leonard, 1956). Although it was certainly, in part, a response to these rapidly increasing numbers of students attending colleges and universities that college student personnel work was born, it was not this factor alone that led to its origin as is often assumed. It was also a response to the changing time, a period of reform that was influencing education at all levels as significantly as it was other elements in American culture. As will be related in the next section, *Student personnel work originated as a part of a reform movement and reflected much of the reform and progressive spirit as it continued to develop.* But, as is so often the case, it was also a response to conservative concerns as well. These conservative concerns were generated largely out of parents' values for the care and protection of their offspring, who were often living out of the home for the first time.

Summary

In the beginning America was almost entirely agricultural and a nation of great distances. Before the Civil War, land was the major focus for development. By 1890, however, 30 years following passage by Congress of the Homestead Act, the frontier had all but disappeared. Although close ties continued with Europe that affected American intellectual life, the United States remained isolated in international affairs. At the same time, the nation was quickly becoming an industrial power, and in nearly all fields of study that were influencing culture and the educational system there was a rapid expansion of knowledge. The Morrill Federal Land Grant Act of 1862 influenced the growth and development of universities and, in particular, brought rural America closer to the developing scientific culture in the country.

This was a nation built with a belief in strong individualism, but in practice the tenacious support of families and communities was an essential ingredient of its relentless expansion. Colleges became a part of this supportive system and functioned as extensions of the family. This uniquely American relationship between colleges and their students had its beginnings in a period before there was a nation and has never been completely abandoned. The needs of a new and rapidly growing nation would create a new role for higher education. Within the economic, political, and scientific changes taking place, there was a reform movement beginning that would influence the future of American higher education. As colleges and universities grew in enrollment and size, logistically it became impossible for the president and a few others to manage all they felt responsible to do in the lives of students. A division of labor was begun that would eventually lead to the development of a major segment of higher education known as college student personnel or college student affairs.

Chapter II

The Age of Reform
(1900–1949)

Reforms at Harvard guided by Charles W. Eliot were taking place in the 1870s (Gruber, 1989). The appointment at Harvard in 1870 of Ephraim Gurney as the first college dean is often pointed to as the beginning of college student personnel work. Gurney's duties, however, were largely that of an academic dean, and it was not until 20 years later, when the deanship was divided into what was essentially an academic dean and a student affairs dean (Brubacher & Rudy, 1976), that boundaries for the profession of college student personnel really began to develop. There is no evidence that either event occurred with great fanfare or celebration. It seems to have simply been a practical way to deal with the growing dimensions of administering a college. At the same time, there was a reform movement underway that affected education from its lowest to its highest level and that reflected the rapidly changing culture and society in America.

The purpose of Chapter II is to gauge the influence of this reform movement on the changing American society and upon higher education and the budding profession of college student personnel work. To do this, some of the more important characteristics and events of the first half of the twentieth century that describe the struggle that took place between Conservatives and Progressives will be presented. This section will look at the influence of Darwinism on philosophy, politics, and the intellectual

17

and social life of the nation. It will briefly consider the developing roles of transportation and communication and the labor movement that were resulting from the continuing change of the nation from an agrarian society to an industrial one. Although the Great Depression and the New Deal politics of Franklin Roosevelt would have an enormous impact upon the time, they would not negate the significant influence of the Reform Movement on higher education and the infant profession of college student personnel. It is important to know something of the nature of these elements to understand how they were reflected in higher education. The development and nature of college student personnel work with its strengths and weaknesses cannot be understood apart from this social milieu of which higher education was a part. Chapter II will conclude by looking at the development of college student personnel during this reform period as a part of progressive education movement and particularly at the important role of the document entitled *The Student Personnel Point of View* (1937, 1949) in reflecting this influence, which would reach forward even into the present day.

Progressivism

Hofstadter (1965) characterized the Progressive Era as the Age of Reform. He meant by "Progressivism" the broader attempt toward criticism and change that was "everywhere so conspicuous after 1900, when the already forceful stream of Agrarian discontent was enlarged and redirected by the growing enthusiasm of the middle-class people for social and economic reform" (p. 5). This Progressive movement took place during a period of rapid and sometimes turbulent transition from the conditions of an Agrarian society to those of a growing urban structure. The tradition of American democracy developed on the farm and in small towns. Its central ideas were rural in sentiment and constructed with rural metaphors (e.g., grass-roots democracy). Americans were taught that rural life and farming were something sacred, and a certain complacency and self-righteousness existed in rural thinking that was challenged by the rise of industrialism (Hofstadter, 1965).

At the same time, a breakdown in the religious homogeneity of the population was occurring. Until 1800 American democracy had not only been rural but primarily Yankee and Protestant in ideology. Until this time immigrant groups were too small and too scattered to have a major influence on the social order. But, with the rise of industrialism there began a 40-year migration of European peasants whose religious traditions, language, and sheer numbers made assimilation impossible. The Progressive movement was heavily influenced by the native population's reactions to the arrival of the immigrants.

The needs of the immigrants and the beliefs of the natives resulted in conflict between two very different systems of political ethics, the American Yankee-Protestant versus European traditions. One was founded upon the Yankee-Protestant political tradition and upon middle-class life that argued politics ought to be conducted in accordance with principles and abstract laws that were superior to and transcended personal needs. It further expressed a common feeling that government must be largely a task to moralize the lives of individuals, whereas economic life should be intimately related to the stimulation and development of individual character. The other system was founded upon the European heritage of the immigrants, upon their unfamiliarity with independent political action, their conditioning to hierarchy and authority, and upon the urgent needs that grew out of their migration. This system took for granted that the political life of the individual would result from family needs and interpreted politics and civic life as personal obligations and placed strong personal loyalties above allegiance to abstract laws or morals. "It was chiefly upon this system of values that the political life of the immigrant, the boss, and the urban machine was based" (Hofstadter, 1965, p. 9).

The Progressive era involved conflict between the two codes supported on one side by the highly moral leaders of Protestant social reform and on the other side by the bosses, political professionals, and immigrant masses. The conflicts of the period aroused strong passions because they resulted from different views of politics, of morals, and religion. Progressives felt all of society was threatened not only economically but by moral and social degeneration and the weakening of democratic institutions. They believed the nation could be redeemed, however, and there was a hopeful mood during the early years of the twentieth century.

As Goldman (1955) pointed out, the dominant groups in the United States did what dominant groups usually do. Unconsciously they selected from among available theories the ones that best supported and protected their positions and advanced these ideas as truth. Such truths blocked Progressives wherever they tried to advance their programs. Their central argument that government should use its central powers for reform was countered by closely related ideas of economics, religion, morals, psychology, biology, history, law, and philosophy. These ideas are generally known as conservatism.

Conservatives argued that democracy was founded on "self-evident" or "natural" rights, and most important among these rights was "liberty"— the liberty of a person to acquire and keep property without the interference of government, and the liberty of a worker to deal directly with an employer without the interference of a union. Not only did such interferences violate "natural rights," but they were certain to fail because they contravened the laws of economics (e.g., Ricardian "law" that stated the income of workers always tended to the subsistence level because a raise in wages simply meant that the poor had more children who ate up the additional income, and the Malthusian "law" that explained enough food for everyone was impossible since population invariably increased more rapidly than did the food supply). Law was law, and conservative judges simply applied it as the Constitution intended when they struck down reform legislation. Additional support was found in the prevailing theories of biology, psychology, and morals. The mind and emotions were believed to be fixed entities from birth that functioned as they did regardless of the environment. Some people were born to success and goodness and others to squalor and sin. Progressives might have admirable motive in their desire to apply democracy to Negroes and women, but human nature cannot be changed. Conservatives asserted that Negroes and women were created intellectually inferior and morally weaker and nothing could change this fact (see Goldman, 1955). Religion was widely used to support this conservative view.

Reform Darwinism versus Conservative Darwinism

At the heart of this issue lay the expanding views of Darwinism, science, and education. "Social Darwinism became a specifically Anglo-American cultural artifact that was held to be much more influential in the United States than anywhere else" (Bellamy, 1984, p. 6). Herbert Spencer (1864, 1876-1897) was undoubtedly the best spokesman for Darwin's theory. He transformed the biological "laws" of evolution into social "laws" and seemed to make science say what every conservative wanted it to say— that all species of organic life had evolved and were still evolving by a process of the survival of the fittest. According to Spencer this was also true for social institutions. "Existing social institutions were therefore the 'fittest' way of doing things, and businessmen who bested their competitors had thereby proved themselves 'the fittest' to enjoy wealth and power" (Goldman, 1955, p. 71). Although poverty and corruption were undoubtedly evil, they could only be corrected by a centuries long evolutionary process. This form of Social Darwinism Goldman (1955) referred to as Conservative Darwinism, and it was the standard doctrine of the late nineteenth century preached from the pulpit, taught in the university classroom, and espoused in the newspapers.

Conservative Darwinism was a well articulated and carefully integrated set of ideas for protecting the status quo. Spencer taught that Evolution was not only a biological phenomenon but a cosmic one as well. The emergence by 1870 of evolution as the best known term for the transmutation of species was a tribute to Spencer's impact because the popularization of the word and concept were due to him and not Darwin (Bellamy, 1984). Although Spencer's works were widely read by American intellectuals of this period and would undoubtedly have had a strong effect on their own, they were made even more influential by the "energetic discipleship" of William Graham Sumner, who held a professorship of political and social science at Yale from 1872 until his death in 1910 (Cremin, 1961). He, too, believed that those who held power did so because they were the fittest and their success in society, through competition, was the most eloquent proof of this fact. Like Spencer, he supported curricular reform in education but was pessimistic about any real influence education might have on the social process (Cremin, 1961).

If a person is not in a position of power or influence and does not have the economic advantages of the elite, what does the person do? It was the Progressives who worked out a new philosophy more compatible with the conditions of opportunity and democracy. Progressives were children of the nineteenth century, too, and they found it difficult to shake their own heritage and create ideas that were really new. It was Conservative Darwinism itself, however, that suggested the reform reply (Goldman, 1955). At the center of the Darwinian theory was the idea of continuous evolution in relation to environment. As Goldman (1955) pointed out, Conservative Darwinians had recognized evolution up to the present and then for all practical purposes called a halt by saying that it was over and everything would remain the same or, if it continued, it would do so as a slow process of change, and every level of life, social as well as biological, would equally benefit so no real shift in the social structure would occur. They advocated ideas that were proposed as timeless and not dependent upon any environment and talked as if Truth were absolute. Why not really believe in full-blown evolution and insist that within certain environments, if the need were sufficient, that contemporary institutions could and should change rapidly? Why not see Conservative Darwinism as simply an idea that supported the people who "had" against the people who "had not"? Why not work out a Reform Darwinism that did not discredit the theory of Darwinism but dissolved the hold that the powerful groups held in maintaining the status quo? In fact, Reform Darwinism could claim to be and soon was claimed to be even more scientific than previous claims for Conservative Darwinism. Reform Darwinism was the natural response of those who felt locked out of opportunity and were angry and frustrated with the status quo. By the 1890s many young academics were seeking Ph.D.s in Europe, particularly in Germany where they came under the influence of an historical approach that prepared them for participation in Reform Darwinism. Some went to England where the attack on Spencer's Social Darwinism was far more developed than it was in the United States at this time.

Politics

The period between 1900 and 1914 produced a movement toward democracy and reform. It was not led by any one group or set of leaders but rather came from a large number of diverse elements such as the agitation of Populists, the reform governors of whom Robert La Follette in Wisconsin was an example, the influence of socialism, the efforts of "mudrakers" in the popular literature, and the work of political and social thinkers.

The fight against "Bossism" was conducted on both city and state levels. Initiative and referendum laws were advocated and passed in many states. Workmen's compensation acts were present in all but five states and territories by 1920 and laws to protect women and children in the workplace were passed. By 1914 six more states granted full suffrage to women and both political parties endorsed equal suffrage in 1916. In 1918 Woodrow Wilson appealed to Congress for federal action; and in 1919 Congress passed the Nineteenth Amendment (the woman-suffrage amendment), which was ratified during the political campaign of 1920.

At the Republican Convention in 1900, Theodore Roosevelt accepted the nomination as vice president on the Republican ticket, and in September of the following year became president when President McKinley was shot and died eight days later. Roosevelt was reelected in 1904. At 43, Roosevelt was the youngest man to hold the office of president of the United States. His administration was generally characterized by national assertion in foreign affairs but tentative in its results on the domestic front (Hacker & Zahler, 1952).

The Hay-Bunau-Varella Treaty of 1904 gave the United States rights to the area on which to build the Panama Canal, and the Canal was opened to traffic in 1914. Interventions to restore peace in Central America were made and although benevolent, they disturbed many Latin American people. In Europe and the Far East Roosevelt claimed a place for the United States among the great powers and won the Nobel Peace Prize in 1906 for mediating and arranging for a peace treaty between Russia and Japan that was signed in 1905. The dispute over the Alaska-Canada boundary was settled in 1903.

Between 1904 and 1906, Americans on the West Coast of the United States demanded restriction of Japanese immigration, and the AFL urged that the Chinese Exclusion Act be applied to Japanese. In 1906 an order segregating oriental children in the San Francisco public schools evoked a formal protest from the Japanese government. In return for a promise to deal with Japanese immigration, pressure was brought that succeeded in changing the school order to limit only persons who spoke no English or were over-age for a given grade from ordinary classes. Japan agreed to grant no passports to the U.S. for Japanese laborers but did permit immigration of wives, former residents, children of residents, or settled agriculturalists (Commager, 1949). One result was a large increase in the Japanese population in California.

The year 1912 represented a peak for political reformists. The Democratic platform emphasized tariff revision and control of monopolies, but it also favored evaluation of railroads, currency legislation, anti-injunction laws, and presidential primaries (Faulkner, 1948). The Progressive Party had a long list of political and social reforms and was more radical in its stance than others. The Socialists again nominated Eugene V. Debbs for president, declaring the capitalist system had outgrown its historical function. Woodrow Wilson was elected, and although he was a minority president as a result of the split between Theodore Roosevelt and Taft, the majority of the voters desired reform and, in this perspective as a Progressive, Wilson represented the popular will. He was reelected in 1916 on the slogan "He kept us out of war."

Politics and diplomacy during the post World War I years were characterized by a return to the strong isolationism of earlier years (e.g., refusal to sign the Versailles Treaty, to accept a mandate over Armenia, to conclude a proposed defensive alliance with France and Great Britain, to join the League of Nations or the World Court). Resurgent nationalism was motivated by a desire to avoid European involvement and by resentment toward European criticism aimed particularly at what was characterized as "crass materialism" (Faulkner, 1948).

The changed attitude toward immigration is illustrative of the strong nationalistic sentiment that existed. Various groups wanted to substantially reduce immigration (e.g., on the west coast there was fear of the "yellow peril"; some scholars of population feared a "racial deterioration"; some feared the increasing numbers of foreigners were preventing "Americanization" and endangering the preservation of American traditions) (Faulkner, 1948). As a result of the strong influence of organized labor, Congress in 1882 had already prohibited Chinese immigration. Legislation in 1891, 1893, 1907, and 1917 excluded immigrants for moral, mental, and physical reasons, in addition to excluding anarchists, vagrants, paupers, and contract labor. In 1917 Congress passed a literacy test over Wilson's veto, and in 1921 passed the Emergency Quota Act limiting immigration in any one year to 3 percent of the number of each nationality according to the census of 1910. It was reenacted in 1922 (see Commager, 1949, pp. 315-317, for a summary of the Immigration Restriction laws of 1917 & 1921). In 1924 an act was passed establishing a 2 percent quota of the number of any nationality residing in the United States in 1890 with the exceptions of Canada, Mexico, and the independent nations of South America, although it was to be enforced only until 1927 when a "national origins" quota could be substituted that would ascertain by government experts the real origin of the American people as constituted in 1920. Immigration officials were to apportion among the nationalities immigration accordingly, with the total number limited to 150,000 a year. Because the task was impossible, Congress postponed its implementation until 1929. By 1930 it was clear that the goals of restricting immigration were achieved, with only 48,500 admitted during that year (Faulkner, 1948).

Waves of immigration and expansion of the middle class stimulated growth of American higher education (Goodchild, 1989). Descendants of these immigrants sought higher learning and would continue to do so in increasingly larger numbers throughout the century. There was an almost immediate response, however, by those already present to limit the numbers of those who were still coming, as Wechsler (1989) pointed out. There were also clear efforts by some to keep "undesirable groups" out of higher education, to limit access to poor, female, Jewish, and Black students and, if admitted, to socially segregate them (Wechsler, 1989). College student personnel would become increasingly involved with the efforts to democratize American higher education and would see much of its energy in later years directed toward helping to integrate higher education and developing multicultural campuses.

Social

Prohibition experiment. Prohibition was probably the most remembered experiment to control the social life of the time. As Faulkner (1948) noted, it was not a sudden uprising but the culmination of a movement for temperance and prohibition that had been going on for at least a century. The Volstead Act was passed over Wilson's veto in 1919 and was, perhaps, the most unpopular law ever enacted, with the result that it was intentionally and consistently violated, and the consumption of alcohol became a major characteristic of the college campus. It was not until 1933 that repeal of the Eighteenth Amendment was achieved and liquor control returned to the states with federal protection for the dry states (see Faulkner, 1948, for a good description of this subject). Alcohol consumption has become a widely practiced tradition on the college campus, particularly in fraternities and social groups (see Kuh & Arnold, 1993), that has been left to the supervision primarily of police and student affairs staff.

Jazz Age. Although usually portrayed as a more frivolous time, the most important accomplishment according to the historian Slosson (1930) was "The outstanding achievement of the American school during the period of 1914 to 1928 . . . to make secondary education almost as universal as the previous hundred years had made primary education" (p. 43). High school students that numbered 1,500,000 in 1914 had grown to nearly 4 million in 1926. The growth in numbers, plus additions to the curriculum and expansion of facilities, caused the cost of education to double between 1920 and 1926. Although dominated by college entrance requirements, efforts were also made to expand vocational training.

Newspaper publishing was becoming more a business and, with increasing competition for advertising, many did not compete. From 1914 to 1924, 2,000 newspapers in the United States ceased publishing. In a competitive structure, however, "chain newspapers" prospered (e.g., Hearst chain specialized in "yellow journalism," Scripps-Howard group tried to maintain a tradition of liberalism). Tabloid newspapers specializing in pictures and stories of sex, sensational murders, and the lives of the rich and famous were developed.

The trend in magazine publishing was similar, but two new industries that would influence the culture of the United States grew rapidly. By the end of the 1920s, nearly 23,000 movie theatres with a combined seating capacity of over 11 million sold 100 million admissions a week. Talking-pictures introduced in 1929 and 1930 kept this new venture growing. After 1920 radio, supported largely by advertising that amounted to $100 million a year, grew into eight networks made up of 561 stations that created intense competition. In 1927 Congress established the Federal Radio Commission to provide some order in this business. It is difficult to estimate the amount of influence that these two new media had, but it unquestionably was considerable and growing (see Slosson, 1930).

The realm of literature and art also did well during this postwar period (e.g., Norris, Sinclair, Dreiser, Fitzgerald, Hemingway, Dos Passos, Anderson, Faulkner in fiction; Edgar Lee Masters, Lindsay, Sandburg, Robinson, Frost, Lowell, St. Vincent Millay in poetry; Eakins, Homer, Sargent, Rivera, and Orozca in art; O'Neill, Anderson, and Sherwood in drama; Louis Sullivan and Frank Lloyd Wright in architecture; and Gershwin, Copland, Sessions, in music).

Periods of growth and change are seldom if ever limited to only a few areas but are observed in every realm—business, science, the arts, education—and this period was no exception.

Industry

The Census of Manufacturers in 1909 stated the worth of manufactured products in the United states as over $20 billion as compared with $8 billion reported in the Census of 1907 for Great Britain. It was estimated that Germany in 1913 produced between $11 billion and $12 billion worth in products. The United States, however, consumed a larger portion of its manufactured products at home than either of the other two industrial powers. In the decade before World War I, Great Britain exported roughly one fourth of its manufactured products whereas the United States exported less than one tenth of its manufactured products (see Faulkner, 1948, 1954, & 1957).

The second decade of the twentieth century saw new levels reached in the percentage of increase in capital, wages, and value of products produced (capital, wages, and value of products from 1914 to 1919 advanced 95 percent, 158 percent, and 157 percent respectively). Although manufacturing from agricultural raw products remained dominant, by 1914 the manufacture of iron and steel had risen from fifth to second place, and for the first time automobile production and repair appeared in the top ten. It is worth noting that in 1860 the leading industry in the United States was flour and meal; in 1914 it was slaughtering and meat packing; and in 1929 it was motor vehicles (Faulkner, 1954). By 1929 cigars and cigarettes had become one of the top 15 industries in the United States, whereas flour and other grain-mill products had dropped from first in 1860 to fifteenth in 1929. The use of high tariffs continued although the internal policy of the federal government remained largely *laissez faire* until the 1930s. The lack of government control coupled with freedom in interstate commerce created strong stimulants for industrial growth.

The time of mass production had arrived. It was developed from earlier knowledge (Eli Whitney used it to manufacture guns in the 1790s) but did not take hold until sufficient progress in technology occurred, adequate capital was available, and a national market large enough to absorb the product existed. Mass production required mass consumption. Industries that developed mass production in the United States were responding to the basic needs of people for food, clothing, and metals for machinery, transportation, and other uses (Faulkner, 1954).

The Ford Motor Company led the way using a moving assembly line process that produced 1,000 cars a day by 1913, reducing the basic price of the Model T Ford from $950 to $290. At the same time, the minimum daily wage at Ford increased to $5 and the workday was reduced from nine to eight hours in 1914. The oil industry that actually began during the Civil War became dominant as a result of the use of internal combustion and Diesel engines.

The 1920s were a boom era. Whereas the population increased by only about 12 percent, industrial production nearly doubled (e.g., in 1917, 500 million barrels of oil were produced and in 1923, 1 billion). Both national and real income per capita increased substantially during the 1920s, and worker productivity almost doubled. A decline in birth rate, restriction of immigration, and increased application of science and technology that resulted in mass production and scientific management influenced industrial efficiency. The radio industry had a phenomenal development in the 1920s, and building construction was booming. Undoubtedly, advertising and installment buying were stimulants to this boom economy. Conservative estimates of the number of cars sold on installment in 1927 are approximately 60 percent, and 15 percent of all goods were being sold on the installment plan by the end of the decade.

Labor

The labor movement grew out of the people collecting around large factories that brought the wage earners together in cities where they could become an organized force. A democratic system facilitated by rapidly developing communication and transportation systems aided its growth across the nation. The labor unions' success during the first 50 years of the twentieth century was due in large part to aggressive leadership, the wage earners' desire for security, and the development of collective bargaining. Although the creation of a labor political party was rejected by union leadership, they did use their political influence with state and national legislatures and made clear progress in bargaining with employers. The struggle with a conservative judiciary, however, was a somewhat different story. The right to strike, boycott, or picket had been unfavorably viewed by the courts for years, but with more progressive public sentiment a gradual change occurred. The right of the state to regulate work hours under its police power was established. Labor continued to bitterly oppose the use of the injunction in labor disputes.

By the 1930s all states had some type of child labor legislation enacted and some new opportunities for women were opening although they continued to be exploited. In 1914 the number of women working in manufacturing was about 1,500,000 and in 1950, about 3,545,000. The belief finally prevailed that women, like children, needed the protection of the state to regulate pay, physical injury, and other working conditions. The first minimum wage law was passed in Massachusetts in 1912 (Faulkner, 1954). By 1942 laws protecting women and children and providing for workmen's compensation for accidents accompanied by other social legislation regulating work conditions and raising the worker's standard of living were enacted. From 1865 forward, with the exception of the depression years of the 1930s, the standard of living of the American worker continued to increase.

Transportation and Communication

The development of transportation and communication technology would help transform American culture and revolutionize business, and it would bring the American college campus much closer to the homes of students attending. Not only would students see a wider number of possible institutions from which to choose, but they would begin visiting campus ahead of time, and parents would be able to visit campus more often, too.

Consolidation of railroads reached its peak in 1906. Seven groups controlled over two-thirds of the railroads. At about this same time, changes in technology occurred. Electricity or the Diesel engine began replacing steam power. After World War I, railroad service was improved by the use of the Diesel engine, streamlined cars, greater comfort, and higher speed.

The most significant development, however, was the gasoline motor car. The development and expansion of this mode of transportation by Ford and others that would ultimately change a culture occurred between 1914 and 1929 (Faulkner, 1954), and it produced during this same period a large increase in highway construction.

The birth and development of aviation occurred at about the same time. Early development was the result of its military value, but rapid development of commercial aviation followed in the 1920s.

The telegraph line had spanned the nation since 1862 and was expanded rapidly in following years. But, it was the telephone that dramatically changed communication and impacted the culture, perhaps, as significantly as the automobile. Whereas in 1880 there were 34,305 miles of telephone wires in the United States, by 1952 there were 159 million miles. In 1900 the American Telephone and Telegraph Company (AT&T) reported 855,000 telephones in use. By 1915 AT&T boasted 9,172,000 telephones in service. It had become standard equipment for the middle class home.

The great development of the postal service occurred after 1860. Rural free delivery was commenced in 1896 with 87 routes. By 1950, however, there were 32,619 routes covering 1,493,365 miles. In 1918 the federal government with the use of army planes began the transportation of mail by air between New York and Washington, and in 1938 every railroad in the country was established as a mail route.

Business

In the rural areas during most of the nineteenth century, the country store was the place to purchase nearly everything a person needed. In the city it was the department store. The creation of rural free delivery facilitated the rapid development of the mail order house (Montgomery, Ward & Company founded in 1872 and Sears, Roebuck & Company founded in 1895 grew rapidly in the late 1990s and expanded again after the establishment of the parcel post system in 1913). Mail order purchasing became as common as buying at the country store. The development of the automobile extended a person's purchasing radius, and it made possible frequent trips to the nearest town or city rather than the previous limit of a few times a year. As a result the country store was forced to specialize in the immediate necessities and mail order houses began in 1926 to open retail outlets in many small and medium sized cities. Mass merchandising increased lowering prices and the ground was prepared for the chain store, which has continued ever since. In 1948 there were over 6,000 different chain stores that combined conducted one-fourth of the total retail sales of the country (Faulkner, 1954).

Advertising became a way of life with newspapers, magazines, radio, and later television receiving most of their financial support from this source. A large expansion in installment buying occurred during the 1920s and 1930s. Foreign commerce continued to grow. Transportation services continued to expand as settled areas of the country were further developed for agricultural use, and new mineral resources and oil reservoirs were tapped. The combination of a rapidly growing population and a high protective tariff, however, was changing the United States from a predominantly agricultural nation to an industrial one. With products to export, foreign trade grew and the federal government continued its efforts to stimulate commerce and foreign trade.

The boom years of the 1920s were nurtured by new and relatively new industries whose products were in constant demand. The automobile industry (estimated 4 million jobs), road construction ($2 million a year spent), the development of radio and household electrical appliances that soon became necessities rather than luxuries were prime examples. In turn, the demand for electrical power grew. Although three decades of federal legislation existed designed to curtail monopoly and insure competition, consolidation continued through the 1920s with little interference from either the judicial or executive branches of government.

The Great Depression

It is generally agreed by most economists and scholars that the depression of the 1930s has been the most severe in our history. There is minimal agreement about its causes, however. The reform attitude that existed during the first part of the twentieth century culminated in the Federal Reserve Act, the Clayton Antitrust Act, and the creation of the Federal Trade Commission. It was believed that this legislation would prevent monopoly, stimulate competition, and establish rational management of the nation's finances. But, as the decade of the 1920s closed, it was clear this legislation had failed to achieve its objectives. Consolidation existed in almost every type of business, and it was particularly evident in industries that had developed since the early period of consolidation (e.g., automobiles, chemicals, aluminum, motion pictures, radio, and electric-power utilities). Business consolidation continued and the level of capital was strengthened; but the power of organized labor declined and the prices for agricultural products continued to drop, with no comparable decrease in manufactured goods, and taxes increased. Considerable capital had been used for industrial development, but it was not converted proportionately into wage and salary and, therefore, was not spent on consumer goods. Employment did not keep up with capital development or the population growth. Some industries overexpanded and others never fully recovered from the postwar economy. In addition, the European economy had not recovered from World War I, and could not buy a sufficient amount of goods from the United States to help the situation. The industrial boom stimulated an unprecedented amount of speculation that resulted in the stock market crash of October 29, 1929, and that was followed by economic decline that continued unabated until the spring of 1932 (see any number of American histories or special sources written on this period such as Schlesinger, 1959; Kindleberger, 1986; Brunner, 1981; or Watkins, 1993).

Although much is written about this period and the New Deal of Franklin Roosevelt, certain conclusions seem reasonable. The extent of the decline in the economy was crippling. Business fell to 60 percent of normal, exports to their lowest level in 30 years, banks failed in large numbers (1,400 failed in 1932), and unemployment rose to between 13 million and 17 million people. Roosevelt engineered a four year battle against unemployment, insecurity, and economic distress with legislation that became known as the "New Deal" and was in reality an effort toward a planned economy (Faulkner, 1948). It began early with a call for legislation to regulate agriculture and followed two months later with a request for legislation to organize industry and commerce under federal authority. The principles underlying the "First New Deal were that the technological revolution had rendered bigness inevitable; that competition could no longer be relied on to protect social interests; that large units were an opportunity to be seized rather than a danger to be fought; and that the formula for stability in the new society must be combination and cooperation under enlarged federal authority" (Schlesinger, 1959, p. 179).

Roosevelt's financial program, completed largely during his first term, had three goals: (a) control inflation, (b) banking reform, and (c) better supervision over the security commodity exchanges. There followed banking legislation (e.g., Emergency Banking Act of March 9, 1933; Glass-Steagall Act of 1933), National Industrial Recovery Act (NIRA), June, 1933, to provide employment and stimulate industry, legislation to relieve unemployment (e.g., Civilian Conservation Corps, Emergency Relief Act, NIRA that established the Public Works Administration, Workers Program Administration that provided employment for as many as 8,500,000 persons), the Social Security Act of 1935 to provide for workers in their old age, and the National Labor Relations Act that the Supreme Court upheld in 1937. Agriculture was supported by the Farm Relief and Inflation Act, Agricultural Adjustment Administration (concentrated on reduction of cotton, wheat, corn, and hog production that was later extended to beef, dairy cattle, peanuts, rye, barley, flax, grain sorghum, sugar beets, and sugar cane). Extreme draught in 1934 and the dust storms in 1935 were cause for the creation of the Soil Conservation Service in 1935 and the Soil Conservation and Allotment Act in 1936.

The New Deal moved primarily to prevent further disintegration of the economic system by achieving balance between agriculture and industry, wage earner and employer, consumer and producer. Although many moved in support of such programs reluctantly, the emergency was so great that few opposed it openly for some time; and Roosevelt and the Democratic Party were overwhelmingly supported in the next elections.

The Great Depression of the 1930s produced a program of government support for scholarly activities in the social and humanistic fields (Curti, 1989; Watkins, 1993) and, while jobs were scarce, encouraged many to remain in student status.

World War II

World War II involved the world in the most lethal war in history. Only with Churchill's leadership did Britain avoid a disaster similar to France. The development and coordination of the production capacity of the

United States under Roosevelt's leadership was the major factor in achieving victory for the United States and its allies.

In World War I, the United States transported two million men to Europe where they relied heavily on English and French equipment with which to fight. In World War II, the United States sent four million men to different places in the world; and, in addition to equipping them, also outfitted other allied forces. Other results included hospitals, camps, roads, machinery, and medicines. During the war a number of products were cut off or in scarce supply, requiring U.S. industry to find other means for producing needed products (e.g., the synthetic rubber industry was created from scratch). Perhaps among the many results of the single greatest production effort the world had ever known, however, was the development of the atomic bomb that could be produced by assembly line techniques (see Miller, 1958).

Although American mobilization and concentration on the War was never as complete as that of Germany, Britain, or Russia, and American losses in human life and material were not as great as that of the enemy or the Allies, it was undoubtedly the most difficult war in the American experience to that time. Pearl Harbor united the nation more completely than any other previous event in our history and resurrected a sense of purpose that has been retained to the present day, fueled by the responsibility for being the first user of an atomic weapon. It also led to the confinement of 112,000 persons of Japanese origin, two-thirds of whom were American born, and the loss of their homes and property.

World War II brought to a halt higher education as it had been known with the induction of millions of people into the armed forces and other phases of the war effort. Not only were many potential students occupied fighting a war, but faculties were depleted as well. It did not close down institutions of higher learning, however, and scientific activity, particularly in support of the war effort, was continued. Franklin Roosevelt's decision early in World War II to use the talent and facilities of the universities rather than build separate laboratories for war research would have a major impact on the future role of higher education in American society, creating a university-government partnership. Women and African Americans as a class experienced significant changes as a result of the war effort, too (Chafe, 1991).

The war completed the nation's economic recovery, putting millions of people to work in industry or inducting them into the armed services. Few periods have experienced such prosperity, and this prosperity produced social change that continued into the postwar years. In 1944 Congress enacted what is known as the "G.I. Bill of Rights." In addition to providing billions of dollars for veterans' medical care, for housing through federally guaranteed veterans' mortgages, it made a college education and professional training available to qualified veterans almost fully at government expense.

As early as 1941, Franklin Roosevelt and Secretary of State Cordell Hull sought support for a permanent world organization. The final details of the United Nations Charter were arranged in the spring of 1945 at a general meeting in San Francisco with delegates from 46 nations in attendance. The first meetings of the United Nations were held in London in 1946, but the world organization was soon permanently located in New York City. Although often limited to being a "debating society" in which the voices of even small nations could be heard, it did on occasion rise above the interests of individual nations to influence efforts for world peace. Perhaps the greatest failure of the United Nations was its inability to control the use and production of atomic weapons. This led to a world wide arms race particularly among so called super powers that has continued to this day. Despite the inadequacies inherent in its structure and its failures, however, it is difficult to consider where the world might be without it.

Truth and Knowledge

What began in the 1890s increased rapidly during the first two decades of the twentieth century. Reform and Conservative Darwinists both believed in the involvement of biological and social structures. They differed, however, in their view of the means and the speed by which it should happen. Intellectuals and professionals deserted the "stand-pat Conservatism" of the Civil War era and joined the "main stream liberal dissent" and gave it both moral and intellectual leadership (Hofstadter, 1965, p. 149).

In the midst of this fluctuating climate, the American clergy worked out a Reform Darwinian interpretation that linked religion to reform (Goldman, 1955). The clergy had been clear losers in the competition for status, resulting in a decline in the influence of the ministerial role and a lowered standard of living. Their turn toward reform and social criticism may have been as much a result of their suffering the living conditions a lowered status produced as it was their concern for social problems and a desire to improve the world (Hofstadter, 1965). While the power and influence of the clergy was falling, it was rising for the academic as evidenced by the following: Richard Ely's (1894-1895) reform attack on orthodox economics; Thorstein Veblen's publication in 1899 of *The Theory of the Leisure Class*; Edward A. Ross' sociology that was clearly Reform Darwinism in character and dismissed Conservative Darwinism as a rationalization of greed; Franz Boas' anthropology that destroyed any argument for absolute ideas, and particularly for racism; the development of professional teachers of the law as an independent group outside of the field of practicing law that influenced the young men graduating from the good law schools to develop a social view of their function as lawyers; Charles A. Beard and Arthur F. Bently's political science that saw the state as an instrument that registered the social pressures brought to bear upon it by various interest groups; and John Dewey's efforts in philosophy to convert ideas into social change.

The election of 1912, for the first time, pitted two progressives against each other for the office of president of the United States. The former professor, Woodrow Wilson, defeated Teddy Roosevelt; and Wilson quickly sent many reform bills through Congress. But his program, perhaps, was best symbolized by the appointment at the end of his first term of Louis Brandeis to the Supreme Court. Brandeis was not only the first progressive to be appointed to the Supreme Court, but he was also the first Jew and the first Zionist (Goldman, 1955).

During this period Americans witnessed: Freud's first lecture at Clark University in 1909; the introduction of modern art to New Yorkers at the now legendary Armory Show in 1913; Walter Lippmann's first two books published by 1914; the scientific alteration of training in agriculture to an extent previously unprecedented, and after 1905 the steady rise in numbers of students studying agriculture in land-grant colleges until by the First World War they almost equaled the number of engineers; the LaFollette era (synonymous with progressivism) in full swing in Wisconsin during the first decade of the twentieth century (by the time he left for the Senate of the United States in 1906, the name of LaFollette was magic in Wisconsin); organization in 1881 and reorganization in 1886 of the American Federation of Labor and labor unions that had become an established fact with a membership reaching 1,676,000 in 1904; Upton Sinclair's novel *The Jungle* (1906) that dealt with the stockyards and was perhaps the most powerful in its immediate effects, although there were other influential novels, such as Frank Norris' *The Octopus* (1901), picturing the struggle between farmers and the railroad, and *The Pit* (1903), a story of grain speculation in the Chicago exchange.

Philosophical Orientation

During the twentieth century there have been three recognizable orientations. These three orientations were Traditionalism, Positivism, and Experimentalism. Traditionalists believed in an absolute separation between the person and the physical world, between mind and matter, and denied the validity of evolutionary theory. Positivists viewed the person as a machine whose behavior could be predicted and in time controlled, but saw humans as an inherent part of nature. Experimentalists differed from the first two, drawing upon the philosophical thought of naturalism, empiricism, and American pragmatism and attempted to build a theory of education that included the new social sciences. Experimentalists rejected the traditional dualism of man-nature, mind-body, individual-society and viewed science to mean human beings are an integral part of nature. These three recognizable orientations have affected education at all levels, and student affairs as a part of higher education is no exception, as will be shown. Partly as a reaction against progressivism and the evolutionary and scientific movement and partly as a result of the effect of World War I on social and moral values, the authority of tradition put new vigor into fundamentalistic views (Butts, 1955). Events like the various attacks on the schools for their secular and godless character and the Scopes Trial in Tennessee illustrate that fundamentalism was still a powerful force, particularly in the rural areas. Liberalism and progressivism made progress toward influencing some religious beliefs between World War I and World War II with the help of science. After World War II and again after Vietnam and the 1960s, there occurred a resurgence of neo-orthodoxy in some Protestant churches and theological schools. In addition to sectarian religious attitudes, there were other strong philosophic views that did not profess sectarian religions but did stand for strong religious values. Continuing from a historic view of idealism, rationalism, and dualism, a conservative philosophy of nature has maintained itself through most of the twentieth century. In general, this movement involved a defensive reaction to social and scientific theories. It repudiated the use of the social and natural sciences in the activities of life and took positions not too unlike the philosophy of Plato, Aristotle, and medieval Scholasticism. Traditionalists believed in an absolute distinction between human beings and the physical world, between mind and matter, and, in the extreme, denied the outcomes of evolutionary theory that the natural and social sciences had labored to establish. At that time, this focus paralleled traditional faculty psychology and presented human nature as a separate entity from other forms of life because it possessed a conscience, reason, sense of beauty, and religion. Traditionalists believed that moral consciousness is a part of a human being's original environment. Some even held that religious instinct is universal in humans and such qualities go beyond any ability of the scientific method to describe. They desired to introduce order into a chaotic world by appealing to a higher and fixed realm of values that lie behind the flux and flow of experience and, therefore, believed that the intellectual powers of discrimination and judgment were the main purpose of education (Butts, 1955). The curriculum in schools, colleges, and universities should therefore be predominantly intellectual in content and be free of worldly matters introduced by science and technical studies, from practical experience, and from the use of the freedom of interest and choice by students as a way to achieve effective learning.

Both as a response to the growing body of scientific knowledge and as a reaction to the traditionalists, many educators in twentieth century United States found in modern science their standards of authority and methods of work. This second orientation relied upon the Newtonian conceptualization of science and the Positivism of Auguste Comte and Herbert Spencer that described the universe as a machine or an elaborate clockwork mechanism, fully logical and predictable in its functioning with which supernatural and rationalistic explanation were inappropriate. Ascending to the next step, they assumed that human nature could be studied and analyzed by scientific methods with as much precision as physical phenomena. Negating the dualistic conception of human nature, *Positivists* presented the human being as a complicated machine whose behavior could be predicted and eventually controlled with accuracy and certainty once the blueprint was completed by scientific study. Although more complex than other animals, humans were an inherent part of nature. Much could be learned about human behavior from the scientific study of animals, however. Most American psychologists were brought up in a climate of scientific realism during the first half of the twentieth century (Butts, 1955).

Knowledge in the field of psychology was developing so quickly that only a few points can be noted here. Experimental and scientific methods that began in the nineteenth century developed rapidly. The work of

Thorndike (1898, 1913-1914) at Teachers College, Columbia University, was a prime mover and example of this. His insistence that learning was highly specific was a direct attack upon the "faculty" psychology that supported the concept of mental discipline. His laws of learning—by exercise and satisfying effect—led to the development of connectionist psychology that refuted the doctrine of mental discipline. Another development of this period was the creation of applied psychology to help with industrial and educational guidance, personnel selection and training, advertising, and other phases of social living. Clinical, abnormal, and later counseling psychology grew in direct response to the demand for help in a society more aware of deviation from normal behavior, and at the same time psychiatry was developing to deal with the physiological bases of this variant. Behaviorism, the most extreme approach to human beings as measurable mechanisms, gained widespread attention after World War I. Behaviorists eliminated consciousness, will, and sensation as constructs and argued for the simple measurement of the observable behavior of humans. They built most of their work on the conditioning process, beginning with Pavlov and her work with conditioned responses (Ray, 1964).

Another important psychological development that would become an important tool for use by student personnel professionals in counseling and career guidance was the continued work in applying scientific method to constructing objective and standardized tests. It became one of the popular trends of the 1920s and 1930s and was viewed as a way to make education scientific. In the years between 1905 and 1908, the French psychologists Alfred Binet and Theodore Simon (Binet & Simon, 1985; Wolf, 1973) conceived the idea of an intelligence scale, and soon educators on both sides of the Atlantic, but particularly in the United States, began to recognize that the scale concept could be applied to intelligence, aptitude, and achievement. Almost immediately, test-makers undertook to develop instruments for appraising virtually every aspect of educational practice (Cremin, 1961, 1988). During World War I, group tests of intelligence and aptitude for the Army were developed, and heavy use was continued in World War II. It was assumed that intelligence tests measured inherited capacity and not achievement—assumptions that were being questioned by the 1930s. World War II further generated the practice and development of testing to help meet the need for specialized skills and assignments (e.g., pilots, navigators, bombardiers). Following World War II, the development and use of tests in counseling and guidance activities and for entrance into college, graduate, and professional schools expanded and continues to the present day.

Ironically, the earliest challenge to the mechanistic view of the universe was issued in the early part of the twentieth century by science itself (Lucas, 1985). The work of Einstein, Planck, Bohr, Schrodinger, and Heisenberg among others began to question the assumption of an objective physical reality that lay as a basis for all previous scientific thought. The belief in a universe that extended through space and time and faith that the universe is directly accessible to investigation by a detached observer was disrupted. Particles were found to lose the essential characteristics of matter and to become like patterns of waves, raising questions with the idea some held that elementary particles constituted the ultimate components of physical reality. Increasingly, physics resorted to mathematical probabilities to describe circumstance rather than any physical constant. The verdict of the new physics was that supposed constituents of matter could not be understood in anything corresponding to physical terms. Simply stated, the structure of matter is not mechanical (Lucas, 1985).

A new point of view developed that differed from the traditional, religious, and philosophical outlook and, also, from the positivist science that most psychologists were following. This third system of thought became primarily known as *"experimentalism"* and was influenced by the work of William James, George H. Meade, Charles S. Peirce, and John Dewey (Childs, 1956). Under the long-term leadership of John Dewey, experimentalism drew heavily upon philosophical ideas in naturalism, empiricism, and particularly American pragmatism, and added new evidence from the social sciences, anthropology, psychology, and social psychology in a brave effort to design a philosophy suitable for the twentieth century. The significance of the experimentalist position for education was that it attempted to construct a theory of education that assimilated the new social science disciplines (Butts, 1955). To achieve understanding of individual behavior and to develop desirable goals for education, experimentalists believed a person must study the culture in which he or she functions. The most important characteristic of American culture was seen in its social ideals of democracy and the intellectual ideals of a free and disciplined intelligence. Experimentalism rejected the traditional dualism of man-nature, mind-body, individual-society and interpreted the findings of science to mean that human beings are an integral and essential part of nature. Humans, Experimentalists declared, are not discreet and separate from society, but as a result of participation in the social structure develop as unique personalities. Therefore, human nature was viewed as not fixed but developed in reaction to its culture, and life was a continual interactive adjustment between the individual and the surrounding environment. Behavior resulted from conditions that disrupted the equilibrium between the individual and the environment causing tension or conflict in the individual and motivating the individual to restore equilibrium by acting on the environment.

The effects of this philosophy on education at all levels were significant. It emphasized (a) achieving a greater linkage between schools in both the local and larger community, (b) the growth and development of the unique personality through experience in interaction with the environment, and (c) the wholeness of the human organism in the responses it makes. It argued that many more students should receive the opportunity and benefits of a higher education in a free society, but its emphasis on the individual student was also saying that students should not be allowed to get lost in the masses of new students who were attending schools and colleges.

Early College Residence Living

These were the early years of student personnel work; its preschool years, so to speak, in which thinking was carried out through images and symbols that did not necessarily maintain logical relationships with one another. The ability to distinguish between perceived qualitative or quantitative change and actual change had not yet developed. Student housing can best illustrate this point, perhaps, in that it was second only to student discipline as a major function for college student personnel work. In the religiously dominated colonial colleges, student housing was a necessity not only because of the young age of students, 14 to 15 years, but because everything more or less took place under one roof and was supervised by the same person(s). As the age of students was raised in subsequent years, largely as a result of the extension of the educational process and child labor practices, colleges still retained their residential character as a part of the process necessary to produce a properly educated person. For women it carried an additional protective expectation. Residence halls remained an integral part of most colleges and universities until the late nineteenth century when the influence of German higher education was injected into American higher education by a number of returning scholars who had achieved their graduate study in German institutions. These returning scholars were interested in scholarship, science, and research, and brought back with them the ideals of Continental European education. They advocated that students were mature individuals and that it was not the proper or necessary role for colleges and universities to be responsible for their out-of-class lives. They believed in the principle of *Lernfreiheit*, the freedom of the individual to learn what he or she wishes, and interpreted it to mean that students were responsible for obtaining their own education. Faculty were responsible for student learning while they were in the classroom. Housing college students became less important and even phased out in some institutions of higher learning. There was an early reaction to this viewpoint, however, that undoubtedly was influenced by the long and continued influence of the English residential colleges on American higher education. Although strongly denounced by some of his contemporaries, William Rainey Harper in 1892 assigned more than one half of the cubic space of the original University of Chicago buildings for use as residence halls (Brubacher & Rudy, 1976). He continued his efforts through the establishment of a house system that was founded on residence halls that were to have their own heads, counselors, and house committees. Columbia University built its first residence hall in 1896, and in 1907 Woodrow Wilson attempted to raise $2 million to establish residential quadrangles at Princeton. He was unable to persuade potential donors or alumni (who feared the loss of their eating clubs as a result) to his plan. Cornell University added residence halls in 1914. Housing units were already in place at Harvard and Yale. Women's colleges had always housed their students on campus and, as a result of staff who migrated to other institutions, they were a strong force of advocacy for residence halls (Mueller, 1961).

Residence halls were also a logical extension of the disciplinary responsibility over student lives delegated to the early student personnel offices. It was not a progressive versus conservative issue, however, and as many progressives could be found on one side of the issue as the other. College student personnel staff were not the determiners of policy. They were largely hired to carry out the educational design of the president and the institution and seem not to have reasoned very much, if at all, about it. Student personnel staff, however, were undoubtedly integrating the experience as the field matured.

It should be pointed out that residence living became less important to the complex research university as a part of its educational program as time progressed. It does illustrate the early attempt to create progressive learning experiences while retaining a conservative framework within which to do it. Results were mixed and have continued to be mixed. Student housing was also supported by middle-class values and, because of its early relationship with student affairs, had much to do with the integration of a middle-class value structure in student affairs ideology. It was a clear result of parents' desire for institutions of higher learning to remain an extension of the family.

Growing Complexity

At the beginning of the twentieth century, the elective system in colleges and universities was seen as the solution to problems with the college curriculum. A growing volume of knowledge and the increasing number of students seeking a higher education in a new democracy had led to a wide acceptance of this method, but it soon became burdened with specific requirements (e.g., hours, credits, prerequisites). As new programs were rapidly added, the maze became increasingly complex. Both conservatives and progressives agreed that there were problems with the free elective system, that too many highly specialized courses with narrow subject matter had been created, but they differed considerably about what the common elements should be and how the solutions could be achieved. For example, the growing general education movement that proposed to provide greater integration through stressing common bodies of knowledge ranged from the conservative proposals of Robert Maynard Hutchins (1936b) at the University of Chicago to the experimentalist proposals of progressive education that followed John Dewey. Between these two extremes, most college educators achieved some type of compromise between the principles of election and prescription. Revisions were generally aimed at (a) revision of course requirements, (b) giving more attention to individual students, and (c) breaking down narrow subject matter fields and developing the study of larger, more related areas of knowledge (Butts, 1955).

During this period between World Wars I and II, college student personnel was developing both its philosophy and its practice. The continued development and expansion of student housing was best represented by the program at Harvard and Yale in the late 1920s made possible by the support of the millionaire philanthropist Edward S. Harkness (Brubacher & Rudy, 1976). It resulted in units called "houses" at Harvard and "colleges" at Yale to house between 250 and 300 upperclassmen under the direction of resident masters and faculty. Each unit included its own dining room, common room, library, and athletic facilities, with students reportedly assigned on a heterogeneous basis with regard to race, creed, economic status, geographical origin, or field of specialization. But, a problem existed that has repeated itself many times since. The money donated was for buildings only, and staff and program needs had to find support elsewhere.

The reading of this literature leads the writer to conclude that, despite the many worthy efforts made to develop residence hall living for college students, its ideals were seldom fully realized. Although by 1939 three-fourths of the institutions evaluated for accreditation by the North Central Association reported efforts to vitalize their student housing facilities (Brubacher & Rudy, 1976), there is evidence to indicate that a growing number of less visible college students were residing in noncampus housing. It has been the small liberal arts college with its traditional residential campus that has come closest to achieving residence hall living in its more ideal state.

A Broadening of the Profession

Concern for the welfare of the individual student brought about the addition of other student personnel functions such as placement centers, health services, and counseling. In some locales, colleges placed intramural and some intercollegiate athletics under student personnel management. Student activities and student government were also growing areas of focus by student personnel staff.

Fenske (1980) has indicated that it was this period, specifically from the end of World War I to the beginning of the depression of the 1930s, that held the greatest promise for full integration of student personnel with the vital functions of higher education. He clearly felt that this did not happen nor has it happened any time since. He further stated that the depression of the 1930s "struck a crushing blow to the student personnel movement's attempt to reintegrate academic and character development on the nation's campuses" (Fenske, 1980, p. 21). The evidence for this interpretation is questionable. It is clear that the battle lines over what should be the nature of higher learning were once again drawn. The economic depression of the 1930s created a willingness in people to reassess their social and educational philosophy. On one side of the debate was Robert M. Hutchins (1936b), president of the University of Chicago, and his followers. Hutchins believed that human nature was the same everywhere and intellectual excellence was always the proper aim of education in all societies. This was a different conceptualization compared to nineteenth century mental discipline and resembled more that of Aristotle or St. Thomas Aquinas glorifying the life of the mind. "Education implies teaching. Teaching implies knowledge. Knowledge is truth. The truth is everywhere the same. Hence education should be everywhere the same" (Hutchins, 1936a, pp. 66-67). Science could not be ignored, but the educational priority was clearly placed on philosophy. One of the very first to disagree with Hutchins' *Higher Learning in America* was John Dewey (Brubacher & Rudy, 1976). Dewey saw in it a threat to the intellectual freedom of learning in higher education. A pupil of Dewey's, Sidney Hook (1946), further questioned the rationalist-humanist position and disagreed with their conception of human nature and its application to educational theory. The most serious difference that Dewey and Progressives had with the Chicago school of thought was about the relationship of theory to practice. They did not believe that concepts could be taught or learned separate from the context that they represented. They drew their more flexible premises from democracy, progressivism, and pragmatism. Undoubtedly, higher education became what it is today as a result of striving to meet the needs of the people in the United States, and development of this philosophical position carried over into the growth of student personnel work. This debate was not made moot by the depression, as Fenske (1980) believed. Although a number of student personnel functions were curtailed and in many instances even eliminated, as was true in other areas of higher education, it not only survived but continued to develop its rationale.

Student Personnel Work as Progressive Education

The most clear indication of the influence that progressive education had on student personnel work is seen in *The Student Personnel Point of View* published in 1937 by the American Council on Education (ACE) as a result of a conference sponsored by ACE and attended by both faculty and practitioners. This document defined student personnel work and presented a statement of purpose that was distributed widely to members of the higher education community. Although already in the latter stages of its life as an organized movement, *The Student Personnel Point of View* is as clear an embodiment of the progressive education philosophy as can by found in higher education. It stated that imposed upon educational institutions was ". . . the obligation to consider the student as a whole—his intellectual capacity and achievement, his emotional make-up, his physical condition, his social relationships, his vocational aptitudes and skills, his moral and religious values, his economic resources, and his esthetic appreciations" (ACE, 1937, p. 1). In short, it emphasized the student as a whole rather than in intellectual training alone, and it prescribed 23 "services" that an "effective educational program includes—in one form or another— "to achieve this end (ACE, 1937, p. 3). It emphasized that not only should students be helped to select and gain admission to an institution suited to meet their needs, but that they should be helped to find appropriate employment upon leaving college. Clearly, reflecting the social ideals of democracy, college was a part of the "opportunity" in this land, and students should be helped to succeed with it in every possible way. The document is also a strong statement of middle-class values emphasizing supervision in almost every phase of student life. Reflected throughout the document was the Experimentalists' assertion that human beings were not discreet and separate from society but developed as unique personalities as a result of participation in the social structure. It embodied the Experimentalist's philosophy of achieving greater linkage between institution and community, of the growth of a unique personality through interacting with the environment, of the wholeness of the human organism, and of the individual student not being allowed to get lost among the masses of students.

Although the *Student Personnel Point of View* reflected the Experimentalist's clear rejection of the mind-body, individual-society, knowledge-action dualism, it did not escape the "in class-out of class" dualism that continues to plague the field. The best it could offer was coordination between instruction and student services and to call for research that would, kin addition to student out-of-class life, also study faculty-student relationships—but only "outside of class." In almost every respect it was a remarkable document, but it did establish the concept of "student services" that has continued to haunt the field to the present day. The concept of a service organization does not support a professional image, and, in time, each service unit would establish its own boundaries to achieve survival.

A little over a decade later ACE sponsored a review of the 1937 document. A committee of 12 student personnel practitioners and faculty was convened in 1948 under the Chairmanship of E. G. Williamson, and they issued a revision of the original "brochure" (American Council on Education, 1949). The resulting revision was an eloquent and almost passionate continuation of the Experimentalist philosophy that had undergirded the original document.

> The student personnel point of view encompasses the student as a whole. The concept of education is broadened to include attention to the student in well-rounded development—physically, socially, emotionally and spiritually as well as intellectually. The student is thought of as a responsible participant in his own development and not as a passive recipient of an imprinted economic, political, or religious doctrine, or vocational skill. As a responsible participant in the societal processes of our American democracy, his full and balanced maturity is viewed as a major end-goal of education and, as well, a necessary means to the fullest development of his fellow-citizens. From the personnel point of view any lesser goal falls short of the desired objective of democratic educational processes, and is a real drain and strain upon the self-realization of other developing individuals in our society. (pp. 1-2)

In addition, the new document noted three objectives that were adapted from the 1947 Report of the President's Commission on Higher Education: (a) "Education for a fuller realization of democracy in every phase of living," (b) "Education directly and explicitly for international understanding and cooperation," and (c) "Education for the application of creative imagination and trained intelligence to the solution of social problems and to the administration of public affairs" (ACE, 1949, p. 1). Undoubtedly, they reflected the nation's experience with the just-concluded World War II.

The revised document achieved a better balance between the individual and the environment, and between the concept of a developing society and a developing individual. It emphasized concepts of "optimum development of the individual" (p. 3), "individual's full and balanced development" (p. 3), "development is conditioned by many factors" (p. 6), and "the college should make optimum provision for the development of the individual and a place in society" (p. 11). This was the period that saw the beginnings of the human potential movement, and this emphasis on the developing student is first evidence of the beginning of the student development focus in student personnel.

The Student Personnel Point of View (ACE, 1949) seemed to attempt a decreased emphasis on the term "services," substituting in some places words like "program" (p. 3), "Elements" (p. 11), and "functions" (p. 14); but it by no means eliminated this concept nor did it resolve the "classroom" and "out-of-classroom" dilemma. In fact, it seemed to extend it and, if anything, broaden it into a curricular-cocurricular dualism. Despite these inherent weaknesses, this was a strong and literate statement that would stand as a rationale and foundation for the field and remains amazingly contemporary in many of its ideas. Before student development would become the guiding philosophy for the field that it is today, however, it was necessary for further integration of knowledge to occur that would mature the profession and its thought.

Summary

The twentieth century began with a battle being waged between the progressives and the conservatives. The impact of Herbert Spencer upon American intellectuals was considerable, and progressives worked out a new philosophy more compatible with democratic ideals. Reform Darwinism was a response designed to break the lock of conservatives on the door to opportunity for everyone, and a period of democratic reform followed. Despite the Great Depression, the period between the two world wars was one of growth in new knowledge and a growing reliance upon scientific discovery.

Although at one point the German influence had its advocates in higher education, it never really took hold in the United States. Families sending their youngsters away to college had strong expectations about the care and supervision they would receive. As a result student residence living and the disciplinary process were the major stones upon which College Student Personnel built its foundation. It was not until 1937, at the peak of the progressive education movement, that it created a rationale for itself with the document *The Student Personnel Point of View*. This statement unquestionably was a product of progressive education, which had grown out of a reform movement begun around the beginning of the twentieth century thereby making College Student Personnel a child of a reform movement. Like children, however, it was expected to be seen and not heard by the rest of higher education. But, like children, too, it performed in this manner only externally and would provide internally a strong force for reform and change in higher education that continues to the present day.

Chapter III

The Modern Era

Chapter III will trace the events that have occurred after World War II. It will show that student affairs has continued to develop within an Experimentalist philosophy and, despite conservative criticism and press, that student affairs has maintained a reasonably progressive approach to education. A review of the 50 years following World War II demonstrates that the human world has become much more complex, it is more subject to rapid and substantial changes, and changes of a significant nature are no more predictable today than they ever were.

The opening of higher education to nearly everyone who might seek it helped bring about a democratization of higher education and society. New cultural perspectives have created new interpretations of social developments and a belief in relativism about truth (Appleby et al., 1994). The nature of what is believed to be the truth about the nation's social, political, and economic developments and educational system of which student affairs is a part goes a long way to explain beliefs about present conditions.

Throughout the history of the United States, Americans have generally believed they have a distinct mission to impart their values and beliefs to the rest of the world. Although all countries strive to put the best face possible on their military and diplomatic behaviors, the United States seems to feel more strongly than others the need to see their involvement in the world as altruistic and in the best interest of freedom and democracy for all people (e.g., the Mexican War of 1846-48 was clearly provoked by the United States to secure large amounts of land but was characterized as the fulfillment of its mission to extend democracy to those without it; World War I was fought as a war that would "end all wars" but a victory by England and France over Germany was clearly economically and politically in the best interests of the United States). There is a deep reluctance in the United States to use arguments of self-interest as a basis for foreign policy, but other nations have operated with few such constraints. Following the conclusion of World War II, the Soviet Union and the United States saw their foreign policies involve a combination of self-interest and ideological principles, but historians suggest that principles were far more important in the formation of American foreign policy than they were for the Soviet Union (see Chafe, 1991; Diggins, 1988; Matusow, 1984). U.S. presidents have had to remember when conducting foreign policy, and even entering war after being attacked, to place a moral interpretation on this action much higher than simple self-preservation. This writing is not the place to analyze the role of moral issues in the conduct of foreign policy by nations, but it is sufficient to say that at the conclusion of the war the Soviet Union and the United States had a different view of the world and their own self-interest.

Roosevelt had used his considerable political skills to negotiate with the Soviet Union, but Truman took a much tougher stance. The international situation was like a poker game, Truman told one friend, and he was not going to let Stalin beat him (McCullough, 1992). The atomic bomb was perhaps the most significant issue that influenced not only the end of the war but the negotiations and political maneuvering that followed. The final breakdown of United States-Soviet relations resulted from the failure to achieve agreement on international control of atomic energy. The first six months of 1946 saw a series of events, war-like in nature, that were accompanied by inflammatory rhetoric. In March of 1946, Winston Churchill accompanied by Truman declared in Fulton, Missouri, that "from Stetting in the Baltic to Trieste in the Adriatic, an iron curtain has descended across the [European] continent." The Truman Doctrine and the Marshall Plan formed the major thrust to the implementation of U.S. foreign policy that was aimed at preventing a Soviet Union takeover of Europe. In 1947 Russia moved quickly to establish communist governments and achieve complete control of Eastern Europe. Russia instituted a year-long blockade of all supplies to Berlin to protest the West's decision to unify its occupation zones in Germany and institute currency reform. Before the end of spring, the Brussels Pact brought together the major Western European powers in a mutual defense pact that a year later provided the basis for the North Atlantic Treaty Organization (NATO). The cold war had begun.

The cold war can best be seen as an ideological conflict between the two major powers in the world, the United States and the Soviet Union. The Soviets interpreted events through Marxist-Leninist ideology that tended to result in their perception of any stable situation as "inherently contradictory and thus pregnant with the seeds of inevitable conflict between communism and capitalism" (Diggins, 1988, p. 72). The United States drew upon Wilsonian principles that declared national self-determination, representative government, free enterprise, and free elections have universal relevance. As a result, Russia claimed to defend "socialism," whereas the United States believed it was defending the "free world." It was within this climate that the Truman Doctrine was proclaimed—the commitment of the United States to assist any country struggling against the forces of communism.

In 1945 the formation of the United Nations offered the greatest hope for peace. In 1947 a decision to focus on Europe as the main defense perimeter led to the development and implementation of the Marshall Plan. The program called upon European nations to cooperate in a plan of mutual assistance to the best of their ability, and pledged the United States to contribute substantially to whatever remaining aid was necessary, which was estimated to be roughly $17 billion. The plan was to succeed in achieving its two objectives of integration and restoration and laid the foundation for what was later to become the European Common Market. It succeeded, too, in achieving its political objectives. By facilitating industrial recovery, it reduced the danger that prolonged economic chaos would undermine democratic government in Western Europe. A policy of containment that was constructed around the theoretical constructs of George F. Kennan influenced Truman's cold-war diplomacy.

At the same time, Mao Tse-tung was demonstrating that communist movements could succeed independently of Moscow despite what communist theory had indicated and that peasants could win revolutionary struggles on their own without the support of urban workers. In 1949 the world learned that China had been overrun by communism. As a result, between the Union of Soviet Socialist Republics (USSR) and China, approximately 13 to 14 million square miles of land mass and more than 750 million people, an estimated one-third of the world's population, were controlled by communism. At the conclusion of World War II, Korea was divided at the 38th parallel. The USSR controlled the area north of this line and the United States the south. In June, 1950, North Korea sent seven divisions and 150 tanks to attack South Korea. Truman immediately saw the invasion as an act of aggression that must be resisted or other communist leaders would be encouraged to undertake similar actions. Although Truman went before Congress to explain his actions and marshalled the support of two-thirds of the nation, he acted without official congressional approval. The U.N. Security Council, with the Russian delegate absent, condemned the invasion and called upon the world to assist South Korea. A number of nations did send combat divisions (including the British Commonwealth countries, France, Greece, Turkey, Belgium, the Netherlands, the Philippines, and Thailand), bringing into direct full-scale conflict for the first time in the cold war the forces of the communist and noncommunist world. Objectives of the U.N. forces were never defined, however, and many countries sent only token forces, making the war (although undeclared) largely an American effort. It would be the first modern war that the United States failed to win, ending in stalemate and frustration with a truce finally achieved in July, 1953, with the 38th parallel established again as the dividing line (see Diggins, 1988).

Postwar Years

Political Climate

After Franklin Roosevelt's death, Harry Truman had pledged to carry forward the liberal policies of the fallen president. The legislative program of social reforms he proposed to Congress in 1945—a full employment bill, a higher minimum wage, and national housing legislation—seemed to be evidence of this. But, his approach and political style were different. He appointed to his cabinet both conservatives and moderates in an attempt to improve relationships between the executive branch and Congress. Although Truman repeatedly urged Congress to enact an agenda of reform, his appointment of businessmen, corporate lawyers, bankers, and military men to important government posts made liberals uneasy. In the 1946 fall election, Republicans won control of both the House and Senate and the road to rapid social reform seemed closed. Labor quickly became disillusioned by Truman's seeming nonsupport. Franklin Roosevelt's economic bill of rights (i.e., national health insurance, full employment, improved social programs) was all but lost.

Many had seen the threat of communism influencing policies of the New Deal, but after World War II the politics of anticommunism achieved a new high. The House Committee on Un-American Activities (HUAC), first established in 1938 to investigate anti-American propaganda, was made a permanent standing committee; and the Smith Act, passed in 1940, created the means to prosecute anyone who even advocated communism. The Truman Doctrine to fight communism abroad was to expose all subversives, and the efforts of government officials such as J. Edgar Hoover of the Federal Bureau of Investigation (FBI) supported the HUAC in its work to identify communist influence in American society, attracting widespread media attention. Disregard for civil liberties was frequent, and the politics of anticommunism dominated American political life after 1948. Over a four year period, Senator Joseph McCarthy of Wisconsin terrorized Washington; and in 1950, shortly after the beginning of the Korean Conflict, Congress, over Truman's veto, passed the McCarran Act, which required communists to register with the government, revoked the passports of anyone suspected of communist sympathies, and established authority to construct concentration camps to contain subversives in the event of a national emergency. Any activity or program that could be characterized as deviating from total conservative Americanism was open to attack for reflecting the communist party line. Whether it was civil rights groups or the women in New York fighting to retain day-care centers or modern art, any effort to achieve social reform was sufficient to make a person, in Joseph Mccarthy's words, one of those "egg-sucking phony liberals," one of those "communists and queers," one of those "pinkos" (Rovere, 1959). American foreign policy was designed to contain the Soviet Union and was supported from within by a fear of anyone who might give support to communism. The result was a moral and social rigidity that thwarted any real social reform for some time to come.

Intellectuals, many of whom were in colleges and universities, were not the primary target of McCarthy's constant attacks. He was after bigger game, but universities were often targeted by right wing critics and, when caught in the line of fire, it delighted his followers (Hofstadter, 1962). It was part reaction to social status and part a "reflection of the old Jacksonian dislike of specialists and experts" (Hofstadter, 1962, p. 14). The intellectual climate on college campuses was affected by this reactionary response.

Although large numbers of GIs were on the college campuses, the attention of Americans was directed elsewhere other than on the problems of education. There were major concerns about support for higher education. Truman appointed the Zook Commission in 1946 to make recommendations about higher education. Much of the Commission's time was centered on increasing educational opportunity and how far the Commission should go in proposing remedies for discrimination and segregation practices. Attention was given to recommendations to reorganize higher education and develop statewide systems of tuition-free community colleges. The Office of Education (OE) used the results of the Zook Commission to focus primarily on creating a student aid bill that would include undergraduate scholarships and graduate fellowships to be administered by state commissions as agents of the federal government. A loan program was also proposed. So much concern existed about details of the bill that it did not reach Congress until August of 1950, where it fared no better than had attempts to pass elementary and secondary education bills (Kerr, 1989).

Truman's opposition to the McCarran Act, the House Un-American Activities Committee, and McCarthyism in general was courageous behavior, and he took McCarthy on fearlessly in states like Massachusetts where McCarthy had a strong following. Truman's integrity as a person was unquestionable. His administration was not without its share of corruption, however, and it was a major campaign issue for the Republicans in the 1952 election. Although later to become something of a folk hero, he was never a popular president during his term of office, and his final years were difficult. His plans for national health insurance were opposed by the medical profession and federal aid to education was only successful later when the Russian space program shocked the United States into action. He had appointed a civil rights committee that produced a report used by his administration to support civil rights and end discrimination. He demonstrated his belief in equality as a principle to be sought. He could take pride that the postwar economic collapse expected by many did not occur. Incomes instead were rising and, with the G. I. Bill, eight million Americans had attended college (McCullough, 1992).

The 1952 election not only elected Dwight D. Eisenhower as president but gave Republicans control of both houses (48 to 47 in the Senate and 221 to 212 in the House). The Democratic candidate, Adlai Stevenson, showed considerable moral courage during the campaign speaking out against McCarthy, but Eisenhower had coordinated the allied invasion of

Europe in World War II and had the advantage of an image that included both "hero" and strong leadership. Eisenhower refused to criticize McCarthy's anticommunist crusade. Eisenhower's running mate, Richard Nixon, was discovered to have been receiving secret political contributions from a group of wealthy Californians that produced the now famous "checkers" speech by Nixon on television in which he referred to his daughter's dog. He told the audience that regardless of what people thought they were going to keep the dog. Image, however, was becoming important in national politics. General Eisenhower presented a warm and winning smile, dignified poise and personal charm, and above all the ability to reassure people that in their beliefs they were safe from the confusion that surrounded them. "Ike" was the invincible war hero at a time when the country was divided over progress toward concluding the Korean Conflict and wanted a leader to restore stability and confidence in the country.

The Eisenhower administration was characterized by his own personal style that was notable for its refusal to engage in controversial issues. He was skillful in turning what seemed to be mistakes to his own advantage, and he was in full control and knew what he was doing in his term of office. He failed, however, to use his considerable political power to deal with important social problems that would haunt the country long after he was out of office (e.g., civil rights, poverty, medical care).

Americans were concerned about the threat of radioactivity in the event of an attack by a foreign power or an accident at home in the handling of one of the powerful weapons of mass destruction in the U.S. arsenal. British author Neil Shute (1957) wrote *On the Beach*, which was later made into a movie depicting the final days of human existence resulting from a thermonuclear war. In 1957 Congress began hearings that would lead to new knowledge and information about the effects of radiation. The Federal Civil Defense Administration distributed one million copies of a pamphlet about radioactive fallout. Throughout the country there was an effort to maintain a civil defense program in which many colleges and universities participated, with food, water, and medical supplies stored in what was hoped were safe places in the event of such an emergency. It was not unusual in many institutions of higher learning for students to walk along underground corridors and see such supplies stored in clearly labeled boxes. Many families built bomb shelters. It was estimated that about 5 percent of the population may have had bomb shelters or had made structural changes or additions to their homes to prepare for survival, and another 20 per cent had stockpiled food and emergency supplies (Diggins, 1988).

Business and the Economy

The pace of social reform in the immediate years after World War II was exceedingly slow and a disappointment to many minorities and women who had expected to continue the movement toward equality commenced during the war. The country's economic prosperity was another matter.

The growth of the American economy was the single most impressive development of the postwar years. Between 1945 and 1960, the gross national product grew 250 percent, and the average real income for American workers increased as much as it had in the previous half century. The nation entered a consumption period that Rostow (1990) referred to as the "high mass consumption" stage of economic development. Short-term credit grew from $8.4 billion in 1946 to $45.6 billion in 1958, and nearly 60 percent of the American people were defined as having achieved a "middle-class" standard of living by the middle 1950s (Chafe, 1991). By the end of the decade, 75 percent of American families owned a car and a washing machine, and 87 percent owned their own television (TV) set. The G. I. Bill provided guaranteed loans to veterans to establish businesses or buy a home at low interest rates or to pursue an education. The government was primary sponsor of the efforts that achieved discoveries in science and technology that generated new industries (e.g., nuclear physics, electronics, chemicals, aerospace), and these industries experienced tremendous growth. This period saw the beginning and development of a new industry in computer technology after Harvard University produced the first general purpose computer in 1944 that consisted of 500 miles of wire and 750,000 parts. It was to be rendered obsolete, however, only two years later by the introduction of the first electronic computer. Career opportunities were rapidly changing. The number of factory workers fell 4 percent during the 1950s; clerical workers increased by 23 percent; engineers increased by 370 percent; and scientists by 930 percent.

As a result of cold war tensions and the commencement of fighting in Korea in 1950, government continued to be a primary source of support of new jobs and further research and development. In 1956 the nation's economy "crossed the line from an industrial to a 'post-industrial' state with white-collar workers outnumbering blue-collar workers for the first time" (Chafe, 1991, p. 114). Organized labor began to weaken as it grew conservative and focused on the traditional approach to unionism. Salaried middle-class workers increased 61 percent, and a new managerial class was emerging. The economy was becoming dominated by a handful of very large corporations like General Motors and American Telephone and

Telegraph (AT&T). Ford Motor Company in 1956 went public selling stock to more than 250,000 investors. The age of the organization had arrived. William Whyte in his book *The Organization Man* (1956) warned of the dangers of individual managers subverting themselves too much to the organization and of losing the values of individualism. In the same vein, Riesman, Glazer, and Denney (1956) warned of the loss of "inner-directedness" as a result of the social dominance of the group to which the person related and "other-directedness" becoming the basic characteristic of the new middle-class.

A housing boom resulted as marriages doubled and easy housing loans were available through the Veterans Administration (VA) and Farm and Home Administration (FHA). Between 1950 and 1960, more than 13 million homes were built in the United States and 18 million people moved to the suburbs, whereas the population increase during this period was only 28 million. Levittown communities in Pennsylvania and New York came to symbolize the uniform four-room box-like houses built on uniform streets inhabited by people of the same social class and age group. The move to suburbia increased the need for the automobile and between 1945 and 1960 the number of cars in the country increased 133 percent. In 1956 Congress appropriated $32 billion under the Highways Act to construct 41,000 miles of highway. During this same period, advertising increased 400 percent (three times the nation's annual investment in higher education) and a new culture of consumerism was developing (Chafe, 1991). As John Kenneth Galbraith (1958, 1967) indicated, producing firms sought to control, manage, and shape market behaviors so that they in fact created demand for the products they produced. Rostow (1990) argued that when human beings reasoned that their physical environment was "subject to knowable consistent laws" they began to "manipulate" it to their economic advantage (p. 90). Unemployment was at a low level and the lowest unemployment rate was reached during the Korean War, 1950-1953 (Vatter, 1963). A good portion of the new consumerism resulted from increased opportunities for recreation (e.g., four million boats were purchased in the 1950s), and people in large numbers traveled both at home and abroad. The motel industry income increased by 2,300 percent between 1939 and 1958.

Social Life

The symbol of social life in suburbia became the outdoor barbecue grill, with almost every household owning at least one. Suburban life was shaped within an environment of tract house developments that faced on a common street and often with a shared backyard. Picture windows provided a view of everyone's movements, and new residents were greeted by the "welcome wagon." Evenings in good weather witnessed a community walk in which neighbors discussed everything from problems with their lawn to what was new at the school their children attended, and those who did not emerge from their homes to participate were viewed as strange and unfriendly. Suburban community life was structured around cooperation and volunteerism. Parents came together to work with and support school activities (e.g., need for new playground equipment or library materials) and church membership grew to 110 million before 1960. If so desired, between school and church, a family could have little time left for anything else. Bowling leagues, couples groups, potluck suppers, and car washes to raise funds for youth activities or other needs at church or school, and recreational groups were designed to bring people together and maintain the community structure.

Social critics lamented the loss of individualism and the machine like nature of community social life, its churches, schools, and resulting conformity. But, as other observers noted (e.g., Bell, 1960; Whyte, 1956), people lived in these communities for rational reasons, not the least of which was they were a good buy, providing the best in living accommodations for the least money. The "organization man" often gave allegiance to the organization itself and development of the workers' professional skills in order that he or she might earn the "where withall" to indulge his or her individuality at a later time. Whatever the problems with the social order at the time, it did not seem to lack dynamism or turbulence albeit a turbulence "born, not of depression, but of prosperity" (Bell, 1960, p. 94). Wherever order of one kind or another evolves, a counter force will soon develop.

The family theme and the baby boom reflected certain of these conflicts during the 1950s. The baby boom was the single largest growth industry of postwar America, and during the 1950s the population of the United States increased by nearly 30 million people (e.g., the birthrate of third children doubled between 1940 and 1960 and tripled for fourth children). The public school enrollments exploded, increasing by 10 million. Many social critics viewed the family to be controlled by children and the dominant ethic in child rearing as "permissiveness."

The same picture portrayed a return to a polarized sex role system in the family (fathers at work and mothers at home raising the kids). What Betty Friedan (1963) later labeled "the feminine mystique" was viewed as the standard for American culture. Marriage and homemaking were re-created as the proper role for women (e.g., many college newspapers described the coed of the time as a failure if she were not engaged to be married by her senior year) and the portrait of the female as the foundation of the home was both a social and religious expectation. No other job was more important or more rewarding than that of housewife and mother. Woman was viewed as the necessary counterpart of the organization man without which he could not reach his full potential and achieve good mental and physical health (Chafe, 1991). But, a major change was underway that would produce for many women confusion, frustration, and conflict over their role. Women were entering the market place for a variety of reasons, not all of which were economic. Faced with a sense of unfulfillment, many women wanted to participate in the world beyond the home. During the period between 1940 and 1960, the number of women employed doubled and 40 percent of all women over 16 years of age worked outside the home. During the 1950s the employment of women increased at a rate four times greater than men, and the proportion of wives employed during this decade doubled from 15 percent to 30 percent by 1960.

Despite the rapid increase of women in the work place, they were not achieving equality. The majority were concentrated in clerical positions with little possibility for promotion, and those who had risen to higher level positions were often not taken seriously nor paid the same wage for the same work as men (Halbertstam, 1993). Alcoholism, consumption of tranquilizers, and the divorce rate were on the rise. But, clearly a major change was underway and by the 1960s over 50 percent of women college graduates were employed. The entrance of the woman into the market place was necessary for many families to achieve middle-class status, and by 1960 in over 10 million homes both the husband and wife worked. This was a 330 percent increase over 1940. The majority of women entering the market place were over 35 years of age, had completed their primary childbearing responsibilities, and were contributing to the comfort and security of their family and to college funds for their children. They were not competing with men for jobs or seeking careers in the real sense. On the other hand, women for the most part reported they enjoyed their jobs and the recognition of being useful, and the opportunity to be with other people. For many women a new pattern was emerging in which they worked before having children to help with the mortgage or other family expenses and after a few years raising the children reentered the world of work to help achieve prosperity for the family. Clearly, the social order was growing more complex and the role of women was reflecting both the social and economic pressures of a culture that offered them little improvement in equality or independence.

The impact of television on the culture was almost too comprehensive to describe. Whereas in 1950 only 3 percent of rural homes had TV, by 1960 over 80 percent possessed a television set. By 1960 almost 600 commercial and noncommercial stations were broadcasting to 45,750,000 households. People could watch the same shows and receive the same messages. Many people saw major league baseball for the first time. Attendance at movies and nightclubs dropped. A whole new set of heros was created on the television screen (e.g., Don Larsen's perfect game; Bobby Thomson's miracle home run; Lucille Ball, Jackie Gleason, and Milton Berle in early situation comedies [sitcoms]; game shows such as the "$64,000 Question;" Clint Walker in "Cheyenne" and James Garner in "Maverick" recreated the Old West). Jack Benny simply moved his program from radio to TV. From the beginning television entertainment was seen as "family entertainment" and was structured by a scheduling framework that took into account the audience, commercial value, and FCC regulations.

But the new industry was also terrorized by the anticommunist hysteria that resulted in a blacklist of actors and artists across the country. This also produced what is sometimes referred to as television's "finest hour" when CBS newsman Edward R. Murrow and his producer, Fred Friendly, putting up their own money to pay for an advertisement for the program, directly confronted McCarthyism using footage from McCarthy's own statements to show how the Senator from Wisconsin thoughtlessly and rashly attacked people's character and destroyed their careers as a result. It marked the turning of the tide against the smear tactic and gave others the courage to respond.

In the 1950s the car was the most prized possession; and shopping centers, multilevel parking lots, drive-in-theatres, and motels were developed to exploit the needs created by this instrument of mobility. A high school dropout, Ray Kroc, in San Bernadino, California, put together an efficient food stand to turn out french fries, beverages, and fifteen-cent hamburgers, which became the McDonald's fast-food empire that would be emulated by others.

Sports events attracted increased attention and rising attendance. Professional athletes became role models, and TV commercials produced revenues that would make possible new franchises and later result in spectacular player contracts. Johnny Unitas, Bob Cousy, Willie Mays, and

Joe Louis, seen in the home on the TV screen, became celebrities, although not wealthy, as contrasted to the multimillion dollar contracts that were to come later.

Music was available to everyone. Technology was producing the jukebox and sophisticated hi-fi sets that stimulated the recording industry and with television catapulted singers like Elvis Presley and the Beatles into universal fame. Modern jazz became a serious art form, perhaps best exemplified by John Coltrane and Miles Davis. But, jazz was to be nearly drowned out by the rise in popularity of rock 'n' roll. The Italian conductor, Arturo Toscanini, organized the NBC Symphony Orchestra and along with Serge Koussevitsky of the Boston Symphony, Otto Klemperer of the Los Angeles Philharmonic, George Szell of the Cleveland Orchestra, and Bruno Walter of the New York Philharmonic-Symphony reawakened America's interest in classical music and the ballet. The composer/conductor, Leonard Bernstein, not only went to television to explain the complexities of music, but enlarged the concept of music with the popular Broadway musical, *West Side Story* (Diggins, 1988).

Marlon Brando, James Dean, and Montgomery Clift were new film stars that in a similar fashion were changing acting methods and emerged as existential film heroes (e.g., *On the Waterfront, East of Eden, From Here to Eternity, Rebel Without a Cause, The Wild One*). Marilyn Monroe and Brigitte Bardot became sex symbols, and sex was undoubtedly what launched *Playboy* magazine that began publishing in 1955.

Truth and Knowledge

The 1950s was a difficult period for writers and intellectuals. Many of them had been shaped by their experiences as teenagers or college students during the depression. On the one hand they were charged with failure to have warned the public about the evils of totalitarian government and were soft on communism, whereas on the other hand they were accused of being too hard, leading the American people to create a climate for a McCarthy and his witch hunts.

The literature of the period explored a theme of the individual versus the system in which the person under the illusion of independent action is controlled by others and is made aware of the lack of control over his or her own destiny (e.g., see Ellison's, 1952, *Invisible Man*). No matter what the person does, she or he is caught in the web of the all powerful organization, and attempts to escape only lead to other equally enmeshed circumstances (see Bellows, 1953, *The Adventures of Augie March*; or Heller, 1961, *Catch-22*). Golding's moral and symbolic novel, *Lord of the Flies* (1955), was introduced to college students in the later part of the decade.

Salinger (1951), perhaps more than any other, was able to identify the struggle going on between the individual and the culture with *The Catcher in the Rye*. But, the novels of this period were contradictory, and "modes of imaginative endeavor were almost totally discordant" (Klein, 1969). The novel became nihilistic, existential, apocalyptic, psychological, and explored the loss of self. Among notable examples were Truman Capote's *Other Voices, Other Rooms* (1948); Bernard Malamud's *The Assistant* (1957); James Baldwin's *Go Tell It On The Mountain* (1952) and *Nobody Knows My Name* (1963); Nabokov's *Lolita* (1955); and William S. Burroughs' *Naked Lunch* (1959). Hemingway published his last work, *The Old Man and The Sea*, in 1952. Faulkner and Steinbeck continued publishing into the 1950s but without the acceptance accorded their previous efforts. Some novelists poked criticism at college life (e.g., Malamud, 1961, *A New Life*; R. Jarrell, 1954, *Pictures From an Institution*; McCarthy, M., 1952, *The Groves of Academe*; Ellison, R., 1952, *Invisible Man*).

Existentialist philosophy going back to Søren Kierkegaard was modernized in the drama and literature of Sartre and Camus (e.g., see Camus, 1956, *The Fall*; and Sartre, 1947, *The Age of Reason*), and its influence was later felt in psychology as well (see May, Angel, & Ellenberger, 1958). Sartre and Camus believed that the human being is always in process and people are always projecting themselves from one moment in time to another seeking immortality and immutability. Existentialism was not so much a comprehensive philosophy as it was an endeavor to grasp reality. Recognizing that death and life are interdependent, it stresses that although physical death terminates a person, it can give a vital meaning to life. The most a person can achieve is to be aware of the choices he or she makes and choose with integrity. Living is choosing, and the awareness of possibility is all a person can expect. Without the awareness of possibility, existence results in despair.

Frankl's experience in German concentration camps during World War II led him to develop his own version of existential analysis that he called logotherapy (see for example Frankl, 1963). There was a movement away from Freud toward other modes of therapy such as existential analysis. Existential writers seldom agreed about anything, however, and would have repudiated the "existentialist" label. The only thing they had in common, indicated Kaufmann (1956), was a marked aversion to one another. The one essential feature shared by all existential thinkers was their perfervid individualism, and they refused to belong to any school of thought. Although very few novels, plays, movies, or other writings focused directly on the themes of existentialism, it was a vital force in creating the intellectual atmosphere in which people sought to understand their own condition. As diverse a group of people as can be imagined shared in the effort to understand and interpret the chaotic condition of a world nearly destroyed by war (e.g., Humphrey Bogart, Camus, Sartre, Jackson Pollock, James Dean, Arthur Miller, Saul Bellow, Joseph Heller).

Reinhold Niebuhr, protestant theologian and one of the founders of the Americans for Democratic Action (ADA; an organization that consisted of former New Deal liberals, labor leaders, civil libertarians, and academic intellectuals), argued that the error of both communism and capitalism was to have replaced the reality of sin and evil with an 18th century belief in reason and progress (Diggins, 1988). Niebuhr (1947) believed that God is inscrutable, the meaning of history is incomprehensible, and cursed by original sin, human beings are on their own and must accept power and human corruption from the source that it originates. Arthur Schlesinger used Niebuhr's concepts in *The Vital Center* (1948) to defend both the liberal and radical traditions of social conflict and to expose the sentimentally ignorant such as Henry Wallace who saw a farmer's utopia in Russia. Morgenthau's (1951) *In Defense of National Interest* used Niebuhr to confront Senator Taft's position that the American Cold War policy was motivated by unselfish idealism.

McCarthyism threatened and divided American intellectuals during the 1950s. Arthur Miller's play *The Crucible* (1954) was an attempt to make Americans more aware of the evil of false accusation and the very thin line between delusion and reality by using the Salem witch trials of the 1690s as a setting. William Buckley's *National Review* and Irving Howe's *Dissent* were both founded in 1954-1955. Buckley was the Laissez-faire conservative and Howe the more socialistic liberal. The Eisenhower administration suited neither of the two editors, however.

Curiosity about sex focused attention on two postwar publications produced by Alfred Kinsey and his colleagues at the Institute for Sexual Research at Indiana University, *Sexual Behavior in the Human Male* (1948) and *Sexual Behavior in the Human Female* (1953). Filled with graphs, charts, and tables, these two publications directed thought toward behavior that made many individuals uncomfortable, particularly when the female study was released; and politicians persuaded the Rockefeller Foundation to withdraw support of Kinsey's Institute for Sexual Research.

Much as in the arts, the American community of scholars was significantly enriched by the emigration of scientists and scholars escaping the Nazi dictatorship. In the free and technologically advanced society of the postwar United States, this influx of some of the best scientific minds in the world began to flower. The Hungarian physicist Edward Teller, who developed the hydrogen bomb; the great physicist Albert Einstein; psychoanalytic and psychologic theorists such as Erik H. Erikson, Bruno Bettelheim, Karen Horney, Erich Fromm; and social theorists and economists like Franz Neumann, Hans Morgenthou, Theodor Adorno, Herbert Marcuse, and Hannah Arendt are but a few examples.

In art, "The New York School" that emerged in the late 1940s and was center stage by the mid 1950s was influenced by refugee artists who brought with them the influence of cubism and surrealism. But abstract expressionism was to be the unique American contribution to the world of art and was developed by artists like Willem de Kooning, Mark Rothko, Franz Kline, and Robert Motherwell. The most notable abstract expressionist was, perhaps, Jackson Pollock, who amazed the art world with his new method of floor painting in which he laid unstretched canvas on the floor and circled it in bursts of energy dripping and splashing brilliant layers of color that reflected off one another in striking fashion. With abstract expressionism, New York replaced Paris as the art capital of the world.

A similar theme was being produced in drama with plays like Samuel Beckett's *Waiting for Godot*; Eugene O'Neill's *The Iceman Cometh* and *Long Day's Journey Into Night*; Tennessee William's *The Glass Menagerie*, *A Streetcar Named Desire*, and *Cat On A Hot Tin Roof*; and Arthur Miller's *All My Sons*, *Death of A Salesman*, and *The Crucible*.

Historians explored several themes. Schlesinger (1945), *The Age of Jackson*, identified liberty with conflict and struggle; Boorstin (1953), *The Genius of American Politics*, exulted the American people for their ability to derive knowledge and value from nature and their interaction with the environment rather than ideological doctrines as the Europeans did; Hartz (1955), *The Liberal Tradition In America*, analyzed why class conflict had not developed in America; and Miller (1954), *The Crucible*, saw liberty having emerged from the Puritan experience and admired it for its intellectual richness. Totalitarianism and World War II had a strong impact on American historians (Chafe, 1991; Cremin, 1988; Diggins, 1988).

Theology and religion in the 1950s witnessed a struggle between the liberals and the conservatives, between the orthodox and the unconventional. By the end of World War II, many Christians of varied beliefs were persuaded that totalitarianism was the political sickness infecting modern intellectual thought that had eliminated God. Nietzsche (1967) had spoken of "the death of God," and this was explored more fully by intellectuals during this period and was seen not so much as anti-Christian as post-Christian. The thesis was that when God becomes a cultural accessary of a human ideal God dies. Existentialism originated in Christianity but, if a person is what he or she wills herself or himself to be, there is no longer a need for a justification in God (Vahanian, 1957). The Christian can appeal to God and rely on God's justification, but for many existentialists (e.g., Sartre) no such possibility was available because God was dead. For others, however, it was possible to correlate existential uncertainty with Christian revelation (e.g., Bultmann, 1960; Tillich, 1957). The modern view seemed not to deny the existence of God, but at most affirmed God's absence. The human being asks questions and seeks some correlation with appropriate answers that go beyond the substance of the question itself. Existentialism, however, seemed to make it impossible to identify God and the human person.

The philosophy of pragmatism was waning, and many younger thinkers were moving toward existentialism to find answers to the human predilection for evil and self-destruction. Dewey had believed that education would provide the answers to all human problems, but the disillusionment and even despair experienced by many as a result of totalitarianism led to a number of European refugees who had come to America to seek meaning elsewhere (e.g., see Arendt, 1951; Kaufmann, 1956). Existentialism became the intellectual fad of the period, and "being and nothingness" and "you have no essence, only existence" were bandied about both the classroom and cocktail party discussions. But, the more orthodox, trained and educated with the Bible and the Torah, saw this leading to chaos and moved strongly to express their disagreement with what they viewed as the fraud of liberal tolerance. This movement was to contribute to a developing polarization of liberal and conservative views extending well beyond the realm of religion and theology.

A mystic search for salvation was occurring among young intellectuals that were to become known as the "New York intellectuals" in the East or the "Beatniks" in San Francisco. Although Beatniks were the offspring of the New York intellectuals, they often clashed over the means of their expression. They did, however, share in common a distaste for politics and the society of this period. But, Beatniks expressed their rejection of the social order in life, as well as in literature. They repudiated the conventions of marriage and family, roamed and explored the life of sexual freedom, city night-life, and wore slovenly clothes and sandals. The men grew beards and the women wore little makeup; and they avoided work of any kind, as characterized by Maynard G. Krebs in the sitcom "Dobie Gillis." They were to appeal to a large segment of college students who saw in this life a way to rebel against the conventions of their elders.

World War II gave black writers some of their first opportunities to challenge the government and society. Many black writers had grown up in the South and then moved to New York City where they were emersed in Harlem life and the exotic world of jazz. Even when they wished to avoid the issue of race in general and blackness in particular, it was always there in their writing. Richard Wright published his first novel, *Native Son* (1940) followed by Ralph Ellison's *Invisible Man* (1952) and James Baldwin's *Go Tell It On The Mountain* (1952).

Civil Rights

In Topeka, Kansas, on a September morning in 1950, Oliver Brown was refused permission to enroll his daughter in their neighborhood school. The school principal cited a law in Kansas (and in 16 other states) that required black children to attend segregated schools and referred them to an all-black primary school one-half hour bus ride away. The National Association for the Advancement of Colored People (NAACP) filed suit against the Topeka Board of Education claiming violation of Linda Brown's rights under the equal protection clause of the Fourteenth Amendment. On May 17, 1954, the Supreme Court of the United States issued their soon-to-be-famous unanimous ruling that declared school segregation unconstitutional (*Brown v. Board of Education*, 1954). The Court declared that the doctrine of "separate but equal" had no place, thereby overturning the historic precedent established in *Plessy v. Ferguson* in 1896.

The initial response to the *Brown* decision was good, and beginning steps were taken in many areas to achieve compliance with the Court's decision (e.g., in Topeka, Kansas, where the court case originated, desegregation was smoothly implemented). But, soon massive resistance developed in many areas, particularly where the black population was large. White South Carolinians, for example, successfully resisted for a decade court orders directed at various "black-belt" regions; and in Prince Edward County, Virginia, a white school board closed its public schools rather than desegregate them.

Although the Supreme Court can define law, it soon became clear that it required the president of the United States and other elected officials to act if the court order was to be implemented quickly and effectively. Eisenhower, who enjoyed a strong position of moral authority and political strength, chose not to place himself and the federal government fully behind the civil rights movement. Instead, he refused to endorse the *Brown* decision, claiming it was his responsibility to execute the law, not to comment on it. He repeatedly refused to act when numerous incidents occurred to block court ordered integration of schools (e.g., when the University of Alabama expelled its first black student, Autherine Lucey, in direct violation of a federal court order), and he remained silent even when violence occurred (Chafe, 1991). Despite the urging of several advisors and many civil rights leaders, Eisenhower refused to issue a statement condemning the breakdown of law and order in Mississippi after Emmett Till, a 14-year-old black male, was lynched in 1955 because he was accused of leering at a white woman. Instead, he chose a policy that supported his conviction that the federal government should be passive on controversial social issues and that it had no right to interfere in the affairs of local governments. Nor was Eisenhower interested in addressing discrimination based on sex.

Not everyone shared this same belief, however. There were strong supporters of civil rights in the U.S. Senate (e.g., Hubert Humphrey of Minnesota and Lyndon Johnson of Texas) and within the Eisenhower administration (the Attorney General's office first headed by Herbert Brownell, Jr. and later by William P. Rodgers advanced the need before Congress of a strong civil rights bill). The Civil Rights Act of 1957 did little, however, to address the real problems of job discrimination, school desegregation, or access to public accommodations. Opponents such as Richard Russell and Henry Talmadge of Georgia and Harry F. Byrd of Virginia were successful in emasculating the bill. In some states like Alabama, the NAACP was outlawed and resistance grew as evidence indicated the federal government would do little in opposition. Several governors seized on the opportunity to further their political purpose. Even in a more moderate and progressive state such as North Carolina, Luther Hodges did much as Orval Faubus had done in Arkansas to avoid integrating the public schools. Although federal district judges in the South were upholding the Supreme Court's decision on desegregation, sometimes in the face of angry threats from white opposition, their orders were being circumvented by a number of strategies (e.g., admit a token few blacks that fell far short of real integration, organizing classrooms according to "ability groups" that resulted in the two races attending at different times of the day, creating a lengthy and complex registration process that dissuaded black families from enrolling their children).

Only when Governor Faubus of Arkansas defied federal court orders and withdrew the state National Guard rather than asking the president to put them under federal authority, leaving Little Rock open to mob violence, was Eisenhower forced to respond to uphold the law by sending 1000 paratroopers of the 101st Airborne Division to Little Rock to assure that black students were able to enter Central High School. During the last three years of the Eisenhower administration, however, the number of school districts even attempting token integration fell from 712 to 49 (Chafe, 1986). The bifurcation point was reached with a single act by a single person, Rosa Parks, a black seamstress, who in 1955 refused to move to the back of the bus she was riding in Montgomery, Alabama. Word of her arrest stimulated black leaders into action, and the Montgomery bus boycott was organized that lasted 381 days in which black people refused to ride the buses, exerting nonviolent economic pressure. It was to be the foundation for the civil rights movement of the next decade. By the time the Supreme Court declared that the Montgomery buses must integrate, a new force had been born. It also spawned the Southern Christian Leadership Conference (SCLC) led by Martin Luther King, Jr.

Higher Education

John Dewey liked to forecast during the later 1930s and 1940s that the time might soon come when progressive education would be so fully accepted as good education that the adjective "progressive" would be dropped by reform-minded people. This seems to have generally occurred during the period following World War II (Cremin, 1988). By the late 1940s and the 1950s, "progressive education had become the conventional wisdom in the United States" (Cremin, 1988, p. 241).

World War II was a major turning point in higher education that has been equaled only by the establishment of land-grant colleges under the Morrill Act in 1862. Up until World War II, colleges and universities had maintained the illusion, if not the reality, of being separate, single purposed communities with clear boundaries between their world and the world beyond. They prided themselves on their autonomy and independence and saw their mission as preparing young people for a world that was yet to be. If ever the ivory tower existed, it came tumbling down after the war, especially in the research universities. World War II stimulated the transformation of American higher education, particularly in the concept of service (Cremin, 1988). Congress passed the Serviceman's Readjustment Act of 1944, usually referred to as the G. I. Bill of Rights, that led to the popularization of higher education. An enrollment increase occurred that almost overwhelmed many institutions as they sought to provide faculty, classroom space, and particularly housing for the new student (which was largely male, older, more mature, and more involved with family responsibilities than the traditional age college student). The readjustment legislation was designed primarily to placate organized veteran interests and to manage the effects on the economy and society of rapid war-time demobilization. It was to have results, however, that reached far beyond its original intentions. One result was growing tension between the commitment to the creation of knowledge and the commitment to its popularization. Progressives believed in the promise of science and the specialization it cultivated, but they also believed in the popularization of learning as the only sure foundation of a democratic government (Cremin, 1988, p. 255).

From 1930 to 1957, the number of higher education institutions increased from 1,409 to 1,850 but enrollments more than doubled from 1,101,000 to 2,637,000 (Bureau of Census, 1957, pp. 210-211). By 1960 the view was generally accepted that every American had a right to higher education, along with life, liberty, and the pursuit of happiness (Handlin & Handlin, 1970). Veterans achieved better in their academic pursuits than expected, and the expanding postwar economy was able to absorb them when they graduated. The list of vocations for which a higher education could prepare a person grew in large numbers (e.g., community colleges prepared mechanics, hairdressers, office workers, and x-ray technicians; and senior colleges prepared computer programmers, television writers, film makers, systems analysts, police officers, hotel managers, etc.). The system of higher education was called upon to transmit and discover knowledge at an unprecedented rate and in new areas that would have civic, national, and international impact. Just as progressivism had generated a differentiation of curricula in high schools during the early part of the twentieth century, so would its effects be seen in higher education after World War II and into the 1960s and 1970s (Cremin, 1988, pp. 252-253).

This was, perhaps, nowhere more true than in college student personnel work.

After World War II, with the infusion of large amounts of federal money into the research universities, individual units within these institutions (i.e., schools, colleges, departments, and institutes), particularly those in the natural sciences and medicine, became powerful and in some cases very independent groups. This growing alliance with the federal government led to what Clark Kerr called the "federal grant" university (Kerr, 1963, p. 49). Harry Truman had established a Commission on Higher Education in 1946. Its report, *Higher Education for American Democracy*, indicated a change in American thinking about higher education. The commission argued that American colleges and universities could no longer consider themselves merely instruments for producing an intellectual elite; rather they would have to become "the means by which every citizen, youth, and adult is enabled and encouraged to carry his education, formal and informal, as far as his native capacities permit" (President's Commission I, 1947, p. 30).

The commission stated in its report that at least 49 percent of the American population had the mental ability to complete at least 14 years of schooling and that at least 32 percent could complete an advanced liberal or specialized professional education. It pointed to the historic gap that had existed between the educational potential of the American population and the actual enrollments in colleges and universities and recommended an immediate doubling of enrollments in higher education from the 2.3 million of 1947 to 4.6 million by 1960. The commission went on to recommend that (a) each state create the means to plan new institutions of higher education; (b) an immediate expansion of community junior colleges be achieved; (c) the federal government establish a program of undergraduate and graduate scholarships based on need; and (d) federal legislation be passed to combat the historic patterns of discrimination in higher education based on race, gender, and income.

Congress ignored the commission's report. No hearings were held and no laws or appropriations resulted; but states did create planning mechanisms, the number of community colleges grew rapidly, and the federal government later provided large scholarship and loan programs. Enrollments rose from 2.7 million in 1949-50 to 3.2 million in 1959 to 8.6 million in 1970 and to 12.1 million in 1980 (Snyder, 1987), and some small steps were occurring to combat discrimination.

On October 4, 1957, Americans learned that a Russian satellite had been propelled into space and was traveling 18,000 miles per hour, thereby circling the earth every 92 minutes. Americans were shocked, humiliated, and a little frightened that their lead in technology was being preempted. Although the Russians had warned the world of their plans to launch missiles into space, Americans had refused to believe they could catch up and forge ahead so quickly. This satellite, named Sputnik, that was successfully launched into space marked a dramatic change in technology and the world view. Eisenhower was attacked for his lack of leadership in science and technology. Up until this point, Americans had been unwilling to match Soviet expenditures on research and development in space technology, but six months after this stunning event, funding to develop space technology was increased from one half billion dollars to $10.5 billion.

The United States was not as far behind as many feared and the public was led to believe. A group of former German scientists had been brought to the United States secretly near the end of the war. Led by individuals such as Wernher Von Braun, they had already spent a considerable amount of time working on modern rocketry. Under the process of demobilization, however, Truman and Eisenhower had imposed severe limitations on expenditures in this area, concentrating instead on the development of the atomic and hydrogen bombs. But the United States Air Force had been authorized to move ahead with further development of the Titan missile.

Eisenhower did not like the idea that government would become so heavily involved in research, development, and technology. In 1958 his administration steered through Congress a bill establishing the National Aeronautics and Space Agency (NASA) as his way of meeting the demands of the new space and missile age without giving it to the military.

Leaders like Admiral Hyman G. Rickover were so concerned that the United States would not catch up in the space race that they urged the educational system be revitalized. Eisenhower had promised to make public education a high priority during his 1956 campaign for reelection, but he had done very little to honor this pledge. He quickly agreed, however, to support Congress when it overwhelmingly passed the National Defense Education Act of 1958 (NDEA). NDEA made available substantial loans to college students, established a program for graduate fellowships, and gave assistance to high school counselors responsible for vocational instruction. It reserved highest funding for the teaching of science, mathematics, and foreign languages. NDEA was as successful as the older G. I. Bill. It assisted many young physicists, anthropologists, economists, and historians to obtain a Ph.D. degree. But, in many respects, it was less a commitment to knowledge and learning than it was to "national defense."

Colleges and universities were being transformed from elite into popular institutions and, at the same time, moving from the periphery to the center of public life. The faculty was influencing more what would be taught and how it would be taught. Faculty members were increasingly prepared in a specialty that culminated in a doctorate and were more oriented toward research. As specializations multiplied, the faculties were becoming more diversified although they were still clearly dominated by white, native-born, Christian males. The numbers of women on faculties had been rising slowly until it reached a peak of 28 per cent in 1950 and decreased to approximately 25 per cent by the middle of the 1970s.

The percentage of women who obtained the Ph.D. in 1950 and 1960 (10-12 percent and 16-18 percent as compared to figures in 1930) declined, although the actual numbers increased. A similar trend is noted in the proportion of women students to men students at the undergraduate level. Women decreased from 43.3 percent in 1920 to 35.2 percent in 1958, but in actual numbers undergraduate women increased. By 1956, 2,232,000 veterans had attended college under the G. I. Bill, of whom 64,728 were women. NDEA affected women as well as men and was designed to recruit a broader spectrum of students (Friedan, 1963).

This period of great expansion in higher education affected private institutions of higher learning, too. Among private colleges and universities there were successful campaigns to raise millions of dollars for libraries, laboratories, and residence halls. The expansion of enrollments in private colleges, however, was much more cautious (Havighurst, 1960). Private universities were not immune to the influences of the federal government and responded to government initiative in a manner similar to state institutions. As Clark Kerr pointed out, "the better and more individual the university, the greater its chances of succumbing to the federal embrace" (Kerr, 1963, p. 50). Federal support became a major factor in the operation of many universities, but the bulk of federal research expenditures was directed to relatively few institutions. Six universities received 57 percent and 20 universities, about one tenth of all universities in the United States, received approximately 79 percent of the funds in a particular year during this period (Kerr, 1963). This practice of funding was to gradually spread to a larger number of institutions and with it expanded federal influence as the federal government continued to achieve much of its research for defense purposes in universities.

College Student Personnel

The roots of college student personnel are clearly found in the beginning years of the twentieth century. It budded in the 1930s with the production of the first *Student Personnel Point of View*, but it was not until after World War II that the modern movement in college student personnel (later to be known as college student affairs) began.

The American College Personnel Association was first organized in 1924 as the National Association of Appointment Secretaries (NAAS) and then in 1929 changed its name to the National Association of Placement and Personnel Officers (NAPPO). It was in 1931 during its conference in Detroit that it became the American College Personnel Association (ACPA), the name it retains to the present day. As an effort to strengthen itself, in 1942 the ACPA Executive Council recommended to its membership that they affiliate with Educational and Psychological Measurement (EPM), and ACPA members began receiving in that same year the *Educational and Psychological Measurement Journal*. In 1934-35, ACPA numbered 111 members. In 1941-42, it had 271 members and by 1953 it numbered 1,160 members.

The National Association of Deans and Advisors of Men (NADAM) dates its beginning to 1919 when six men met on the University of Wisconsin campus. Scott Goodnight was elected as chair of the meeting and was retroactively referred to as the first president of the organization. The second meeting was held on the University of Illinois campus, and attendance increased to nine. More important, however, was the decision to continue holding a meeting each year on the campus of one of the members. This pattern continued until the last meeting in the 1920s, which was conducted at the Mayflower Hotel in Washington, D.C., with 76 men attending. Dues of $10 were paid by each member. During the 1930s NADAM developed its first constitution, giving each member institution one vote but inviting as many representatives as an institution might wish to send to the NADAM annual conference.

The creation of the National Association of Student Personnel Administrators (NASPA) in 1951 to replace NADAM was accomplished under the leadership of Wesley P. Lloyd at Brigham Young University. This was part of an effort to broaden the organization's base, and in 1951 it began for the first time to recruit members. The renewed purpose of "the expanded organization was 'to discuss and study the most effective methods of aiding students in their intellectual, social, moral, and personal development"' (Rhatigan, 1991, p. 6). During the 1950s NASPA developed a commission structure, establishing eight by 1959.

The first business meeting of the National Association of Deans of Women (NADW) was held on Thursday, February 24, 1938, in Atlantic City, New Jersey; and the association renamed itself from what was formerly known as the National Association of Deans of Women and Advisors to Girls that had begun in 1916. In 1938 NADW voted to discontinue publication of the *Yearbook*, which had been a convention proceedings issued annually since 1923, and the informal *Bulletins*, which had been issued quarterly since 1926. In their place the members decided to publish a quarterly journal, which made it the first official college student personnel journal. The June edition (first volume) contained much of the former *Yearbook* material. The other three issues of the first volume included articles and summaries of investigations, bibliographies, book reviews, and official commentaries. The first volume also contained a full membership list, including student and associate members. There were 994 paid members as of May 31, 1939. The second volume contained the by-laws of the renamed association. The *Journal's* editor was Ruth Strong.

E. G. Williamson was president of the American College Personnel Association (ACPA) during most of the war years. He served as Dean of Students at the University of Minnesota and was on its faculty. During his second term as president of ACPA, he also chaired the advisory committee of the U.S. Armed Forces Institute and was consultant to the War Manpower Commission. He chaired a special conference, which issued *Counseling and Post War Educational Opportunities*, was elected president of Division 17 of the American Psychological Association (APA), and was active with the U.S. Veterans Administration Committee. Williamson undoubtedly provided much needed direction during this period that helped college student personnel work maintain its role within higher education. Although he attributed his election for two terms as ACPA president to restricted war travel and curtailment of national conventions, his leadership was important to the maintenance of a professional focus for student personnel in higher education. He and Esther Lloyd-Jones were the representatives of the two major philosophical orientations in college student personnel preparation programs during the 1950s, he at Minnesota and she at Teachers College, Columbia University.

The revised document, *The Student Personnel Point of View* (ACE, 1949), provided the needed philosophical and intellectual base for the profession to develop. It was truly a remarkable document that reflected the progressive spirit of student personnel work for at least the next 25 years. The committee, brought together in June of 1948, was comprised of 12 leaders in the field of higher education and student personnel work. Women, who had clearly influenced the field of college student personnel by their work and numbers far greater than in most professions, were represented by only three members on this committee. For this time, however, that was undoubtedly progress. On the committee were three former presidents and one future president of ACPA. E. G. Williamson (president of ACPA from 1941-45) chaired the committee. The other two past presidents were Esther Lloyd-Jones (president from 1935-37 and a member of the committee that had produced the original document in 1937), and Daniel D. Feder (president from 1945-46). Willard W. Blaesser would be president of ACPA in 1957-58, and Williamson also was later to serve as president of the National Association of Student Personnel Administrators (1966-67) and the American Personnel and Guidance Association (1967-68).

During her later years, Lloyd-Jones related how she had, with the help of W. H. Cowley (also on the committee), done much of the writing of the document. Although undoubtedly influenced most by Lloyd-Jones, the document was able to bridge philosophical differences that would later develop between what was labeled a "specialist" orientation represented by the University of Minnesota and a "generalist" approach represented by Teachers College, Columbia University. The revised document retained the Experimentalist philosophy that was the strong base for the original document. Its further development was influenced by the 1947 President's Commission on Higher Education Report that reflected the country's experience with the recently-ended World War II. Perhaps the most notable change in this document from the original one was the better balance that was achieved between the individual and the environment and between the concept of a developing society and a developing individual. The emphasis reflected in this document on developing human beings to their fullest potential was to be a strong influence in all of education for some time to come.

In 1952 ACPA became Division One of the American Personnel and Guidance Association (APGA) and the *Personnel and Guidance Journal* replaced *EPM* as ACPA's official journal. The organization in 1945 began publishing its own organ of communication, the "Personnel-O-Gram" (P-O-G) and, of its proposed 1955-56 budget of $1,925.00, it allotted $1,300.00 for publication of what was the forerunner of its own journal. Thelma Mills from the University of Missouri, who served as president of ACPA in 1949-50, started the *P-O-G* with the help of Fred McKinney, who was also at the University of Missouri.

In 1953 ACPA's 26th annual meeting was held in conjunction with the first overall APGA Convention at the Conrad Hilton Hotel in Chicago. By this time ACPA had organized 12 committees to guide its work, of which the following six were new: (a) Committee to Review Editorial Policies of, and Advisory Relationships with, Student Newspapers; (b) Committee on Constitutional Revision; (c) Orientation Programs; (d) Special Committee to Consider Matters of Interest to Clinical Counselors; (e) Student Eligibility Requirements for Participants in Co-curricular Activities; and (f) Committee on Recording and Retention of Student Disciplinary Records. This last committee included representatives not only from ACPA, but from the National Association of Deans of Women (NADW), the National Association of Student Personnel Administrators (NASPA), and the American Association of Collegiate Registrars and Admissions Officers (AACRAO). The composition of the committee reflected the efforts at cooperation made by the several professional organizations representing college student personnel that would be an on-again, off-again endeavor over the next 40 years. The committees appointed gave a clear indication of the concerns of the profession for its role during this period. The convention program held the next year in Buffalo with its theme as "Integration of Student Personnel Services in the College Community" indicates, too, the search for a proper role in higher education that the student personnel profession was experiencing at that time.

World War II had created an "unprecedented demand for psychological services" to assist with the creation of a wartime army from civilian draftees and volunteers, and after the war, psychologists helped meet the large demand to return veterans to civilian life (Whiteley, 1984, p. 9). The Veterans Administration (VA) contracted with colleges and universities to assist the millions of veterans returning to civilian life, particularly with problems of personal and vocational adjustment. Forced to seek outside help with this work to help guide exservice men and women into a new life, older, already established graduate training programs at institutions like Teachers College, Columbia University, the University of Minnesota, and

Ohio State University were reorganized and expanded to train people to fulfill this need (Pepinsky, Hill-Frederick, & Epperson, 1978).

The evidence is clear that although there was diversity in the work and interests of college student personnel professionals, as evidenced by committees of the various professional associations representing the field and the planned discussions held during national conventions, there was also a strong counseling base and influence, particularly in the preparation programs. This is, perhaps, best exemplified in the several ACPA presidents during this period who also served as presidents of the Division of Counseling Psychology (Division 17) of the American Psychological Association (APA). E. G. Williamson, ACPA president from 1941-49, was the first Division 17 president of APA as well as president of NASPA and APGA; C. Gilbert Wrenn was ACPA president 1947-1949 and Division 17 president in 1951; Harold Pepinsky, president of ACPA 1955-56, was Division 17 president of APA in 1957. Both Barbara Kirk and Ralph Berdie served as ACPA president during the 1960s and were also elected president of Division 17, APA.

Many individuals carried membership in both associations, as well. Division 17 was chartered as a division of APA in 1944 and named "Division of Personnel and Guidance Psychologists." It was renamed several times, ending up with its present official designation "Counseling Psychology" in 1953. Many of the Division 17 founding members had common affiliations outside of the new organization. Hugh Bell, Edward Borden, John G. Darley, Mitchell Dreese, Frank Fletcher, William Gilbert, Milton Hahn, Francis Robinson, Winfield Scott, Dewey Stuit, Donald Super, Edmund Williamson, and Gilbert Wrenn were university faculty and administrators. George Bennett and Harold Seashore were in the business of producing and marketing psychological tests. Nearly all of these individuals, however, had concurrent memberships in two other organizations—the ACPA and the National Vocational Guidance Association (Pepinsky et al., 1978). For example, C. Gilbert Wrenn was president of the National Vocational Guidance Association (1946-47), president of ACPA (1947-49), and founding editor of the Division 17, APA, *Journal of Counseling Psychology*. Of the Division's 369 members in 1948, 165 or nearly 45 percent of its members were employed in college or university settings, with almost two-thirds of this group in college counseling centers (Whiteley, 1984). Harold Pepinsky, president of ACPA 1955-56, represented the apparent trend in the 1950s to solidify counseling and student affairs work through research and publication. Pepinsky and his wife, Pauline, published their book *Counseling: Theory and Practice* in 1954, which was a major work in the counseling field. (See Appendix for a list of the past presidents of the four major associations.)

The programs and discussions held at national conventions indicate that college student personnel was searching for its proper role in higher education during this decade. Although confined within the perimeters of the college campus with very little opportunity to transfer its practice beyond higher education, college student personnel was struggling to define itself as a unique profession. There was already under way consideration of professional ethics, as a discussion at the 1954 convention in Buffalo indicates, and a preconvention workshop at the Detroit convention in 1957 was held to study the role and future of ACPA in higher education. The perceived need and strong press of the environment to be all things to all people would create an uncomfortable schizoid existence for occupants of the field and thwart its efforts to define itself clearly. The need and failure to define itself within the traditional framework of other professions was to plague the field for years to come.

Although there may have been disagreement and confusion about the proper role of student personnel within the house of higher education, there can be little question concerning its importance. With the popularization of higher education and the massive influx of students following World War II, as much or more was required to meet student needs outside the classroom, particularly in the area of housing. Presidents had little time to worry about the day-to-day problems of students, and faculty had little inclination to do so. Nearly everyone gave lip-service to the importance of the "extracurricular" life of students, but presidents were busy building and expanding their institutions and faculty were generally ill-prepared and too busy with the demands of their disciplines to respond to student needs in these areas. For most faculty and administrators, the less they heard from students outside the classroom or off the athletic field the better they liked it; and they left the management of this vast area of student life to the deans of men, deans of women, and deans of students and their staffs.

Not only were the old areas of admissions and housing growing more complex, but the areas of counseling and vocational guidance and student health were organized into units that counseled, tested, helped students make important choices about careers, and treated their minor health needs; and new areas such as financial aid were emerging. Psychology was clearly the basic training for most of the practitioners in the field and nearly all of its leaders, but it was applied in any number of ways as the content of preparation programs and the writings used by the field indicate.

A new breed of student personnel professionals was gaining ascendancy in the field at about this time. This group was best characterized, perhaps, by their efforts to create an umbrella organization under which the various developing specialties providing service to students could be unified; and by developing a research literature on which to base practice in the field.

Robert Callis, ACPA president 1959-60, perhaps represented best the new breed of student personnel professionals that would carry over into the 1960s. He, along with five other ACPA members, attended the American Council on Education (ACE) meeting in Chicago in 1958 as well as the usual meetings of APGA. He presided at the ACPA convention in Cleveland, Ohio, in 1959 at which time the Personnel-O-Gram was renamed the *Journal of College Student Personnel,* a quarterly publication of scholarly work with Charles Lewis as its first editor. Lewis would serve in this capacity until 1964 and later as president of ACPA in 1969-70.

Literature Effecting the Field

A substantial literature was developing in the field during the period after World War II. The American Council on Education produced a series of "brochures" covering a range of topics that encompassed most of the concerns of the field during this era. The series, "Personnel Work in Colleges and Universities," began in 1939 with *Educational Counseling of College Students* (Bragdon, Brumbaugh, Pillard, & Williamson, 1939), included the revised *The Student Personnel Point of View* (1949), and concluded in 1958 with *The Administration of Student Personnel Programs in American Colleges and Universities* by Feder, Bishop, Dysinger, and Jones (Feder had been ACPA president from 1945 to 1947). In addition to the above, this series covered: *Occupational Orientation of College Students* (Cowley et al., 1939); *Social Competence and College Students* (Lloyd-Jones, 1940); *Religious Counseling of College Students* (Merriam et al., 1943); *Counseling and Postwar Educational Opportunities* (author unlisted); *Student Personnel Work in the Postwar College* (Blaesser et al., 1945); *Financial Assistance for College Students* (Sharpe et al., 1946); *Counseling for Mental Health* (Mueller et al., 1947); *The Use of Tests in Counseling* (Darley et al., 1947); *The Teacher as Counselor* (Shank et al., 1948); *Graduate Training for Educational Personnel Work* (LaBarre, 1948); *Helping Stu-*

dents Find Employment (Kirkpatrick et al., 1949); *Housing of Students* (Strozier et al., 1950); *Counseling Foreign Students* (Blegen et al., 1950); *Student Personnel Programs in Transition* (Brumbaugh & Berdie, 1952); *Personnel Principles in the Chapter House* (Rhutman et al., 1953); and *Students and Staff in a Social Context* (Sutherland et al., 1953).

Several books were published that served as texts for course work in various preparation programs in college student personnel: Wrenn (1951) *Student Personnel Work in Colleges and Universities;* Arbuckle (1953) *Student Personnel Services in Higher Education;* Lloyd-Jones and Smith (1954) edited *Student Personnel Work as Deeper Teaching.* Barry and Wolf (1957) later attempted an analysis of some of the major issues in student personnel in their book *Modern Issues in the Guidance and Personnel Work,* and Lee (1959) in an interesting way with his small book *God Bless Our Queer Old Dean* looked at the pattern of activities performed by a dean of students. Hardee (1959) with *The Faculty in College Counseling* documented concerns by the faculty that student personnel was more favored and, as a result, had over-expanded. She wrote with the purpose of integrating student personnel work with instructional programs by intentional and "vigorous, persistent actions" (p. 8). Hardee emphasized counseling in the work of the faculty advisor and the need to view the whole institution and the whole student. In a more specialized vein, Farnsworth (1957) produced *Mental Health in College and University.*

In 1939 Rollo May had written with *The Art of Counseling,* perhaps the first how-to-do-it book on counseling. Soon after, Rogers (1942) produced *Counseling and Psychotherapy.* Prior to this time, psychotherapy was of the view that only properly trained psychiatrists were qualified to conduct psychotherapy. The major focus of counseling psychology was on assessment and diagnosis, stimulated by the psychometric movement (Super, 1955). With this work and Rogers' (1951) most influential book on counseling, *Client-Centered Therapy,* this view was rapidly changing.

Work in psychology and social psychology relevant to college student personnel was appearing (e.g., Snygg & Combs, 1949, *Individual Behavior;* Erikson, 1950, *Childhood and Society;* Festinger, 1957, *A Theory of Cognitive Dissonance;* Horney, 1950, *Neurosis and Human Growth;* Lewin, 1951, *Field Theory in Social Science*). Other volumes of significance published during this period were Hilgard and Bower's (1956) *Theories of Learning* and Hall and Lindzey (1957) *Theories of Personality.*

Attention to group work was growing. Cartwright and Zander (1953) edited *Group Dynamics: Research and Theory* in which conclusions and theoretical interpretations resulting from the research in group dynamics was presented (this volume was to be revised in 1960 and again in 1968). Thelen (1954) wrote an influential book in this field with *Dynamics of Groups at Work*. It should be noted that Strang (1941) anticipated the focus in this area of knowledge with her book, *Group Activities in College and Secondary School*, in which she emphasized the importance of group behavior in a democratic philosophy.

Consideration of research and measurement continued to grow as evidenced by publication of such work as Thorndike and Hagen (1955) *Measurement and Evaluation in Psychology and Education*. But clearly the study of occupations and occupational choice was receiving vigorous and significant attention during this period with the work of Eli Ginzberg and his associates at Columbia University (e.g, Ginzberg, 1952; Ginzberg, Ginzberg, Axelrod, & Herma, 1951). Other important works were by Roe (1956) *The Psychology of Occupations*, Rosenberg (1957) *Occupation and Values*, Super (1949) *Appraising Vocational Fitness By Means Of Psychological Tests*, Super (1957) *The Psychology of Careers*, and Super et al. (1957) *Vocational Development: A Framework For Research* (the first publication of the "Career Pattern Study" a longitudinal research project in vocational development at Teachers College, Columbia University).

The diversity of this literature drawn on by professionals in student personnel reflected the diversity of the field itself and thereby tells the tale of the difficulty that college student personnel would always seem to have in defining itself. In its need to be all things to all people, it never quite looked the same from one campus to the next, and it always seemed to be changing as was the college experience changing.

What Was the Impact of the College Experience?

In 1957 the Edward W. Hazen Foundation published a report authored by Philip Jacob, professor of political science at the University of Pennsylvania. The report described an exploratory study Jacob undertook "to discover what happens to the values held by American college students as a result of the general education they secure in social science" (p. 1). (Although a considerable amount of data was used in this study, it was all data collected for other studies and not gathered for the purpose of Jacob's study.) He concluded that very little change occurred during college "in the essential standards by which students govern their lives" (p. 55). The values that are integral parts of the personality and that students entered

college with remained essentially unchanged when they left college. Jacob
wrote, "They may have modified their opinions on a lot of questions and
learned how to tolerate and get along more easily with people of differing
hues and views. They may have become more self-reliant. They may have
changed vocational plans. But most students remain fundamentally the
same persons with the same *face value judgments*" (p. 55). He did find that
with some students there was substantial change but that this change did
not come primarily from the formal educational process. Rather, he found
it occurred in a few institutions with a distinctive climate that had the
"potency" to affect student values, or as a result of a special teacher who
possessed a strong personal value commitment, or from some personal
experience the student had and integrated with their intellectual development. Although there were points of promise and a few institutions might
claim distinction in this regard, needless to say, this was not what most
institutions wanted to hear or what they had been telling parents happened if they sent their sons and daughters to the hallowed halls of "dear
old Siwash". The report was generalized by many to mean that not much
happened to students during four years of college and, therefore, why
send one's offspring if it was not going to make a difference in their lives.
Jacob helped focus activity already under way in higher education to study
the influence of college upon the student. It seems that at least part of the
prediction William Harper Rainey had made in 1899 that "scientific study
of the student" would develop was occurring (Brubacher & Rudy, 1976, p.
322). How integral a part of the university scientific study of students has
since become is open to question.

Closely following Jacob's study was a report conducted by Wise (1958)
describing students of the day and challenging the stereotypic idea of a
student between 18 and 24 years of age as a late adolescent who regarded
college chiefly as a social activity (p. 2). In 1959 an edited version of a
discussion of a number of invited notables in higher education was published by ACE (Habein, 1959). The focus of this discussion held in 1957
was Jacob's report; and Jacob, who was present, pointed to a need that he
called "experience centered learning." Nevitt Sanford made a plea for the
college research department to get the necessary research done to account
for the changes that occur in college. Jacob also strongly endorsed David
Riesman's conviction that colleges should go forward with a more inten-
sive and significant guidance program.

The impact of Jacob's analysis, along with the overpowering need of
the nation to overtake the Soviet Union in space exploration and reassert

its leadership in science and technology, would affect the future direction of higher education and thereby college student personnel work as well.

Summary

In the years immediately following World War II, social reform was slow. Economic prosperity increased dramatically, and the U.S. became a postindustrial country for the first time. There was a population explosion, and the social order was becoming more and more complex. Within a society that was increasingly emphasizing consumerism, there was a concern for the loss of individualism. But, individualism was not being lost. It was only beginning to focus on other matters. Television would have an enormous impact on the social structure as it produced an image and message seen by millions of people almost simultaneously. At the very moment when the role of woman as homemaker was being idealized, women were entering the labor market in larger numbers, filling not only traditional jobs but seeking professional opportunities as well. For many women a pattern was emerging that made their second income in the family essential to achieve the standard of living desired or, for a few, an alternative to marriage and a family. Issues of civil rights were beginning to enter the courts from the community.

The G. I. Bill passed by Congress in 1944 was having an enormous impact on higher education. Higher education was soon transformed from an experience for the intellectually elite to an opportunity every citizen should consider in developing his or her talents to their fullest extent. A little more than a decade later when the Russians launched the first satellite into space higher education would become an instrument of national defense as the United States initiated a massive program to develop space technology and passed the National Defense Act of 1958 that made available various forms of funding in support of higher education. It would contribute to a period of great expansion in higher education, and college student personnel would grow accordingly. College student personnel, more than any other segment of higher education, was pressed to provide the services that would deliver the burgeoning numbers of students to the classroom on a daily basis.

This was an era of growth leading to increased specialization. Experience in World War II had demonstrated the value of psychological services for educating people in a number of ways that were soon integrated into the civilian society at war's end. Although counseling would continue to be a strong base of knowledge and skill for student personnel work, counseling began to develop into a specialty of its own, emphasizing its psychological nature and seeking a formal identity within the discipline of psychology. At the same time, the base of college student personnel work was broadening to include other knowledges and skills seen as important to its expanding administrative and managerial role. As counseling sought a clearer definition of its role by greater specialization and identity with an academic discipline, college student personnel continued in the progressive spirit to broaden and expand its role but with great uncertainty about where it was leading and what it should mean. Although progressive education as a movement collapsed after World War II (see Cremin, 1961), its spirit clearly continued philosophically to influence the development of college student personnel work. From the beginning progressive education was pluralistic in nature and frequently contradictory, and these same characteristics would continue to plague college student personnel as a field.

Chapter IV

The Decade of the Sixties

The 1960s was a significant period for the nation and for higher education, but it was as a result, perhaps, an even more important time for student affairs. The philosophy and rationale for student personnel or student affairs had been forged in the 1930s and 1940s and proclaimed in the *Student Personnel Point of View* (American Council on Education, 1937, 1949). Along with higher education as a whole, college student personnel had grown and flourished in the 1950s, but the events of the 1960s would test its ability to effectively fulfill its chosen role at a time of extreme crisis and to survive.

The influence of progressivism continued to be a major factor in college student personnel during the Sixties if for no other reason than the *Student Personnel Point of View* was still the basic rationale for the field. Because the influence of progressivism had never been openly acknowledged in college student personnel, its effect was implicit and continued to be so. Progressive education was a part of the reform born in the early years of the century that from its very beginning was pluralistic, contradictory, and closely related to the wider tide of social and political reform. It began as a protest against a narrow view of what schools should be and resulted in educational reform from kindergarten to the university.

Progressivism has been seen almost solely affecting the reform of education kindergarten through the 12th grade (K-12), but it strongly influenced the colleges and universities, too, particularly in the midwest during the early years of the twentieth century and later in the west. As the movement became professionalized, it seemed to lose its reason for being, however, and by the end of World War II was forsaken largely as a repudiation of its emphasis on the individual that was later translated into a life adjustment focus. Although born out of a desire to reform, progressives were not radicals. They were generally moderates who viewed education as instrumental to achieving America's promise (see Cremin, 1961, pp. 161-168).

Progressive education as a formal movement died soon after World War II, but what it contributed to education was irreversible and many of its ideas were continued in the practice of educating youth in the schools and colleges of the nation. This was true as fully in college student personnel or college student affairs work with its emphasis on psychosocial learning as it was in any other part of education.

The 1960s were a tumultuous period for the nation and for higher education. American college students became involved as never before in efforts to influence the choices being made by their government in matters of both war and peace. The civil rights movement and the war in Vietnam would raise moral and political issues that students believed were directly affecting their lives. Efforts to change the response to racial differences at both a moral and legal level reached a peak during this period, and the war in Vietnam became an albatross around the nation's neck.

Many college students set out to correct what they believed were morally indefensible positions in the two situations that frequently brought them into direct conflict with both local and national authority. Student affairs staff members were often caught in the middle, attempting to mediate an almost impossible situation and at the same time struggling with their own moral values over the same issues. They were representatives of the institutions that employed them, but, in their chosen profession, they were dedicated advocates for students. It was a time when student personnel staffs across the country would mediate with student groups and institutional and civil authority in a thankless effort to bring about a positive resolution of conflicting values. It was a time when a number of student personnel professionals would respond in ways that were individual acts of courage and principle. In the end the profession survived, both wiser and stronger, but not without scars from having been perceived as both friend and foe by the institution and its students.

The Kennedy Years

By 1960 the United States had achieved unprecedented power and pres-
tige in the world. Although not always loved, it was respected as the leader
of the free world with its military strength and seemingly unlimited wealth.
For a number of reasons, however, it would search for its own purpose
and direction as a nation during one of the most turbulent decades in its
history.

In 1959 Fidel Castro's Cuban Revolution was openly supported by many
people in the United States. Castro with his guerrilla force seemed to provide a choice that lay somewhere between the communist party that had
been collaborating with the Batista dictatorship and democracy. With a
full beard and in battle fatigues, he became something of a hero and seemed
to give Latin America an answer to problems and frustrations it had experienced for a long time. When Castro achieved power he made numerous
changes that seemed to address the immediate needs of the Cuban people
(e.g., building hospitals, turning barracks into school rooms, increasing the
wages of workers), but within a year he began attacking the United States
in extremely long speeches. He suspended habeas corpus, established military tribunals, held public executions, jailed writers, called off promised
elections, and dared the "Yanqui's" to invade Cuba.

In response Eisenhower suspended purchase of Cuban sugar by the
United States, which was a severe blow to the Cuban economy. But, Castro
arranged with the U.S.S.R. to accept Cuban sugar exports and announced
to the world that he had all along been a "Marxist-Leninist." Although
originally skeptical, Khrushchev now accepted Castro and the *Fidelistros* as
full partners in communism. The fear that the Eisenhower administration
had throughout the 1950s that communism would spread to South America
had happened. The cold war entered Latin America with the enemy only
90 miles away. In January, 1961 Eisenhower left office with his popularity
still very high, although as a result of Cuba and the U-2 espionage aircraft
that had been shot down over the Soviet Union while gathering intelligence data, his foreign affairs program was in serious trouble.

The election of 1960 between Richard Nixon and John F. Kennedy was
very close (a margin of only 118,000 votes). Television became a factor for
the first time in presidential elections with the series of debates between
the two candidates. Although experts felt the content of the first debate
came out about even, Kennedy appeared handsome, cool, and confident
whereas Nixon, recovering from a leg infection, looked tired and nervous.

An important factor in the campaign that Kennedy was able to exploit was a perceived "missile gap" between the United States and the U.S.S.R. The black vote went overwhelmingly to him, too. He was also skillfully able to turn the handicap of his Roman Catholic heritage to his advantage. In October, Martin Luther King, Jr. was sentenced to four months at hard labor for organizing a sit-in at an Atlanta department store. When asked for his response to the situation, Nixon indicated he had none; but Kennedy made a personal phone call to Coretta King offering to help and his brother, Robert, phoned a Georgia judge, thereby achieving King's release on bail. The effort on King's behalf influenced a great many black Baptists to vote for a Catholic.

The Political Climate in the 1960s

In comparison with the 1950s, which was more a time of transition, the 1960s was a time of issues and movements both at home and abroad. It was a time when the liberals gained ascendancy for a period, advocated and enacted a more progressive philosophy and program, and experienced a great reaction to their liberalism as the country divided over basic value differences.

The legislative achievements for the Kennedy administration in 1961 and 1962 were mixed. A number of social programs including expansion of the minimum wage, health care for the aged, federal aid to education, increased social security benefits, creation of a cabinet-level Department of Housing and Urban Development (HUD), and allocation of funds to build up underdeveloped areas of the country were pressed forward. Success was restricted to improvements in social security, expansion of the minimum wage, and passage of an Area Redevelopment Act and a Manpower Training Act. When passed, however, the minimum wage bill excluded 700,000 workers who needed assistance the most; and Congress turned down Kennedy's tax reform proposals, vetoed the creation of a Department of Urban Affairs, rejected his request for stand-by authority to spend two billion dollars on an antirecession public works program, and failed to consider measures for migrant workers, youth employment, and assistance for public transportation. Leadership to achieve federal aid to education needed to help equalize educational opportunity in the country was inadequate.

In 1962 tariff reduction was the Kennedy administration's primary legislative priority. Kennedy believed that rapid economic expansion offered the best way to solve social problems and assure a strong position internationally. With a combination of executive action and legislation, he wanted to eliminate recessions, control inflation, and create sustained economic growth. During the Eisenhower administration, the GNP had increased at only an average growth rate of 2.5 percent (compared with a 7 percent in the Soviet Union). Two recessions and an increase in inflation at the end of the decade indicated a real need for economic improvement. Kennedy had stated repeatedly during his campaign that it was time to "get America moving again."

With the help of Walter Heller, a University of Minnesota economist appointed to chair the Council of Economic Advisors, Kennedy worked hard to achieve full employment through economic growth, to control deficit spending, and achieve tax cuts as incentives. During the first two years of the Kennedy administration, consumer cost increases were held to 1 percent in contrast to a 3.4 percent increase in 1957. The Kennedy Administration persuaded labor unions to accept wage controls calling for an average hourly growth in earnings of only 3 percent a year (approximately the same level as productivity increases). Although Congress rejected the reform provisions of Kennedy's first tax bill, the Revenue Act of 1962 did encourage new investment and plant renovation through easier depreciation allowances and helped promote an increase in economic growth.

Kennedy and Heller believed that steel prices had contributed the most to the increase in the wholesale price index between 1947 and 1958 and that the noninflationary period after 1958 was due directly to the stability of steel prices. As a result of their analyses, both labor and management were urged in the summer of 1961 to achieve a contract that would maintain price stability. Soon after labor unions agreed to a contract that would cost steel companies only a 2.5 percent increase, Roger Blough of U.S. Steel and five other companies announced a large price increase in steel, which was a direct threat to the Kennedy economic policy. Kennedy was infuriated, and he responded quickly and decisively to force the steel companies to withdraw their increase. They were permitted to rise the following year, however.

International relations. Kennedy demonstrated the most interest and decisive action in foreign affairs. The best example, perhaps, of his commitment to innovation was the Peace Corps. It was first mentioned during the campaign in 1960 and was an ideal program to support the view that the United States had a moral responsibility to help save the world. What better way could be devised to carry out this ideal than a program to send young people throughout the entire world to live at a subsistence level and share their existence with Third World people attempting to catch up with the modern world. This program quickly captured the imagination and enthusiastic response of thousands of dedicated young people and, although in the scheme of world events it has diminished somewhat in its luster, the Peace Corps has survived as a viable program to the present time.

The Kennedy solution to combating the U.S.S.R. militarily was to out-perform them. A basic assumption of the Kennedy administration was that every local civil conflict was a microcosm of the larger conflict between the United States and the U.S.S.R. Kennedy wanted elite fighting units like the Green Berets that could move in quickly to deal with "brush-fire" wars where traditional military forces were ineffectual. He envisioned on the one hand the Peace Corps recruiting the best youth to assist in the struggle through education and technical expertise and on the other hand Special Forces that would bring together and train the most daring and tough-minded young soldiers to wage the military and political war against the Soviet Union (Chafe, 1991).

Eisenhower had left a plan to overturn Castro and his government, and Kennedy proceeded willingly. He wanted quick action and, therefore, worked through the CIA and did not consult with the military. In April 1961 the Bay of Pigs operation was a complete failure and was the major defeat for the Kennedy administration in foreign affairs.

In 1961 Khrushchev and the Soviet Union pursued a hard line position on Berlin, seeking a separate peace treaty with East Germany from the other victor nations in World War II. Although by fall of that year Khrushchev dropped his effort for a separate peace treaty, in the mean-time the Berlin Wall had been built dividing the city, and both superpowers announced their intentions to resume nuclear weapons testing. Matters in Laos were also beginning to heat up. In late April 1961 Kennedy went on national television to warn the American people that American troops might need to be sent to Laos.

The most important confrontation occurred in 1962, however, when the Soviet Union took steps to install intermediate-range ballistic missiles (IRBMs) in Cuba, 90 miles from American shores. The world seemed about to go to war. A quarantine to prevent Soviet ships from entering Cuban waters was put into effect, and military action was avoided when Khrushchev agreed to remove the missiles from Cuba under United Nations inspection in return for the United States' promise not to invade Cuba and to remove its missiles from Turkey within five months. Whereas the Bay of Pigs fiasco was Kennedy's greatest defeat in foreign affairs, the Cuba missile crisis is remembered as probably his greatest victory. Idealism was high during this period, particularly among the young, and reinforced by a young president of the United States who called on a new generation to "make a difference" in this world and to carry forward the American revolution. Despite high public support for a military solution in Cuba following the Bay of Pigs incident, this event would raise questions among some college students about the wisdom of military intervention, but college students would soon turn their attention to civil rights issues and would not return to the problems of war and Vietnam until 1969-70.

Civil rights. Although during the early period of his administration Kennedy was slow to fulfill campaign promises on civil rights, by 1963 things began to change. His brother, Robert Kennedy, was more responsive, and as attorney general was adamant about enforcing the law. He believed the Justice Department's failure to implement existing voting rights legislation was scandalous, but on the other hand he favored a gradualist policy of litigation to the explosive confrontations created by groups such as the Freedom Riders[1]. His philosophy did not accept well the disorder created by the demonstrations, and it was also reflecting on the country and the president abroad. The Kennedy administration supported voter registration as the best way to achieve its goals in this area and avoid direct hostility of civil rights opponents in the South.

Although the Justice Department was far more involved in activity to support civil rights efforts than it had been under the Eisenhower administration, it failed to act when violence resulted from these activities, and Blacks were disillusioned by the lack of response. Only when the authority of the federal government was directly challenged did the Kennedy administration act immediately (Chafe, 1991). For example, in 1961 federal marshals were sent to Montgomery, Alabama to ensure the safety of the Freedom Riders. In the fall of 1962, federal troops and marshals were mobilized to assure the admission of James Meredith to the University of Mississippi as a result of Governor Ross Barnett's defiance. Foreign affairs had dominated the Kennedy administration's major attention, and it was not until 1963 that its commitment to civil rights became clear.

In 1963 black people took to the streets in Georgia, Alabama, Mississippi, North Carolina, and Florida. Angry at the refusal of the federal government to act, they were committed by their own action to break down the barriers to equal treatment. Led by the Reverend Fred Shuttlesworth, the struggle was waged in the nation's most segregated city, Birmingham, Alabama, to achieve some degree of equality for black people. In 1963 Martin Luther King, Jr. and the Southern Christian Leadership Conference (SCLC) focused on Birmingham and led silent marches through the city to demand that black people be accorded equal access to public accommodations. Corporate leaders were petitioned to create policies that would provide "Negroes" with decent jobs. But, it was through television that the American people were shocked to see the repressive actions employed by Bull Connor and the Birmingham police force. Using fire hoses and police dogs against women and children illustrated the extent to which a racist culture would go, and, communicated on the nightly news, it did more to bring about a response than almost any other previous effort of the civil rights movement.

Governor George Wallace added fuel to the fire when he refused to admit black students to the University of Alabama in Tuscaloosa. In defiance of a court order, he publicly vowed to "stand in the door" to block the entry of the black students "today, tomorrow, forever." In response Kennedy mobilized federal troops for deployment at Tuscaloosa if necessary and conducted extensive negotiations with Alabama business leaders to achieve compliance with the federal judicial order. Responding to Wallace's vow to prevent desegregation of the University of Alabama, Kennedy placed the Alabama National Guard under federal control and went before the American people to declare his administration fully in accord with the leaders of the civil rights movement.

Wallace made clear during a press conference that he had heard the message and rejected it. Learning from past events, the White House made ready troops in nearby Fort Benning. On June 11, 1963, Governor Wallace made his futile gesture and appeared in the doorway of the University administration building. He replied to U.S. Assistant Attorney General Nicholas Katzenback's reading of the president's proclamation and read one of his own but made no objection when two black students were escorted to their residence halls.

On the same evening, speaking in part extemporaneously, the president stated that it was not a sectional issue, nor a partisan issue, nor even a legal or legislative issue alone.

It is better to settle these matters in the courts than on the streets, and new laws are needed at every level, but law alone cannot make men see right.

We are confronted primarily with a moral issue. It is as old as the scriptures and is as clear as the constitution. . . .

Now the time has come for this nation to fulfill its promise. . . . We face a moral crisis as a country and as a people. It cannot be met by repressive police action. It cannot be left to increased demonstrations in the streets. It cannot be quieted by token moves or talk. It is time to act. (Sorensen, 1965, p. 557)

Previously, on June 4, 1963, Kennedy had ordered a review of all federal construction projects to determine whether blacks were being hired on an equal basis and asked each of his cabinet members to prepare an immediate assessment of what their departments were doing to promote equal employment opportunity. The figures presented by Labor Department Secretary Williard Wirtz were startling. Unemployment for black male breadwinners was three times higher than for white male breadwinners. Only 17 percent of backs had white-collar jobs compared with 47 percent of whites, and black teenagers experienced joblessness at twice the rate of white teenagers. Income for blacks in the postwar years had not improved (in 1959 the median income for whites was $5,600 but for non-whites only $2,900), and Kennedy believed that civil rights would mean little for blacks unless they were accompanied by economic gains.

On June 19, 1963, Kennedy sent to the 88th Congress the most comprehensive civil rights bill proposed to that time. The two basic features of the bill were to ban discrimination in places of public accommodation (e.g., hotels, restaurants, amusement places, retail stores) and to give authority to the attorney general to seek desegregation of public education on his own initiative when a lack of means or fear of reprisal prevented the aggrieved students or their parents from doing so.

Kennedy did not live to see its final disposition. His assassination in Dallas, Texas, on November 22, 1963, affected the United States and the world unlike any other single event in modern world history. In some way he had become a part of everyone's life and existed larger than life. Although there is much that a person might debate and criticize of his period in office, he had taken courageous and decisive actions in the months before his death, creating even more the hope and promise of what was to come but was cut short. With grace and wit and a sense of magic, he had given the country a new purpose and direction and a reawakening to its own strength and potential.

The Johnson Administration

The man who succeeded John F. Kennedy was, perhaps, one of the most complex individuals who ever occupied the Oval Office. During his administration, Lyndon Johnson would experience both the greatest triumphs and the worst defeats of liberal democracy. Extremely ambitious, he learned very early from accompanying his father about his business that success depended upon winning the favor of those with power (see Caro, 1990).

When he entered Congress in 1937, he saw Franklin Roosevelt as his model and became a master at smoothing over conflict, although not necessarily resolving it. When he entered the Senate in 1948, he began accruing power that would eventually allow him to dominate it as no one had before him. He developed to a level of art the skill of consensus making as a means to satisfy an overpowering need to dominate and control. It was this need to both dominate and control that often created his most difficult failures (e.g., he sought a behind the scenes consensus to lead the Democratic Party while Kennedy had been out in the states seeking delegates and achieving visibility that Johnson's strategy did not).

Once in office, however, Johnson called on labor leaders, old political enemies, civil rights leaders, friends, and religious leaders to put aside their differences for the larger good of the country. He moved quickly to turn the assassinated president's program into a martyr's cause. In his first speech to Congress, perhaps the most eloquent one he ever delivered, he pleaded for the prayers and support of Congress and the nation. He quoted Kennedy, "let us begin," and he asked "let us continue."

He masterfully used the emotional intensity of the moment to achieve a wave of action on the nation's most urgent social problems. Although Johnson had been a supporter of Kennedy's Civil Rights Bill, he had believed that it should be held back until Kennedy achieved the rest of his legislative package. But now, he intuitively recognized the urgency of enacting such legislation as a part of the Kennedy legacy.

Political Consensus

Johnson knew how to achieve a consensus. He skillfully portrayed himself as carrying forward the Kennedy legacy and, using his own mastery of legislative politics and the art of conciliation, he managed the 89th Congress to achieve a record of legislation in 1965-66 unparalleled in our history. He placed himself fully behind the tax-cut measure and achieved its passage four months after taking office. It set off the greatest prosperity of the postwar years (unemployment dropped below 5 percent and the Gross National Product increased 7 percent in 1964, 8 percent in 1965, and 9 percent in 1966). He declared "an unconditioned war on poverty" and adopted Kennedy's decision to aid those at the bottom of the economic ladder.

Although he knew his first task was to implement the Kennedy Legacy, he wanted to achieve his own record in his own name and create a place in history for himself. The time had come in America, he believed, to build a "Great Society" and "to prove that our material progress is only the foundation on which we build a richer life in mind and spirit" (see Chafe, 1991, and Caro, 1990). Running for the presidency on his own right against the conservative Goldwater in 1964, Johnson received 61 percent of the popular vote and the mandate he sought.

He believed that a president had to move quickly because every day he was in office he would lose some of his popularity and, therefore, some votes. Over the years Johnson had honed his qualities of leadership to a fine edge (see Caro, 1990, pp. 368-370). He pushed through Congress in 1965-66 the most extensive legislative program ever achieved at one time that included federal aid to education and medicare (long stalled in Congress). The program moved into new areas, too, passing the Higher Education Act of 1965, a housing act that included rent subsidies, a demonstration cities program, aid to urban mass transit, Operation Headstart, manpower training, a teachers corps, new provisions for mental health facilities, environmental safety regulations, truth in packaging, rent supplements, and high speed mass transit. Perhaps the most dramatic example of his leadership was the congressional approval of the Voting Rights Act of 1965.

Two of these bills enacted by Congress proved to be landmarks in the history of American education, the Elementary and Secondary Education Act of 1965 and the Higher Education Act of 1965. The first measure authorized federal assistance to school districts with larger numbers of poor people (often, but not exclusively, people of minority background) as well as assistance for a variety of teaching materials and special services. The second act authorized federal assistance for students attending two- and four-year colleges as well as assistance for the purchase of library materials and laboratory and teaching materials. Title I of the act also sought to attract the efforts of colleges and universities to solve the problems of housing, transportation, health, and employment in the cities, hoping in this manner to create a similar relationship between urban institutions of higher learning and their communities as the Morrill Act of 1862 had created between land grant colleges and their communities (Cremin, 1988).

Perhaps his greatest undertaking was the attempt to abolish poverty in America (the War on Poverty). He moved to join the issues of poverty and civil rights (e.g., in 1965, 43 percent of all black families fell into the poverty bracket earning under $3,000 per year). Although the plight of black Americans was the most obvious, there were many groups of Americans experiencing the grip of poverty. In 1960 the top 20 percent of Americans owned 77 percent of the nation's wealth; the bottom 20 percent owned only .05 percent of the wealth. The top 10 percent earned 28 times as much as the bottom 10 percent. Although a "postwar boom" had benefited many citizens, there had been no redistribution of wealth or income since the end of World War II. The poorest half of the nation received 23 percent of total money income, whereas the richest half received 77 percent. The problem was profound and complex. Issues involving race, class, gender, power, education, and history were involved.

Choosing a course of action was difficult. Redistributing the wealth would necessitate investing funds in the public sector to create jobs, build housing, and revitalize urban slum areas. Extensive tax reforms and the reallocation of economic resources would be essential to overcome flaws in the economic and social structure. This confronted one of Johnson's beliefs that conflict between groups should not be created by requiring one group to sacrifice to achieve improvement for another.

A second approach would be to give those in need enough financial support (e.g., food stamps, health care, rent supplements) that they would be able to climb above the poverty line. The Council of Economic Advisors stated in 1964 that the "Conquest of poverty is well within our power. The majority of the nation could simply tax themselves enough to provide the necessary income supplements to their less fortunate citizens" (see Matusow, 1984).

This approach conflicted with the traditional American way of life, however, that Americans want to earn what they receive, and it would neither motivate nor provide the skills for the poor to escape poverty. Such an approach would be a "dole" or "handout," which Americans had always rejected as demeaning. The third approach was to simply extend the liberal reform agenda and to give individuals a chance to overcome their disabilities and to participate equally in the social and economic life of the nation.

Recognizing that poverty is rooted, in part, in substandard education, inadequate job training, and poor health care, specific programs were designed to address these problems. The unfair distribution of power was not the real problem, but rather, the inadequate availability of opportunity. This model combined approaches to abolish discrimination that would give blacks equal opportunity (e.g., right to vote, to go to school, pursue jobs) free of legal restrictions based on race. The model included sponsored programs that offered incentives to the poor to "provide the social and psychological resources that made conformity possible" to the goals and rewards of an achieving middle-class society (Chafe, 1991). The result was a variety of approaches: rent supplements, model cities, food stamps, Head Start program (education), Upward Bound programs, Job Corps, Neighborhood Youth Corps, and Volunteers in Service to America (VISTA; a domestic Peace Corps).

Interestingly, the choice of this model was the most conservative approach of those considered, and it undoubtedly appealed to Johnson because it offered a way to attack poverty with the lowest possible expenditure of dollars and the least disruption to the existing social system, thereby maintaining the commitment to consensus. Philosophically, it assumed that the problem was not the economy but the character and motivation of poor people.

Community Action Programs (CAPs) were established to create a new attitude among the poor and to encourage them to participate in determining policy for their own local communities ("maximum feasible participation," Matusow, 1984, p. 124). CAPs became the major focus of the War on Poverty, receiving $340 million of the first $500 million of appropriations. Johnson wanted quick results, and this seemed like a brilliant, cost-effective way to achieve it. The strategy backfired, creating the intergroup conflict that Johnson hoped to avoid. Groups of poor people who took seriously the promise that they would have a voice in all aspects of the poverty programs in their community soon came into conflict with their local city governments. When they realized that their role on advisory councils was illusory, they became involved with rent strikes, picketing city government, efforts to take control of local school boards, and exercising power that usually was assumed by established politicians. When the Johnson administration sided with city hall, the poor rebelled. They saw City Hall as the enemy representing the special interests (e.g., landlords and school boards) that schemed to keep them in the same or their current economic circumstances. The struggle developed into one over class differences in power. In reality, CAPs promised social change that they could not deliver.

Despite the problems this created, the War on Poverty did achieve some success. The number of families living in poverty fell from 40 million in 1959 to 25 million in 1968, a decline from 22 percent to 13 percent. Black family income rose to 60 percent of white family income as compared with 54 percent in 1965. Although much of the change may have resulted from improving economic conditions, it is difficult to say that the antipoverty programs did not contribute to the result.

On the other hand, three out of every four living below the poverty line were not affected; and the sick, the elderly, and people with disabilities who existed outside of the "opportunity structure" were largely ignored. The War on Poverty failed because there was not the will to spend the necessary money or to resolve the social conflict that resulted. Appropriations for the Office of Educational Opportunity (OEO) were never more than two billion dollars per year. Solutions to inherited problems pitted one interest group against another, which spelled defeat for consensus politics in the War on Poverty, and, perhaps, ultimately for Lyndon Johnson's presidency. On the other hand, the list of achievements under his administration are enormous, particularly in the area of civil rights, education, medicare, urban development, and social welfare.

Vietnam

It is ironic that a person who prized and valued consensus so highly was presiding over a nation so bitterly divided over a war. On the one hand, the United States was involved with a domestic policy that centered on civil rights, the economy, and creating opportunities for people in poverty; but on the other hand, a war in Vietnam was becoming the focal point of American foreign policy.

The involvement of the United States in Vietnam was not a sudden event or decision but, rather, resulted from a long series of decisions over a period of two decades that were directly affected by the policies and values of the cold war. More than any other situation, involvement in Vietnam reflected the problems of a U.S. containment policy toward world communism that began long before Vietnam but with Vietnam created one of the deepest conflicts among Americans since the Civil War.

The first step in a policy to contain communism occurred in the 1940s with enactment of the Truman Doctrine engineered to contain communism wherever it might be found. The Korean War was the next logical step when North Korean troops crossed the 38th parallel into South Korea and was concluded in stalemate in 1953 with excess of 100,000 American casualties. Asia was the field of battle for the cold war and was as firmly a part of the U.S. defense policy as was the protection of Western Europe. The Korean War established a precedent for bypassing Congress to wage war on executive authority alone. It reinforced a trend in American foreign policy to support dictatorship in the name of freedom and to ignore nondemocratic circumstances in local situations. The Korean War increased the resolve of the U.S. to fight communism everywhere in the world and to strengthen the government's conviction that forceful containment was the only communication the Russians would understand (Chafe, 1991, pp. 253-255).

Determined not to weaken a fragile relationship between the United States and France, Truman implemented Secretary of State Dean Acheson's recommendation to commit 20 million dollars in direct military aid to the French effort to contain Ho Chi Minh and the nationalist movement in Vietnam despite State Department acknowledgement that the struggle was an effort by an overwhelming majority of the Vietnamese people to achieve freedom. Although the French were urged to concede independence for Vietnam as a way to win political support, the French leaders only appointed a puppet leader in an attempt to retain their power. France threatened to withdraw from the European Alliance and withdraw support for the European defense community unless the United States continued to accelerate military aid in Indochina.

Between 1950 and 1954, the United States spent 2.6 billion dollars in the effort to save Vietnam from Communist takeover. By 1947 the British had withdrawn from the Mediterranean, leaving it to the United States to step in and guarantee European stability against the Russians. The French failed in Vietnam, and when they were forced out of Indochina, Dien Bien Phu fell. Again, the United States stepped in to replace a European power, and by 1955 the Vietnam conflict became an American conflict. The Eisenhower administration was confident in 1954 that it could avoid the errors of the French and make Vietnam another example of communist containment, but by 1960 it had repeated most of the errors previously made by the French.

When John F. Kennedy entered the White House, the Soviets were investing billions of dollars in military and economic aid in developing nations (e.g., Aswan Dam for Egypt, steel mills for India, arms for Algerian rebels, arms for Indochina) (Sorensen, 1965). Kennedy came to believe that in Laos and Vietnam there were no "right" answers, only problems to be managed instead of solved (Sorensen, 1965). Although skeptical, he was unwilling, however, to reverse the policy of his predecessor to turn back communism in Indochina.

In December 1961 the Kennedy administration committed increased aid and support for the leaders of South Vietnam. By the spring of 1963, faith in its policy of support of Diem, leader of South Vietnam, was fading, and it acted to support a coup on November 1, 1963. Although Kennedy was clearly beginning to question the continued participation of the United States in Vietnam, he had not chosen to extricate the United States when he was assassinated in Dallas. Lyndon Johnson immediately acted to support the war in Vietnam and "made it his own" (Chafe, 1991, p. 273).

Although Johnson probably had the opportunity as a new president to reverse policy in Vietnam, he chose not to and despite later advice to begin withdrawal, he chose to maintain the existing policy. When he became president, there were 16,000 troops in Vietnam, and they were there as advisors not combatants. Press coverage was minimal and public interest small. During the campaign for the presidency in his own right, Johnson promised not to widen the war, but his election by a landslide in 1964 gave him the confidence to move ahead (Caro, 1990). Johnson believed in the "domino theory"[2] and was determined not to lose out in southeast Asia. By February 1965, his administration concluded the time to act had come and began activity to escalate the war.

As the war was widened, Johnson kept the American people and even some of his own advisors uninformed about decisions to escalate the war. He was able to manage the public's perception of the war by use of the media (e.g., in the televised speech at Johns Hopkins University in early April, 1965, he did not mention that troops had been authorized to engage in combat or that the U.S. was conducting sustained and systematic bombing of North Vietnam). While the war was being escalated, he acted to forestall national debate on the issue for fear that the result would destroy the consensus he had built to pass legislation on medicare and civil rights, which were at a crucial stage of discussion. In so doing, some close to Johnson believed that he not only deceived the American people but himself as well (Chafe, 1991).

By the end of 1967, however, many Americans were beginning to recognize the negative consequences and the probable disaster ahead. In

October 1967, more than 200,000 protesters organized and marched against the war. Where in 1965 civil rights protesters outside the White House had sung "We Shall Overcome" they were now chanting "Hey! Hey! LBJ! How many kids did you kill today?"—a chant he was to hear for the rest of his presidency and remember for the rest of his life (Caro, 1990, p. xxiii). In November 1967 a Gallup Poll indicated that 57 percent of Americans disapproved of Johnson's handling of the war, and Congress was becoming increasingly restive. He found himself caught between the "hawks" on the one hand and the "doves"[3] on the other. It had become his war and, as Kennedy before him, he feared the revival of McCarthyism if he pulled away from any aspect of the cold war. Although he inherited a policy of involvement in Vietnam from Truman, Eisenhower, and Kennedy, he was largely responsible for its radical extension. In the end it would defeat his dream of a "Great Society" and prevent another term as president.

Politics

Signs of a liberal revolt against Johnson and his renomination were appearing in the fall of 1967. Americans for Democratic Action (ADA) came out against Johnson in September and promised to back the candidate offering the best possibility for settlement of the Vietnam conflict. Albert Lowenstein, a 38 year old liberal activist and ADA vice-chair, opened an office in Washington, D.C. and began to organize on college campuses, among members of the peace movement, and among dissident Democratic politicians to deny Johnson the nomination. When Robert Kennedy and other potential candidates chose not to run against Johnson for the nomination, Eugene McCarthy, convinced that someone would have to raise the issue of the war, became a candidate. His popularity as a candidate grew as Johnson's faded with ratings on the Gallup Poll of only 41 percent in November.

In New Hampshire, the first primary state, so many college students were working on McCarthy's campaign that some were asked to stay home. Students ran a canvassing operation for the McCarthy campaign that was the envy of professionals, and 42 percent cast ballots for a Senator that few knew only days before the primary as compared to 49 percent for Johnson.

In March 1968 before the Wisconsin primary, Johnson decided that he could not win reelection and made his March 31, 1968, State of the Union Message the occasion to announce his retirement. "I have decided that I shall not seek, and I will not accept the nomination of my party for another term as your President." He also announced the first step to de-escalate the war. On March 16, after rethinking his position, Robert Kennedy decided to run.

Within a period of less than three months, a series of events occurred to shake even the most complacent person. The Tet offensive[4] in Vietnam had persuaded Johnson to retire and begin a process to seek peace. First Eugene McCarthy and then Robert Kennedy became candidates for president. Three national leaders represented the hopes of people who wished to change American society with economic reform and peace—Martin Luther King, Jr., Robert F. Kennedy, and Eugene McCarthy.

In addition to the cause of civil rights, King became a strong and outspoken critic of the war in Vietnam. He argued that peace in Vietnam was tied to social justice in the United States. Only a few days after Johnson's announcement that he would not seek reelection, on April 4, 1968, in Memphis, Tennessee, Martin Luther King, Jr. was shot dead; and within hours of the event, more than 100 cities all over the nation erupted in violence.

With King gone, Robert Kennedy became for many blacks and poor people the focus of hope. Entering the campaign late, he had angered many liberals and youth who had sided with McCarthy (see Schlesinger, 1978, pp. 904-921). But Kennedy seemed to be the only one who could rebuild the Democratic Party and bring back to it both blacks and whites. He won a decisive victory in Indiana and Nebraska but lost in Oregon where McCarthy was better organized. California then became all important. Kennedy won with 46 percent of the ballots to 41 percent for McCarthy. But, even on the same day and as he was making plans to reach out to McCarthy supporters, he was assassinated with a bullet to the head (Schlesinger, 1978, pp. 921-983). For many people the best hope for bringing the country together was gone. With two dynamic leaders gone and McCarthy retreating to a Benedictine monastery to seek sense of what was going on in his life, the political system was without direction.

Hubert Humphrey, Johnson's vice-president, announced his candidacy for the presidency in late April of 1968, and the Democratic Convention held in late August in Chicago was one of the most unusual and tumultuous ever held. Thousands of youth, most of whom were college students, came to Chicago to demonstrate, or take a last stand for the McCarthy peace movement, or to simply indicate by their presence their dissatisfaction with "old politics."

Led by Abby Hoffman and Jerry Rubin, the Youth International Party

(Yippies) urged the young people to demonstrate, to use guerrilla tactics to create chaos, pitting disorder and the politics of total freedom against the machine-like-discipline of the old politics. Mayor Richard Daly responded by making the city into almost a fortress with the mobilization of nearly 12,000 police and preparing to summon 7,500 national guardsmen to deny demonstrators the right to hold protest rallies, march through the city, or even sleep in the parks. With the help of television, the Yippies stimulated a violent response from the police who lost their control and attacked the demonstrators using clubs and mace and took many to jail.

On the convention floor, delegates had rejected an antiwar resolution three-to-two and were considering further business when the police outside attacked the peaceful demonstrators with little effort to distinguish bystanders and peaceful demonstrators from law-violators. The conflict and division carried to the convention floor where Abraham Ribicoff, Democratic senator from Connecticut, denounced the "Gestapo tactics" taking place outside the convention. Hubert Humphrey's speech accepting the party's nomination for president emphasized "law and order" and seemed to reflect the deep division existing in the Democratic Party.

Richard M. Nixon, the Republican Party nominee, was prepared and well positioned to exploit this division. He focused on the discontent of "middle Americans" who were tired of Hippies, drugs, Black Power, and antiwar protests. Nixon narrowly won the election with 43.4 percent of the vote compared with 42.7 percent for Humphrey. George Wallace, Alabama's segregationist governor, received 13.5 percent, helping to deny Humphrey the presidency. Wallace appealed to the vote of the right with his emotional denunciation of busing, the Eastern establishment, and intellectuals.

By 1969 white middle-class Americans were growing dissatisfied with the emphasis on minorities and the poor. They were incensed when students uttered obscenities at police and authority, attacked the flag, and opposed the Vietnam War. Nixon sensed this and understood how to exploit it. For a brief time (following student protests of the Cambodian invasion) he sought dialogue with protestors who gathered in Washington, but then he quickly returned to a hard-line posture for the 1970 Congressional elections.

Student Movement

In 1940 15 percent of the young people from ages 18 to 22 attended college. By 1965 that number had grown to 44 percent. By the end of the decade, more than 6 million students were enrolled in college—four times as many as in the 1940s. The prosperity of the postwar years made available an increasing amount of money to be invested in the education of American youth. Approximately 75 percent of the students came from families with incomes above the national median. They had been born into and grown up in a world where economic security was a given. They had never experienced anxiety over trying to find work or supporting a family, which so strongly affected the life-view of those who had grown up during the Depression (Matusow, 1984).

Between 1941 and 1958, the number of universities with 20,000 or more students grew from 2 to 31. With a college degree becoming a more important prerequisite for a good job, institutions of higher learning became more essential (but also more vulnerable to public scrutiny). On the other hand, idealism was running high, even for youth, reinforced by the call of a young president for a new generation to "make a difference" in their time (Sorensen, 1965, pp. 263-280).

For students who wanted to be involved, the civil rights movement provided the opportunity to do more than just read about it. For some it meant joining a local Congress of Racial Equality (CORE) chapter and picketing a Woolworth store in a northern city, but for others it meant traveling south. When the Student Non-violent Coordinating Committee (SNCC) called for students from colleges and universities across the country to help with freedom elections in the fall of 1963, many White students saw the opportunity to take a stand they had been wanting to make. Most of these White students believed that the federal government and law enforcement officials would be supportive, but they were quickly disillusioned as they repeatedly witnessed the law used to repress attempts to protest and to support violence rather than reform. They soon understood that the problem was not a few bigots and rednecks but, rather, the systematic indifference and complicity of a social system committed to maintaining itself even if it required brutal oppression (see Knowles & Prewitt, 1970).

When later they returned to the college campus, they brought with them an increased sense for hypocrisy and many began to perceive the university itself as a source of repression and manipulation. For some students the institution was only a microcosm of society controlled by government and industry. As such, it was an issue of moral significance that must be changed even if it meant destroying the institution so something better could arise from its ashes (see *Atlantic*, 1966; Cohen & Hale, 1967).

In the fall and winter of 1964, the new left was rediscovering the meaning and relevance of the *Port Huron Statement* (Students for a Democratic Society, 1962/1990) at what was probably the first major confrontation between students and an institution. It occurred on the Berkeley campus when Berkeley administrators ruled that noncampus political literature could no longer be distributed on the Berkeley campus and political activity would be prohibited along a 16-foot strip of brick pavement at Bancroft Way and Telegraph Avenue, the one place on campus where political activity and fund raising had previously been permitted. At first the issue was simply free speech on campus; and students saw the ruling as arbitrary, a break with tradition, and a violation of open political discussion. Led by Mario Savio, a veteran of Freedom Summer[5] in Mississippi, students responded with massive protests and the Free Speech movement was born.

Each side became resistant and the issues polarized. For students it took on the moral and social dimensions of the civil rights and peace movements. Institutions had become machine-like, treating students more like objects than human beings and in the eyes of militant leaders took on the character of a George Wallace, governor of Alabama, or Ross Barnett, governor of Mississippi. For the institution it represented the need and responsibility to preserve the learning environment and the need to remain above the outside world while at the same time obeying the law (see Lipset & Wolin, 1965, pp. 285-333).

Berkeley was the beginning of protests that multiplied across the country, and soon the large majority of colleges and universities were reporting demonstrations of one kind or another. Students for a Democratic Society (SDS) launched a campaign to organize northern urban areas. Most institutions were less confrontational and less restrictive on political activity than Berkeley had been and allowed SDS activities on campus.

After Freedom Summer, civil rights organizations, particularly SNCC, discouraged White participation in their activities as they moved toward a goal of Black Power. The student movement on campuses might well have run its course in a much shorter time but for the military escalation in Vietnam that fueled student activism for at least the next six or seven years. Many students were able to see for the first time a connection between their own everyday activities and the policies of the government. A large number of universities depended heavily on federal grants, many of which were directly tied to Defense Department research. Companies that manufactured napalm or chemical defoliants used university facilities to recruit new employees, and through Reserve Officers Training Corps

(ROTC) programs universities helped to train military officers who would fight in Vietnam. Because of the direct connections between their own institutions and the government, students were motivated to act. Many male students were of draft age and only avoiding induction into the armed services as a result of student deferments. During the 1960s young men were drafted into the armed forces under the Selective Service System; all males were eligible but individuals could be given deferments based on responsibilities, physical impairment, or educational activities and enrollment in college qualified a person for such a deferment.

By the fall of 1966, individuals in the antiwar movement began to pursue a series of step-by-step actions to match the federal government's policies of escalation in Vietnam (Becker, 1970; Chafe, 1991; Matusow, 1984). They believed that the war in Vietnam was criminal and that they must act together to stop it, even though at great individual risk. Some chose to openly defy the draft and confront the government and its war. Burning one's own draft card was a federal offense and became a symbol of their defiance. Demonstrations of civil disobedience took place at the Selective Service headquarters in Oakland, and throughout 1966 and 1967, the anger, bitterness, and ugliness of the antiwar confrontation with the federal government grew.

In 1967 the National Student Association (NSA) took a position on the Central Intelligence Agency (CIA) and broke all ties with it. For 15 years NSA had been receiving funds from the CIA and at one point it provided as much as 80 percent of NSA's budget. NSA's officers negotiated directly with the agency, but the funds were passed to NSA through a number of foundations.

The CIA had been using NSA and particularly its overseas representative to carry out its activities. Students found themselves caught in a trap between exposing the activity and relationship, risking harm to themselves, or remaining quiet and cooperating with the CIA. The third alternative and the one chosen was to attempt quiet disengagement. Quiet disengagement was not possible at the time, however, due to the nature of the relationship. In an attempt to reestablish its integrity, NSA severed all ties with the CIA giving up all financial support, disengaged from any student group that did not clearly separate itself from the CIA, and demanded an official apology to NSA from the federal government (see National Supervisory Board, 1967). NSA never fully recovered from this incident, however.

As a result of their feelings of alienation from what was taking place, many young people developed habits of dress and a life style that symbolized their search for a new culture that would agree with their politics. In the same manner as SNCC, workers donned overalls to identify with the sharecroppers and tenant farmers of the rural south, many students participating in the war movement chose to grow beards and long hair as a way of separating themselves from the traditional norms of middle class respectability. Rooted in the rhythm and blues, rock and roll, and the folk song traditions of the past, music became their primary symbol and achieved a cultural and political significance that set them apart (e.g., Simon and Garfunkle's "Sounds of Silence" and "Dangling Conversation"; Bob Dylan's "Blowin' in the Wind"; the Beatles' declaration that "All You Need Is Love"; and others like Joan Baez, the Rolling Stones, and Pete Seger).

For some drugs represented another "sacrament" and a marijuana "joint" took the place of alcohol that their parents used for relaxation or escape. They preached the idea of "Being" rather than "Becoming." Living now was more important than getting ahead. By 1967 the new life style had become a sensation and "Hippies" would become a new catchword in American vocabulary. It represented a new set of values, a search for meaning, and a rebellion against conventions that had deep roots in the political disaffection and alienation that was developing between the generations.

By 1967 the student movement reached a crossroads as many adults were joining the antiwar outcry. Several U.S. senators (e.g., Robert Kennedy, D-N.Y. and John Sherman Cooper, R.-Ky.) voted against appropriations for the war, and in the fall of 1967 less than 30 percent of the people approved of the president's policies.

Students were the cutting edge of the antiwar movement. A new wave of protests began in the spring of 1968 at Columbia University when its president, Grayson Kirk, insisted that the university should be "value free" about social issues although Columbia, like many other prominent universities, was tied by contracts to the government policy in Vietnam. In response, radical students led by Mark Rudd denounced the administration and, when Columbia moved to build a new gym on a park overlooking Harlem with a separate back door to the gym for Harlem residents, acted to directly confront both the university's racism and its involvement with the war effort by occupying the president's office and classroom buildings. In the week of April 23 to 30, 1968, SDS and Students Afro-American Society (SAS) led 700 to 1,000 students to seize and occupy five university buildings. They barricaded themselves inside and defied the administration. After six days, with the aid of more than 1,000 police, the buildings were cleared but the campus was in chaos (Cox, 1968).

On May 4, 1968, the Executive Committee of the Faculties of Columbia University requested a fact finding commission to investigate and report on the disturbances on campus. Archibald Cox, professor of law at Harvard University, chaired the commission. "The spark that set off the explosion was an SDS rally on April 23, called to protest Columbia's relation to the Institute for Defense Analysis (IDA), her 'racist policies,' and the administration's placing six SDS leaders on probation for violation of a rule against indoor demonstration" (Cox, 1968, p. xvi). The commission rejected the view that the disturbance was primarily the result of a conspiracy of student revolutionaries, although a few revolutionaries were involved. In the final analysis, the revolt had grown to enjoy the wide and deep support among the students and junior faculty and in a lesser degree among the senior professors. The administration had become isolated from its own structure and fixated on maintaining its own authority. The faculty organization was weak and lacked experience in university governance. As a result, it was unable to counter the administration-student polarization. It was the reluctance of the faculty to adopt a clear position that most alienated the student protestors (Trimberger, 1970). The trauma of the violence that followed police intervention intensified emotions, but support for the demonstrators rested upon broad discontent and widespread sympathy for their position. Stripped of their context and symbolism, the commission concluded that the "avowed objectives of the April demonstrations . . . were inadequate causes for an uprising" (Cox, 1968, p. 191).

A similar pattern was occurring throughout the country. Students occupied Harvard University buildings to protest the university's refusal to take a stand against the Vietnam War or to withdraw its investments in racist South Africa. Harvard president Nathan Pusey took a similar position to the one taken by Kirk at Columbia when he stated that their purpose was to invest in places that were selfishly good for Harvard, and they did not use their money for social purposes. At Berkeley Governor Ronald Reagan called out a battalion of police with armed helicopters and tear gas to confront more than 5,000 students and community residents who had seized a vacant lot and turned it into a "people's park." At Cornell University on April 18, 1969, following a series of events, black students with machine guns took over the student union to demand their rights and communicated they would no longer take things lying down (Friedland & Edwards, 1970). And, at San Francisco State on December 2, 1967, acting president S. I. Hayakawa became a hero for the right when he called out police and National Guardsmen to suppress student demonstrations (McEvoy & Miller, 1970).

The culmination of the movement was reached at Kent State in Ohio in May of 1970. The tone for the confrontation was set when Nixon referred to student demonstrators as a bunch of "bums" during an informal briefing at the Pentagon. His ordering the invasion of Cambodia set off a wave of strikes that swept universities, including Kent State. When Kent State students protested the invasion by rioting downtown and fire-bombing the ROTC building, Governor James Rhodes called out the National Guard and declared martial law. Insisting that they were going to eradicate the problem of student rebels who were "worse than the brown shirts and communist elements" and represented "the worst type of people we harbor in America," Rhodes sent Guardsmen onto the campus on May 4, 1970; and students held a peaceful rally to protest the governor's action. With no apparent provocation, National Guardsmen opened fire, killing four students and wounding eleven. None of the four victims had broken a law, and two of the women killed were simply walking to class. The tragedy was not at an end, however. In Mississippi, police fired for 28 seconds at students in front of a residence hall at Jackson State, killing two. As a number of commentators observed, the enemy without had become the enemy within. Some campuses were closed and students sent home for the remainder of the spring term.

But even as the protests and horror of the responses reached its peak, the New Left was falling apart. After months of protest, some perceived no positive response emanating from those in power and splintered off into varied alternatives, one of which was the tactics of revolutionary terrorism. The most notorious group was known as the Weathermen, "You Don't Need a Weatherman To Tell You Which Way the Wind Blows." They were self-destructive from the beginning, evolving a strong backlash from most Americans who believed that no matter what the issue, law and order was an essential requirement for any civilized process. Indeed, they literally helped destroy themselves: In March 1970 students accidently detonated a bomb in a Greenwich Village townhouse, killing those present.

Most students were growing weary of excessive rhetoric and irresponsible violence, but were despairing of finding an alternative. Frustration with political activism was increasing and many turned to the counterculture with a religious fervor, believing that building a new life with different values, mores, and institutions provided the only answer. Although slogans like "make love not war" indicate that some concern with politics remained, the counterculture became a personal focus with emphasis on liberation in dress style, sex, and attitudes toward respectability replacing activism in the public arena. Constructing communes and emphasizing interpersonal intimacy might have had political impact had they not quickly become ends in themselves. The Woodstock rock festival of August 1969 where thousands of young people gathered in upstate New York to celebrate their way of life is, perhaps, the most graphic illustration of the counterculture movement. Almost every major rock band provided free performances, and for three days and three nights they communed together, experiencing what life might be like totally without restraints (see Dickstein, 1977; Faber, 1994; Reich, 1970; Roszak, 1969).

For some, the counterculture provided fulfillment, identity, and community they had never before experienced. Living together on collective farms, trying to grow their own food, and refusing to "buy into" the establishment's obsession with grades and careers created a profound sense of liberation. For others, however, it became a life of drugs and psychological despair that led to the death of some from drug overdoses (e.g., Jimmi Hendrix, Janice Joplin, Jim Morrison, who were musical celebrities of the counterculture; Chafe, 1991, p. 411). New freedom sought through open marriages and sexual freedom often resulted in the betrayal of trust and destruction of community. Soon the business world moved in to take advantage of the many who were still tied to affluence by catering to their taste in dress and jewelry (e.g., bell-bottom blue jeans, stereos, records, drug paraphernalia). Herbert Marcuse (1964), the New Left philosopher, had written of a new society where the young would mix their efforts to revolt against the status quo with joy and love. In the end, the emphasis on individual self-expression and "do your own thing" did more to fragment the movement than unify it. Such emphasis on individual behavior meant that it was impossible to be responsible for anyone else, and the movement that had contributed so much to Lyndon Johnson foregoing his choice of seeking reelection was losing its direction and force.

College Student Affairs in the 1960s

The old style student personnel dean was on the way out. As the enforcer of *in loco parentis*, a dean was almost always dealing with disciplinary cases resulting from inappropriate behavior (violation of a rule). Old style deans had a tendency to set their own rules but usually administered them with great humanness (e.g., see English & Williams, 1984). Some employed a "fear-of-God" approach, however, and Gestapo-like methods were not uncommon. Usually presidents or university statutes did little to define the roles of personnel deans, and a person could look in vain to find a description of what a dean was supposed to do. In general they were assigned and accepted the duty of keeping the order on the campus (e.g., Joseph Kauffman at the University of Wisconsin-Madison protected the institution's president from having to deal with student protestors vs. the Dow Chemical Company).

Freshman hazing, a tradition throughout the 1950s, was still in vogue and "panty raids" became fashionable on campus, although there is some reason to believe that "bloomer forays" occurred on college campuses as early as 1899 (Loucks, 1961). These events soon became viewed as mob behavior, however, during which identity cards were confiscated and polaroid pictures were taken to identify culprits that were not close enough for university officials to demand I.D. cards.

The attitudes of students about their role as students on the college campus were gradually changing. The issue of due process for college students began to emerge in the early 1960s. Students in many colleges and universities were being suspended or dismissed without "due process." In the summer of 1961, the United States National Student Association (USNSA) adopted a policy statement denying the traditionally accepted *in loco parentis* relationship between student and college administration, and its officers asked the Conference of Jesuit Student Personnel Administrators (CJSPA) to comment on a USNSA proposed statement on Procedural Due Process and Substantive Due Process (see "A Dialogue on Discipline," *NASPA Journal*, 1963).

CJSPA undertook a year's study in 1962-1963 and formalized a drafted response by Fathers Patrick H. Ratterman, S.J. of Xavier University, Cincinnati, Ohio, and Victor R. Yanitelli, S.J., of St. Peter's College at Jersey City, New Jersey. Declaring CJSPA had no intention of entering into debate with USNSA with regard to the USNSA "Due Process" statements, they did in "A spirit of cooperation" offer comments. The comments highlighted the need for balance in the tension existing between freedom and authority and noted that "nothing, not even reason" (p. 10) will eliminate the tension between freedom and authority but that the students' problem will always be learning to understand and accept authority (Yanitelli, 1963).

A year later Ratterman (1964) argued that the relationship between student and institution should be based on an educational contract that would recognize both the "self-responsibility as the student approaches and achieves maturity" (p. 21) and the authority of the institution to adopt rules and policies to achieve accepted goals that would establish a clear authority structure accepted by contract. Arguing that student life on campus could not be handled by administrative rule, he stated, "A significant number of our students will rebel against such an administration" (Ratterman, 1964, p. 23).

In December, 1965 Robert H. Shaffer, Chairman of the Council of Student Personnel Associations (COSPA), sent a memorandum to all presidents of colleges and universities from COSPA. The memorandum recognized that evidence from a large variety of sources indicated on a large proportion of college and university campuses there was "an atmosphere of tension, mistrust, and antagonism among students, faculty, and administrators" (see Letters to the Editor, 1966, *Journal of College Student Personnel*, pp. 258-259).

The memorandum went on to indicate that the "extra-class life" of many institutions continued in a "superficial, isolated, or provincial fashion" and that students were demanding greater "freedom and rights" in an "increasingly aggressive, vociferous, and overt manner" and that students rejected the concept of *in loco parentis* (p. 258). It also recognized a growing dissatisfaction with the classroom experience by both teacher and students. It called for a more rational approach in which all segments of the educational community would be required to participate and work out a process in which both freedom and authority and responsibility would exist. It specified the need for the chief executive officer and the chief student personnel administrator on the campus to encourage "greater integration of extra-class and classroom activities," to facilitate a more effective interpretation of a college education, and to keep channels of communication open to all groups of the educational community "including those expressing antagonistic feelings." It concluded by stating the purpose of the memorandum was to suggest a plan to "maximize educational benefits and minimize harmful effects from what has exaggeratedly been called the 'student revolution'" (p. 259).

But a revolution was underway that was being waged first on the campus and then in the courts to redefine the relationship between students and institutions of higher learning. One court, writing on this relationship in tax supported institutions, declared that a federal court has the jurisdiction and authority to determine (a) what the lawful mission of a college may be; (b) if a student has been denied due process by a college; (c) if a college has subjected a student to individual discrimination (e.g., race or religion); (d) if a college has denied a student his or her federal rights (constitutional or statutory), which are protected in the academic community; and (e) if a college has acted in an unreasonable, arbitrary, or capricious manner (see *Dixon v. Alabama St. Bd. of Educ.*, 1961; Fowler, 1984).

The court went on to say that the mission of a college can lawfully be quite broad indeed, including not only the intellectual development of students but the physical, social, emotional, vocational, ethical, and cultural development as well; but the relationship is not one of *in loco parentis*. Its relationship with students is a voluntary one, educational in nature, and based upon the philosophy and mission of the college. Nor is the relationship contractual according to the court. Although the college has the legal entity of a corporation, students do not forfeit their constitutionally guaranteed rights in order to become students at any college.

A college may establish standards for students, said the court, both scholastic and behavioral, which are in keeping with its philosophy and mission and which do not deprive the student his or her federally protected rights. The college must accord the student "procedural due process" (fair play) in all cases of student discipline. In cases that might result in separation from the college, minimal due process is required: (a) adequate written notice of charges, (b) opportunity for a fair hearing, (c) disciplinary action to be taken only when there is substantial evidence, and (d) opportunity to appeal to the highest authority of the college.

Further, admission to college could not be restricted because of race, creed, or national origin; and student activities or organizations recognized or sanctioned by the college became a part of the college's mission, process and functions and, as a consequence, were subject to the same rules and standards as any other college function.

Writing later and basing his conclusions on the U.S. District Court for Western Missouri's declaration in the case of *Esteban et al. v. Central Missouri State College et al.*, Robert Callis (1969) declared that the authority to govern a college is vested in its board of control, which may delegate authority to its officers, faculty, and students, and, therefore, is not a political democracy that resides in the faculty and/or students. Then he concluded that there were two bases for student discipline: (a) maintenance of order and discipline on campus, and (b) conduct unbecoming of a student. Therefore, disciplining students by a college is "considered a teaching method," and the "analogy of student discipline to civil or criminal court proceedings is not sound" (p. 78).

The trend in disciplinary proceedings was to become increasingly legalistic, however, and institutions were on notice that a new relationship existed with their students even though they were not quite sure what it would mean. Perhaps no segment of the campus community struggled with this changing relationship to students more than student affairs.

The National Association of Student Personnel Administrators (NASPA), with the support of the Edward W. Hazen Foundation, undertook a national study in 1961 to assess students' "state of freedom to express their views of desirable changes" (Williamson & Cowan, 1965, Fall, p. 2; 1966). Key decision makers and student leaders at four-year colleges and universities across the country during the period from fall 1961 to spring 1964 were surveyed. They found that 71 percent of the presidents and 80 percent of the chief student affairs officers agreed without reservation or qualification that "an *essential part* of the education of *each student* is the freedom to hear, critically examine, and *express viewpoints on a range* of positions held and advocated regarding issues that divide our society" (p. 5).

Further, 70 percent of presidents said "abolition of laws prohibiting interracial marriage" (p. 8) could be discussed on their campus (most of the objection to this topic came from presidents of southern institutions), and 86 percent supported "U.S. dissemination of birth control information to underdeveloped countries" (p. 8). Four out of 10 Catholic institutions reported restrictions on birth control topics. Topics that students were almost uniformly free to discuss were "total military disarmament," "abolition of the House Unamerican Activities Committee," "local fair housing legislation," "abolition of prayers in public schools," and "Federal aid to Yugoslavia" (p. 8). Support for student involvement in political campaigning, petitioning public officials, student government association resolutions, student demonstrations, and newspaper editorializing were almost universally supported.

Student editors reported some censorship (15 percent for the period of the study), but none of the editors in Protestant universities or large public universities reported censorship (one-quarter of the teachers colleges and one-third of the Catholic colleges reported censorship, and 50 percent of the student editors reported they were required to submit editorial copy before publication).

Perhaps an indication of the stress existing within higher education and the climate in which student affairs staff worked is revealed in the finding about the degree of welcome three groups of persons (all men) would have had as speakers on the campuses. The first group composed of Earl Warren, Barry Goldwater, Augustus Cardinal Bea, Martin Luther King, Jr., and John P. Humphry, all of "high stature" and "considered controversial in a non-pejorative sense" (p. 11) would have been welcome on over 80% of the campuses with a major difference in regional response to Martin Luther King, Jr. The number of presidents questioning the advisability of any of these five speakers ranged from 4 for Chief Justice Earl Warren to 61 for Martin Luther King, Jr.

A second group that was categorized as "controversial speakers" was composed of eight persons that would have been welcome at only 44 percent to 60 percent of the institutions. They were James R. Hoffa, Robert Welch, Governor George C. Wallace, Barry Sheppard, Frank Wilkinson, Brewster Kneen, Robert P. Moses, and Fred Schwartz. They represented many of the vital interests of the time (i.e., segregation, integration, socialism, congressional investigating committees, anticommunism, pacifism, morality in trade-union leadership) and represented a more sensitive index of campus freedom than the first group. Although each of these controversial speakers, with the exception of James Hoffa, could address students at 80 percent or more of private institutions and more than 70 percent of the large public institutions, these institutions constituted only 13 percent of all the institutions studied. Southern schools were the most restrictive of these eight speakers, whereas New England institutions were the most permissive.

Four listed speakers were generally considered beyond the limits of acceptable student academic freedom. They were George Lincoln Rockwell, head of the American Nazi Party; Sir Oswald Mosley, founder of the British Fascist Movement; Daniel Rubin, member and National Youth Director of the Communist Party; and Malcolm X, New York leader of the Black Muslims (assassinated in New York City February 21, 1965). They represented the more extreme and controversial positions, and an invitation to speak on campus by any one of these four was "almost certain to involve the institution in a storm of protest" (p. 11). George Lincoln Rockwell was the least acceptable, and college presidents indicated that he had spoken at 17 of 757 colleges and an additional 171 presidents indicated he could speak if invited. Again Southern institutions were the most restrictive, with no more than 17 percent of the presidents indicating that any of the four could speak on their campus.

Institutions with strong religious ties were the most restrictive of this group of speakers. For example, Malcolm X could have spoken at 68 percent of the private universities, 61 percent of the large public universities, and 56 percent of the private liberal arts colleges; but only 7 percent of Catholic university presidents would have offered him a platform, and only 21 percent of the Protestant liberal arts college presidents.

The study also found that 42 percent of the campuses surveyed had no written policy about speakers, and the largest percentage of presidents reporting existing policy (77 percent) were in large public institutions. More than half of the presidents of Catholic universities and liberal arts colleges indicated they were guided by tradition or precedents. In making decisions about speakers, presidents at institutions with a written policy, no matter what the stated level of permissiveness, were much more likely to have permitted the invitation than those without codified policy. Of 320 presidents responding to the questionnaire, 27 percent had not permitted an invitation or appearance of a proposed speaker. The reason most often given for doing so was that the person was known to advocate action contrary to local, state, or national law.

There was a tendency to believe that only a few of the students were involved in controversial activities. The respondents from 57 percent of the reporting institutions believed that 10 percent or less of the students were active participants in matters involving controversial political or social issues and in half of these fewer than 5 percent were reported as active. Only 7 percent of the presidents reported that 25 percent or more of their students participated in such activities. Students were found to hold membership in policy-making committees in about 60 percent of the institutions studied, and they possessed a full vote in 84 percent of the committees on which they held membership.

Clearly, freedom to invite speakers to campus was not total and existed on a continuum of from very open (but not totally open) to very restrictive. It represented something of the climate in which student affairs staff worked and in many cases helped shape. It was an indication of the stresses within higher education at the time. The academic year 1964-1965 provided abundant evidence that the climate of student opinion and action was in a state of unrest from the opening day of classes at Berkeley and all across the nation with less publicized incidences.

By 1964 the issue of student rights was being actively debated in colleges and universities and would become even more of an issue as the decade progressed. Many college administrators and some faculty felt an exaggerated view of student rights interfered with the institution's responsibility to seek truth wherever it might be.

Professional Activity

In this decade efforts were made among the several college student personnel professional organizations to cooperate with each other in activities to further the profession. In particular, ACPA, NASPA, and NAWDC were involved; but these efforts met with little success due primarily to differences in philosophy, professional focus and identification, and professional jealousy. The best and most successful effort in this direction began in 1958 when the Inter-Association Coordinating Committee (IACC) was officially formed with the American College Personnel Association, the National Association of Women Deans and Counselors, the National Association of Student Personnel Administrators, and the American Association of College Registrars and Admission Counselors as members. IACC met annually at the time of American Personnel and Guidance Association (APGA) meetings. In 1962 the Association of College Unions-International (ACU-I), the Association of College and University Housing Officers (ACUHO), and the Association of Foreign Student Advisers (AFSA) were added to the committee.

In addition to establishing a rotating order among the member associations to chair the committee, IACC established that there would be three representatives from each member association, with staggered terms to insure continuity within IACC; there would be an annual meeting; each association would contribute $50 toward the ongoing expense of IACC; and organizations proposed for membership must have a "substantial proportion of its members" employed in college and universities, be nationally organized, and be accepted by a two-thirds majority vote of current IACC member organizations.

A joint commission on student financial aid made up of representatives from ACPA, NASPA, and NAWDC was formed in the spring of 1962. Representation from the newly formed Mid-West Financial Aid Officers Association was invited to its first meeting in Washington, D.C. on June 25-26, 1962, at APGA headquarters. A second meeting was held at the University of Chicago March 6-7, 1963. The commission spent a great deal of its time at these meetings discussing and making recommendations for changes in the administration of National Defense Education Act (NDEA) loans.

Philip A. Tripp, formerly dean of students at Washburn University in Topeka, Kansas, was appointed specialist in student services for the College and University Administration branch of the U.S. Office of Education in Washington, D.C. in January, 1964. He was to conduct research in the field of college student personnel and consult with college and universities and analyze new programs (*Association News*, 1963). This, along with other government programs such as those supported by the National Defense Education Act (NDEA), was an indication of the degree of involvement of the federal government with higher education.

ACPA had sought to add a member to the APGA headquarters staff to represent college student personnel work, and the American Council on Education (ACE) was planning to employ a person "well-known in student personnel circles" (American College Personnel Association, 1964) to coordinate its program of research in this area. On September 1, 1963, in a move of unusual cooperation, Joseph F. Kauffman, director of the Program of Training for the Peace Corps and formerly Dean of Students at Brandeis University and later to become president of Rhode Island University, was appointed to a combined post as a regular staff member of APGA and as a consultant to ACE. This assignment included the preparation of a comprehensive report on student personnel services, the planning and initiating of regional seminars, the assumption of an active role in legislative affairs, and other related activities (Emmet, 1963).

Representatives of 10 student personnel associations met at Airlee, Virginia, December 8 to 11, 1963, at a conference sponsored by the Commission on Academic Affairs of the American Council on Education. The keynote address was given by Lawrence E. Dennis, director of the Academic Affairs Commission. Discussions during this meeting centered around "Opportunities for Disadvantaged Persons in Higher Education" with particular emphasis on "Negro" students, "Year around Operations of Universities and the Trimester," and "The Student and Social Issues." The conference directed by Joseph F. Kauffman, consultant on Student Personnel Services for the American Council on Education and Director of Higher Education Services for the American Personnel and Guidance Association, was the first representative association conference centered on major philosophic themes. A major change made during the conference was to vote to change the name of the coordinating committee from the Inter-Association Coordinating Committee (IACC) to the Council of Student Personnel Associations in Higher Education (COSPA).

Professional Journals

Every profession has certain anchor points from which its members achieve their identity. The establishment and development of professional journals in the field of college student affairs was a clear indication of its growing professionalism. A professional journal presents and preserves the carefully distilled results of research, practice, and theory development for a profession. It reflects the values that the profession uses to guide and direct its work. In many ways a journal is like a mirror held up to reflect (although somewhat delayed) the professional posture of the field it represents. The profession searches critically for its best profile and strives to present it for all the world to see through its journals.

There were several professional journals in the field of college student personnel at this time: *Journal of College Student Personnel* founded in 1959; *NASPA Journal* founded in 1963; *NAWDAC Journal* founded in 1938. In addition, the *Personnel and Guidance Journal*, founded in 1952, carried in almost every issue something on college student personnel. It is clear from reading the professional journals that the field of "Guidance" perceived most if not all of its participants as "personnel" workers with counseling as a specialty within it.

The *Personnel and Guidance Journal* grew from a distribution of 6,146 copies for its initial issue in October, 1952, to nearly 20,000 copies 10 years later. It was expected that the journal would keep the members appraised of changes taking place and was enlarged from 9 to 10 issues in September of 1963 with volume 32. It published articles directed toward college student personnel professionals, particularly about counseling, appraisal, vocational guidance, and retention.

Beginning with volume 6 in 1964, the *Journal of College Student Personnel* moved to six issues, bimonthly rather than quarterly; and a new editor, Robert Callis, who was then director of the University Testing and Counseling Service and professor of education at the University of Missouri, took over. Under his editorship for the next six years, the *Journal of College Student Personnel* began a gradual and steady movement toward publishing research data based articles. Albert Hood was elected editor of the *Journal of College Student Personnel* in 1969 to follow Callis, and he continued this direction.

The *Journal of the Association of Deans and Administrators of Student Affairs*, or the *NASPA Journal*, began publication in December 1963 with Thomas A. Emmet as editor. It was published quarterly at a subscription rate of $3.00 per year. Perhaps the first research article published in the *NASPA Journal* was Trent's (1966) paper, originally presented at a preconference seminar, examining student development using the Omnibus Personality Inventory. The *Journal of the National Association of Women Deans and Coun-*

selors had been published since 1938 and, like its host, was dedicated to supporting the role of women in education. It was often most timely in the topics it considered but was not research oriented.

The *Journal of Counseling Psychology*, which began publication in 1953, also published manuscripts that were important to the field of college student personnel. As counseling psychology entered this decade, it was not clearly focused and was emersed in conflict over its purpose and direction. Many of its leaders were also leaders in the broader field of college student personnel and working on college campuses as student personnel professionals or in preparation programs in graduate education (e.g., Ralph Berdie, University of Minnesota; Thomas Magoon, University of Maryland; Harold Pepinsky, Ohio State University; E. Joseph Shoben, Jr., Teachers College, Columbia University; E. G. Williamson and C. Gilbert Wrenn, both from the University of Minnesota). It was not until 1964, as a result of the Greyston Conference, that Counseling Psychology was to organize itself and focus on its own distinct role and identity as a means of survival in a world of growing specialization.

Student protests. Reading the journals published in the first half of this decade gives a person very little clue about the disturbances happening on the college campuses throughout America. There were articles about violations of criminal statutes or ordinances (e.g., Goldworn, 1965), and numerous statements about students' rights as opposed to students' responsibilities. There was concern among student personnel professionals during the early years of this decade for suicidal tendencies among college students and about relationships with the faculty (see both the *Journal of College Student Personnel* and the *NASPA Journal* for these years).

One of the earliest articles on marriage counseling appeared in the *Journal of College Student Personnel*. The article traced the development of marriage counseling at the University of Minnesota since 1945 with the return of service veterans to the college campus (Neubeck, 1960). Predicting academic achievement was becoming important (Baumgart & Martinson, 1961). One of the first articles appearing that discussed racial and religious discrimination was authored by Trueblood (1961) and confronted student personnel professionals with the issue of discrimination in higher education.

The indirect response to student unrest in the professional literature seems to have been aimed primarily at better advisement to student groups. Problems with student activities on campus received considerable print (e.g., Ratterman, 1964), and one of the first responses in the journals was an article by Trueblood (1960) about the counseling role in group activities. Social fraternities felt threatened by their critics and almost every issue of the professional student personnel journals presented an article about their effectiveness and relationship to higher education. It was not until 1965 that the journals began to directly reflect the turmoil existing on the campuses. Two of the very first articles to do so were by Butler (1965) and Wise (1965). Butler looked at students demonstrating for increased freedoms, and W. Max Wise, then associate director of the Danforth Foundation, looked directly at the campus disruptions in a thoughtful analysis of what had led to modern higher education. Wise pointed out the deep suspicion that had developed between able students and faculty and administrators, and analyzed the background and development of the "new balance of power" created on the campuses. By the late 1960s, however, articles in the student personnel professional journals about violence on the campus were quite common. For example, excerpts of a report commissioned by the Forbes Committee of the Regents of the University of California to evaluate causes of unrest at the University of California and make recommendations to the Board of Regents was printed in the *NASPA Journal* (Byrne, 1966).

Drugs. Writing about drug use followed much the same pattern as writing about student unrest. In fact, it would seem from the evidence in the journals that student personnel professionals and other campus officials often saw the two going hand-in-hand. Concern about the use and abuse of drugs by students was growing, NASPA initiated a drug education project in September, 1966, and a growing amount of the literature was being devoted to the problem. Next to alcohol, marijuana was by far the most popular drug in use on campuses, followed by lysergic acid diethylamide (LSD). Hard drugs (i.e., narcotic, hallucinogen, or stimulant-causing addiction) were rarely reported in use. Bound up with social and moral concerns, health and psychological implications, and conflict between generations, student attitudes reflected defiance of any applied authority from college administrators or the older generation in limiting their experimentation. It was no longer a simple matter of right or wrong, legal or illegal.

Discrimination. The writing in the journals reflected the attitude of the time toward both gender and race. Some awareness of the impact of women in the field was creeping into the literature. For example, in 1960 the *Journal of College Student Personnel* published excerpts from a statement from the Commission on the Education of Women of the American Council on Education: "It is that most young people have not been informed that the role of home-maker can well be combined with other creative endeavors and responsibilities" (Association Exchange, p. 27). The impact of the women's movement was only beginning to be felt at this time, however.

In 1966 the *Journal of the National Association of Women Deans and Counselors* had one of the earliest issues dealing with black students and their problems. It was not until 1968 that a Black Task Force Committee was established and funded by ACPA to implement a report made by J.B. Jones of Texas Southern University. In 1969, Harper wrote one of the first accounts of what the black person's experience in a white university was like from his own experience and why black students were revolting against the racist structure of most universities (Harper, 1969).

Sexual behavior. The growing sexual freedom was receiving increased attention from nearly everyone. When parents sent their children to college, they expected much the same care and protection in these matters as had the previous generation. Student personnel staffs were again the professionals positioned to take the brunt of the changing social mores. Much was being written about the subject, and some groups were attempting a rational approach to the question. For example, the Group for the Advancement of Psychiatry (1966) illustrates an effort to use what was then known about human sexual development and recommend guidelines for college policy towards sexuality. Their discussion considered pregnancy, abortion, and homosexuality. Abortion was illegal, and homosexuality was considered a deviation but not of direct concern to college officials so long as it was practiced with discretion. The view was, however, that it "usually constitutes a conscious or unconscious distress signal and should normally result in referral to the psychiatrist for evaluation" (p. 138) and, thereby, was recognized as a deviation that required careful evaluation. Sexuality was considered in this writing as a biological drive that went through normal development and affected human development in many ways. A General Session of the 1961 NAWDC Convention was devoted to the topic "Changing Sex Standards," and the January 1963 issue of the *Journal of the National Association of Women Deans and Counselors (26)* was devoted to the same topic.

One writer felt that student personnel administrators were expected to deal with student sexual expression in incompatible ways (Gross, 1968). They were expected to administer college policy and support traditional sexual morality with restrictive rules and punishment (a coercive and punitive role), whereas on the other hand, they were to broadly stimulate education and personal development of students' sexual development.

A journal ultimately becomes a historical document, reflecting the path along which the profession journeys and the means by which it arrives at its present status. As the 1960s progressed, three journals began to emerge as the primary sources for professional literature in the field. They were the *Journal of College Student Personnel* and the *NASPA Journal* followed by the *Journal of the National Association of Women Deans and Counselors*.

Professional Associations

A second indication of the growing professionalism of the field of college student personnel or student affairs was the continued development of the professional associations themselves. The associations provided for the organization and support of the professional journals. The two associations that were clearly the most representative and broadly defined were ACPA and NASPA with a third organization, NAWDC, limited to women only. Professional associations in student personnel, however, to this day have been unable to combine forces and work together in more than a limited fashion except through a third umbrella-type organization that seemed to neutralize differences and focus on specific issues and problems. COSPA performed this function for a number of years.

ACPA. In February, 1962 ACPA had a membership of 3,027. New York State had the most members, 353, followed by California with 220. The majority of the Association members were from the populated Eastern states and the Midwest, and ACPA membership endorsed candidates for president of the Association from the Eastern and Midwestern states with one from California. There were four women and six men elected as chief executive officer of the association during this decade (see Appendix).

The ACPA budget for 1960-61 (approved on April 14, 1960) totaled $7,805. The largest item in the budget, $3,400, was for the *Journal of College Student Personnel*. ACPA held its 35th annual convention in Chicago (April 16-19, 1962) and the 10th as a division of APGA with a program theme "Climate for Learning" that would continue to symbolize ACPA's efforts to find a legitimate place in higher education. It also indicated that learning as a theme would be looked at from a variety of perspectives throughout the entire history of the profession.

Melvene D. Hardee, professor of higher education at Florida State University, was instrumental in commencing the commission system in ACPA during her year as president-elect in 1961-62. This was the beginning of a much larger involvement by the membership of ACPA in governance of the association. The ACPA mid-year meeting in November 1969 provided the first opportunity for a joint meeting of commission chairs and the Executive Council of the Association. ACPA in 1970 held its 43rd national conference in St. Louis, Missouri, and its first conference separate from APGA since APGA was organized. The major reason given for holding a separate conference was the growing size of the APGA convention and the difficulty finding appropriate housing even in major cities. Although true that the APGA convention was scheduled for New Orleans and convenient housing promised to be particularly difficult, as Charles Lewis, 30th president of ACPA, would comment later, the move was in part at least a compromise to avoid a vote on ACPA withdrawal from APGA. In 1972 Lewis would become executive director of APGA and served as its chief executive officer until July 1983.

ACPA maintained its ties with APGA and continued to grow. The organization budgeted $15,350 for 1962-1963 but only $14,900 for 1963-64. Regular ACPA members paid $22 in dues and a $2 assessment instigated in 1956. ACPA received $4.50 of this $24 and APGA retained $19.50 to support its various activities. The assessment was increased by $2 in 1968 to meet inflationary costs and increased publication frequency and size of the *Journal of College Student Personnel* (Hoyt, 1968).

NASPA. The National Association of Student Personnel Administrators continued to flourish. Despite its name change in 1951 from the National Association of Deans and Advisors of Men (NADAM) to the National Association of Student Personnel Administrators (NASPA) and efforts to recruit members for the first time, the "old boy" reputation continued to follow the association with some justification. Women were very slow to associate themselves with the organization. It was not until 1966 that a woman, Patricia Cross then of Cornell University, was appointed to the NASPA Executive Committee and another 10 years would pass before a woman, Alice R. Manicur, would become the first woman president of NASPA.

In 1958 the annual NASPA conference was attended by more than 300 persons and in 1959 the dues were increased to $25.00 for each institutional member. The *NASPA Journal* as it appears today was introduced in 1963. It was not until near the end of the decade that individual memberships were provided for by the organization. Three classes of membership were established: institutional, individual affiliate, and subscribing. Affiliate members would have voting rights as provided in the by-laws, but major decisions and election of officers were determined by voting delegates only.

Undoubtedly heavily influenced by the nature of its membership, perhaps, no other organization in the student affairs profession at this time was more attuned to the general administrative issues than was NASPA. This is clearly reflected in the early issues of its new journal (e.g., printing extracts from the Byrne Report in 1966). On the other hand, ACPA seemed more broadly oriented overall with its concerns for the practice of student personnel at all levels of the profession.

NAWDC. In 1966 the National Association of Women Deans and Counselors celebrated its fiftieth anniversary, reminding its members that it was the only personnel and guidance organization that was a department of the National Education Association (NEA). NAWDC had chosen to remain an independent organization when APGA was formed in 1952. Only the National Vocational Guidance Association was older than NAWDC. NAWDC had set out to recognize and support the role and work of women in education and particularly women in student personnel work because it was not being done elsewhere. It was one of the first, if not the first, professional organization to take a stand on civil rights (Fley, 1966). In the next decade, it would change its name to the National Association of Women Deans, Administrators, and Counselors (NAWDAC), and continue to provide a reference point badly needed by women, who were generally overlooked professionally almost everywhere else.

Counseling Psychology. Designated as a division of the American Psychological Association (APA), this group had grown to membership of 1,211 by 1963, an increase of over 61 percent from 1950. At the same time, however, only about 19 percent of the persons responsible for counselor education were members of Division 17, and 56 percent were not even members of APA (Whiteley, 1984). Although growing and with its own professional journal, it still had a ways to go before becoming fully representative of counseling professionals.

Professional Training

Following the growth of professional associations and professional journals, a third element establishing student personnel or student affairs as a
profession was the growing concern given to professional preparation.
Selection and training of "student personnel workers" was receiving increased attention as articles in the professional journals in the field indicated (e.g., Hill, 1961). Even questions of accreditation for student
personnel work were raised (Penney, 1961).

Concerns about professional preparation were not new, however. In
the early 1950s, the ACPA Professional Standards Committee surveyed a
selected group of 33 training institutions about "Standards of Admissions to Graduate Training Courses in Student Personnel Work" (Kamm,
1954, pp. 362-366). Responses were received from 21 institutions. A wide
divergence in selection standards was discovered, with some programs
following general graduate school requirements that included vigorous
testing and screening to others that allowed almost everyone who applied
the opportunity to prove themselves. The Miller Analogies Test was most
frequently mentioned as a standardized screening instrument, and nearly
one half insisted on related experience prior to beginning study for the
doctorate. The committee acknowledged the need for standards recognized by the field that emphasized "a high level program of selection and
admissions, influenced minimally by such factors as supply and demand in
the profession, and the institution's need for students" (p. 365). In 1955 an
APGA committee studied professional training, licensing, and certification and reported that over 205 institutions had preparation programs for
school counselors (Cottle, 1955). By 1961 "Standards for the Preparation
of School Counselors" were published in the *Personnel and Guidance Journal*
(pp. 402-407).

In 1963 COSPA appointed a committee on Professional Development
to study the need and make recommendations for professional training. A
draft was studied on February 25, 1964, at Indianapolis, Indiana and revised November 17, 1964 at Chicago, Illinois (see *NASPA Journal*, 1965,
pp. 45-47). This draft attempted to define the purpose of the "College
Student Personnel Profession" to satisfy both those of a "specialist" and
"generalist" philosophy. It outlined the functions of college student personnel to include administration, education, and professional development
and declared an interdisciplinary approach to preparation for the profession with a professional core that included study of the characteristics of

the college student (including the differing life patterns of men and women), history of higher educational institutions as social settings, principles and techniques of counseling, principles of administration and decision making, selection and inservice training of staff, communication with other areas of the institution, group dynamics and human relations skills. The study of student personnel work in higher education was to include an overview of orientation, college union programs, student activities, financial aids, housing and food service, health services, counseling services, foreign student programs, religious programs, fraternities and sororities, athletics and intramural programs, placement, alumni relations, current social and legal issues, and professional ethics and standards. Practicum, internship, or field work with college students was required in the core but could be taken in the area of specialization.

In early 1965 APGA established an interdivisional committee to study the training of student personnel workers in higher education. Divisions represented on the committee included the American College Personnel Association (ACPA), the Association of Counselor Education and Supervision (ACES), and the Association of Student Personnel Administrators in Teacher Education (SPATE). At the annual convention in 1965, the ACPA Executive Council instructed Commission XII of ACPA, Professional Education of Student Personnel Workers, to develop a position on training, which might be a representative view of ACPA in this matter. As a result, there were three documents produced in writing on the subject (COSPA, APGA, and ACPA). Donald W. Robinson was asked by ACPA to study all three documents and make recommendations to ACPA about "possible positions ACPA might take relative to supporting any or all of them" (Robinson, 1966, p. 254).

Robinson found that, with minor exceptions, there was agreement about the substantive areas of responsibility and authority that college student personnel work should include. They agreed explicitly on the following: (a) admissions, (b) registration and records, (c) orientation, (d) college union programs, (e) student activities, (f) financial aids, (g) housing and food services, (h) health services, (i) counseling services, (j) international student programs, (k) fraternities and sororities, (l) placement, (m) alumni relations, and (n) social issues involving students and administration. He found that all three statements agreed that preparation for student personnel workers should include (a) a grounding in the behavioral sciences with emphasis on psychology and sociology; (b) an understanding of higher education principles, philosophy, and administration; (c) a basic understanding of human development, the college student, and college culture; (d) an understanding of college student personnel work through formal course work, practicums, and internships; and (e) preparation in "tool" subjects such as counseling, testing, and research methodology was essential. He found minor differences among the three documents. One difference of interest was that the COSPA statement specified there should be some work relative to the differing "life patterns of men and women" (p. 256).

Robinson judged there was remarkable agreement among the three documents about the desirable training for persons entering the field. He did find, however, that the COSPA statement tended to stress administration more than the other two, the APGA statement tended to focus more heavily on the role of college student personnel worker as a counselor, and the ACPA Commission XII statement fell somewhere between the two. This would reflect directions the respective organizations would take in years to come. Robinson concluded that the ACPA statement was the only statement "presenting a theoretical model relating responsibilities, functions and positions to relevant processes and populations worked with" (p. 256) and most successfully delimited the field, but that agreement among the three documents was quite high. As a result of Robinson's work, the APGA Interdivisional Committee edited their document to reflect the sections of the ACPA document with which they had differed.

For some time universities had been providing graduate training for entrance into the field. Major universities preparing individuals in the field as indicted by doctoral dissertations produced over a 55-year period beginning in 1910 were led by Columbia University with 17 percent followed by Indiana University with 6.6 percent, Michigan State University with 4.6 percent, New York University with 4.6 percent, and Minnesota with 3.1 percent (Gladstein, 1968). Ralph Bedell, Chief, Counseling and Guidance, Institutes Section, Financial Aid Branch, Division of Higher Education, United States Office of Education (USOE), appeared at the request of the ACPA Executive Council to discuss the possibility of securing government money to train college student personnel workers at the college level (Summary, Executive Council Minutes, *Journal of College Student Personnel*, 1962, p. 195). Funds were forthcoming when in 1967 a National Defense Education Act (NDEA) Institute was funded at the University of Missouri, Columbia, with the primary focus on the preparation of student personnel workers for community colleges. Although training was clearly perceived as an important element, it would remain a basic issue for the profession for some time to come. A major problem for the profession was the appointment of individuals, particularly to major administrative offices in student affairs, who had no special training for the profession (e.g., see Rhatigan, 1968).

Ethical Guidelines

The fourth element in the establishment of student personnel as a profession was the development of ethical guidelines for its members. The APGA Executive Council approved the publication of a proposed code of ethics in 1959 (Committee on the Preparation of Ethical Standards, 1959). In 1961 the association set forth its approved "Ethical Standards" (American Personnel and Guidance Association, 1961), in which it referred to professionals as "personnel workers" (p. 106). It covered General Counseling, Testing, Research and Publication, Consulting and Private Practice, Personnel Administration, Preparation for Personnel Work, and it made no distinction to level of education to which it applied.

Expanding Student Services

Student health services. In 1969 a joint committee from the American College Health Association (ACHA) and the American College Personnel Association (ACPA) issued a report aimed primarily at counseling and psychiatric services on the college and university campus. It was designed to serve as a guide for establishing and implementing good working relationships for the two areas (Committee members were: Lewis Barbed, Henry B. Bruyn, Donald L. Shaefer, Inda M. Gill, and Vernon E. Keye for ACHA; and Edward S. Bordin, Donald L. Grumman, Barbara A. Kirk, Eugene L. Shepard, and Edward J. Shoben, Jr. for ACPA).

The report listed five objectives of college and university mental health services: (a) to provide to the college community, especially the students, formal and informal education in mental health concepts, practices, and care; (b) to provide expert professional assistance to the students who struggle to cope with academic, vocational, personal, and emotional problems: (c) to provide expert professional consultation to the community in matters of human behavior; (d) to provide specialized training for professional and nonprofessional personnel working with college students in the college community; and (e) to promote and conduct basic and applied research both independently and in cooperation with other behavioral sciences. The report implied the difficulty sometimes experienced between

professionals such as psychiatrists and psychologists working coopera-
tively to provide mental health services on campus. It also established a
broad field of service for mental health service that included not only
students but faculty and staff "who are in direct contact with students,"
and consultation for parents.

A leading figure in college health services was Dana L. Farnsworth,
M.D., who came to Harvard University as director of Health Services in
1954 where he served until 1971. He gave speeches throughout the country and wrote to promote college mental health services by sharing the
needs and benefits to be derived from meeting these needs (Farnsworth,
1957). Psychologists were being hired for the first time in the health services in the late 1950s to do "psychotherapy." Ironically one of the first to
break ground in this direction at Harvard was Richard Alpert, who would
later join with Timothy Leary to influence student use of the drug LSD
(Dinklage, Gould, & Blaine, 1992). One of the major accomplishments of
this effort in campus mental health was the development of extensive out-
reach programs to the campus community.

Financial aid. Financial aid officers were struggling with the question of
"How much is enough?" What should financial aid cover? Should it cover
only the "basic fundamentals needed for survival in a healthful manner"
or could it provide for things other than room, board, and tuition (Carlisle,
1962)?

The Problems and Policies Committee of the American Council on
Education meeting in Boulder, Colorado in June, 1960, prepared and published a statement in October of that year clearly stating what was to become the major theme in higher education for some time to come.

> The Basic Purpose of education in the United States is to provide the op-
> portunity for each individual to acquire the knowledge and understanding
> necessary to recognize and discharge the personal and social responsibili-
> ties of life to the full extent of his ability. The function of higher education
> is to pursue this purpose on more sophisticated levels which necessarily
> include the advancement as well as the dissemination of knowledge. (p. 1)

They also began to acknowledge that "Higher Education appropriate
to the times can never be cheap, and will indeed become more expensive"
(p. 2), while at the same time pointing to the very small fraction of the
national income spent on higher education. They recognized the need for
higher education to operate efficiently even though at that time money

and support were still plentiful. They indicated, however, that the most important thing to happen in higher education "is learning: learning to think, to relate, to do" (p. 5). This effort to sharpen the focus on learning would be echoed again and again in the following years from different sources. The statement emphasized the intellectual and classroom nature of learning, however, and did not seem to sense the importance of the out-of-class experience central to student affairs.

Confusion in the Ranks

Curiously, in the midst of this great growth period in higher education and a parallel growth of the profession itself, student personnel/affairs continued to debate its role and bemoan its lack of recognition on the college campus (e.g., see Koile, 1966). It seemed caught with other institutional administrators in the trap of equating respect with power and seeking power through span-of-control.

Voices such as Shoben's (1958), writing in the *Personnel-O-Gram*, seemed lost on all but a few academics in the field in the decade that followed.

> Student personnel workers will probably make their finest contributions by articulating themselves more explicitly with the rest of the educational enterprise, by finding greater commonalities with instructors and investigators, and by broadening both their professional horizons and their basic knowledge. To approximate its ideals most closely, student personnel work must give thought to professional standards, increasing the effectiveness and depth of relevant training, and the selection on an informal basis of those people who can best represent these ideals in their professional services and relationships. (p. 11)

Shoben went on to say,

> The personnel movement is no longer a protest against the neglect of learning opportunities in student life outside of the classroom. It is an organized effort, currently undergoing a significant degree of professionalization, to capitalize on such opportunities in distinctive ways but in the service of the same goals that justify and animate the educational process generally. (p. 11)

The profession, however, would divert a significant amount of its focus and resources to an internal debate over "identity," "specialization," and "proper role." Kathryn Hopwood in her ACPA presidential address (1961), "Who's for the Ark?", voiced concern over the relationship of "generalists" and "specialists" and a fear that specialists were breaking away into separate groups, all doing work in student personnel. It was certainly true in a number of cases that specialties either had or would commence and develop their own organizations (e.g., Association of College and University Housing Officers, Counseling Psychology as a division in APA, Financial Aids Officers, Union Directors). As colleges and universities grew in size from the early 1950s through the 1960s and reflected the American social ideal of individual development and personal fulfillment, they provided expanding opportunities to come together in more single purposed groups that would provide support, identity, and greater opportunity for face-to-face exchanges with professional colleagues.

Counseling as a specialty is a good illustration. Counseling professionals were struggling for identity during a period when Americans believed that they could still have everything and that everyone could achieve personal fulfillment by seeking to develop to their fullest potential. Counselors found themselves with a dilemma. Should they emphasize counseling as APGA did, or should they emphasize psychology as APA did?

The broad term of "Guidance" as in the American Personnel and Guidance Association was still in vogue during the 1960s. Many academic departments used this term in their title. The term "Guidance" seemed too limiting to some and, perhaps, too identified with public school work. A growing number wanted a broader outlook that would include adults in their focus. In general the work of most in the guidance field continued to center around school achievement, job satisfaction, vocational choice and success, the development of vocational interest, and psychological and social factors in career development. Some of the early college counseling centers reflected this emphasis by giving attention to social adjustment on the college campus. On the other hand, others found the term "Personnel" aversive feeling that it sounded too much like industry. It is no wonder that confusion existed within the counseling specialty and the field of college student personnel in general and has not been fully resolved to this day.

At about the same time as counselors were seeking direction, other practices were engaged that further confused the issue of professionalism and identity. Students were being employed as "junior staff" in positions such as student advisors, student teachers, orientation leaders, and residence hall staff members (see Aceto, 1962). Some of the first self-help literature was developed for the peer staff in residence halls (e.g., Nickerson & Harrington, 1968). It was by intent written for student use in training for staff positions in residence halls. It devoted space to psychological concerns such as suicide, and it recognized homosexuality as a practice to be discouraged. The ombudsman for students, patterned after the model in Sweden initiated there in the 1800s, was another alternative offered for working with students that seemed to represent that something more than the normal professional roles were needed (Schlossberg, 1967). It was not unheard of to appoint individuals to the chief student affairs position on campus who were not trained in the field, contributing further to the insecurity and confusion many felt about the profession. In 1967 Williamson asked the question "Is student personnel work a profession in its own status, or is it 'popularity' with students? Or are the professor's assent and students' acceptance the ultimate criteria of the relevance of our profession to the higher learning?" (p. 92). He went on to declare "It is about time we began to emerge in our own right as a relevant part of higher learning, not as an adjunct or even as a repair station for something gone wrong" (p. 92). The issue would not be quickly resolved, however, and would lead some writers in the future to question whether the field was a profession or not. As a result the profession would continue to question its identity and exhibit on occasion confusion and insecurity, particularly within the professional associations. Although the traditional professional associations would support and contribute to the debate over the important issues of the day, leadership to deal with these issues more often than not would emerge from other groups.

In response to students' charge that institutions were impersonal and dehumanizing, educators (including student personnel professionals) began to look for ways to personalize higher education. The Ninth Annual College and University Self-Study Institute held in July of 1967 by the Western Interstate Commission for Higher Education was on personalizing higher education (see Minter, 1967, for papers presented at the Institute). Wrenn (1967) noted that the character of a student personnel program on a given campus was more likely to reflect a strong personality in the life of that campus than it was of what was "known of student needs or the art of administration" (p. 102).

There was increasing recognition, however, of the need to study and understand the campus environment. Yamamoto (1968), in his overview, which examined the college student culture, specified that educational institutions were the result of the social interaction of individuals with one another and were made up of subgroups and subcultures that also functioned in relationship to other social institutions.

Perhaps the most significant document to emerge during the decade for the field of college student personnel was produced by the "COSPA Commission on Current and Developing Issues in Student Life" (Straub & Vermilye, 1968). The commission members contributing to the development of the report included Richard Covert; John C. Feldkamp; Anna Rankin Harris; Charles E. Minneman; Patrick Ratterman, S. J.; Edward Joseph Shoben, Jr.; Wilmer A. Sojourner; Raymond Stockard; Jean S. Straub, Chair; Philip A. Tripp; Dyckman W. Vermilye, Vice-Chair. The report began by stating, "The chief purpose of COSPA is to encourage and facilitate communication among and between the separate (but overlapping) membership of the different associations" (p. 363). The commission set for itself the difficult task of defining the function of higher education for the future and focused its presentation on six points.

First, the commission decried the growing trend that began shortly before World War II when the government recognized the usefulness the academic community would have for its inevitable involvement in the world wide conflict. The commission proclaimed that "unless an institution can maintain itself in a free and uncommitted position, the whole delicate concept of academic freedom itself is jeopardized' (p. 365). The involvement of the "academy" in the life of society would reduce its ability to fulfill the role of social critic (p. 365). They proposed that a restatement of the mission of the university should include at least three functions: Social critic (defined to mean an expression, involving a judgement of its value, truth, or significance, of a reasoned opinion on the matter), implementor of social change, and provider of associates for students as they developed critical facilities through the process of disciplined reflection. It stated: "The University is both a locus and a producer of critics, informed persons who know how to make normative judgments. And, of course, the better the university fulfills the role of producer of critics, the less will be the pressure on it to play the role of social implementor" (p. 367).

The second point focused on the changing relationship between the student and the institution. They recognized that *in loco parentis* was no longer accepted and explored other possibilities, admitting in the end that they had no definitive answer for what the nature of this changing relationship should be. They recognized, however, the shift in emphasis to "learning" rather than "teaching."

A third focus was on the residential experience (housing, dining, etc.). At issue they believed was the extent to which institutions considered the investment of funds into these areas as "important and educationally relevant" (p. 368).

The fourth point raised the issue of student political activities and their tactics. They posed the issue of the "institutional inability to cope with this kind of behavior," and raised the question of how to "make clear the vigor, usefulness, and morality of sheer thought in the modern world on demonstrably human terms" (p. 369); but they really offered no answer to this dilemma.

The fifth focus looked at the effect of student participation on institutional governance and concluded that participation by students "could not be considered fruitfully in any particular institution apart from faculty demands for such participation or apart from the total structure through which a college or university manages its affairs" (p. 370).

The sixth and final point suggested that "student personnel workers" might need to change their style in the relationships they developed and maintained with students, faculty, and administrations and "take positions on matters that once could have been identified as 'emerging issues'" (p. 370), as opposed to simply keeping the store. To this point the document had extolled the virtues of the rational and intellectual aspects of education. It was only near the end that they recognized the affective and interpersonal elements of human behavior and wondered if these were issues that students wanted professionals to address in their preparation to maintain order.

It is a remarkable document, if for no other reason than the language it used to state its position. It was in large part, however, an argument for a return to the traditional mission and purpose of the college and university. It probably reflected the commission's concern with the immediate events of the past several years on college campuses, events that seemed to emphasize the irrational and disregard the intellectual process necessary to pursue ideas. Although it clearly expressed a longing for a return to a more rational order in the institutions of higher learning, it did recognize the social issues challenging the traditional mission that were being voiced primarily by the students that attended the institutions. It recognized openly the issues of Vietnam and the draft as matters of national interest. It argued, however, that the institution, in order to protect the rights of individual faculty to take positions on these issues, could not as an institution commit itself to a particular position. This placed the commission in opposition to the stance that many students believed the colleges and universities should be taking on the social issues of the day.

United States Senator E. S. Muskie from Maine seemed to open the door to student participation in institutional governance when he suggested that a way for institutions to "work themselves out of the current crisis" was to give students "greater voice in the development of relevant and selected courses and curricula" (1969, pp. 248-250). Bloland (1969), on the other hand, expressed concern about the politicizing of higher education organizations. He feared these organizations were attempting to actively influence the shaping of public policy, which directly affected their primary purpose as academic organizations, he believed (e.g., efforts of the Washington based National Association of State Universities and Land-Grant Colleges and learned societies such as the American Sociological Association and the American Psychological Association to establish a public position on the Vietnam War). While organizations like APGA were advocating greater student participation in institutional governance, Hodgkinson (1969) was wondering "Who decides who decides?"; and Mayhew (1969) was speculating about the role of the faculty in the process. It was the beginning of an emphasis on the process being as important as the outcome. Some argued for a return to the traditional role of the institution as a social critic set apart from the world, whereas others were advocating that higher education must be more involved in the world. It is safe to say, however, that nearly everyone involved with higher education was growing fearful of overt violence on the college campus.

Perhaps one of the most sage observations at the time was made by David Riesman in an address to the American College Personnel Association meeting in Las Vegas, March 31, 1969, and later published in the *Journal of College Student Personnel.* He observed that more and more was being demanded of colleges and universities, including student personnel services. He offered as an example the efforts to recruit minorities, particularly black students, and what teaching and support programs cost to maintain these students on the campus. He indicated that according to figures derived by the Carnegie Commission on Higher Education the cost of higher education was going up at about twice the rate of the rise in national wages. He suggested that the growing trend towards "over commitment and under financing" were indications of higher education's ability to eat up resources while at the same time becoming "less and less able to elicit enthusiastic community support" (p. 367). He did not question the commitment of student personnel professionals to action but wondered about the commitment to action "in all directions at once" (p. 369). He speculated on the effort of academic leaders to make the hard decisions and the resulting unpopularity they would experience as a result. His predictions were to come to pass but, perhaps, took somewhat longer than he anticipated.

A combination of utilitarianism on the part of students, political compromise by the faculty, and the availability of financial resources drove the curriculum in the 1960s and 1970s (Cremin, 1988). Colleges and universities clearly moved from being elite to popular institutions by the end of the 1960s. Although still generally referred to as Junior Colleges, growing efforts to promote student personnel work in community colleges, by leaders such as T. R. McConnell and Max Raines at Michigan State University and Jane Matson in California, were also beginning.

The 1960s was the period of the great civil rights struggle in the United States and the beginning of the feminist initiative on most campuses. The majority of students were involved in preparing for their careers and "the good life" ahead. Faculty and administrators were still focused on academic and internal institutional issues rather than issues of societal importance. By 1967, however, this had changed. The eruption of student political activism was accompanied by demands for academic reform. The reform movement was about the achievement of three major goals or directions. First, the curriculum should have relevance and in a committed spirit address the great social issues of the time. Second, students should have a major role, comparable to the faculty, in academic governance. Third, elitism should be eliminated from the lifestyle of the campus and an open egalitarian structure created.

The student demand for relevance was paralleled by the discontent of younger faculty with the curriculum. Courses in street poetry, poverty law, social change, ethics of government, and how to protest effectively (make your voice heard) appeared all over the country as a formal or informal part of the curriculum. New fields of study sprung up (e.g., black studies, women's studies, clinical legal education, peace studies). It was a period of agitation, experimentation, and exploitation of the desire for change.

Student activism in the 1960s, as was the pattern over the previous century and a half (Lipset, 1993), produced an alliance between students and adult protestors. Bitterly divided on the issue of campus unrest, faculties often sympathized and lent support to unrest on campus. Although students were generally the most militant, the most extreme, and the least disciplined, faculty participation in stimulating and supporting the unrest is well documented (Boruch, 1969). Analysis of demonstrations that occurred at 181 institutions during 1967 and 1968 indicated that faculty were

involved in the planning of over half of the student protests that occurred. In nearly two thirds of the protests, faculty bodies passed resolutions approving of the protests.

Although the protests were usually short lived, student personnel staff
were almost always caught in the middle between the faculty-student alliance and the administrative arm of the institution, which often included
the active participation of the boards of control. Like the faculty, there
were many student personnel staff people, usually younger, that sympathized with the student ideology but found themselves in a much more
difficult position than did many faculty who felt little or no responsibility
to respond within the rules and administrative structure of the campus.
Internal governance structure was often ignored by faculty and students.
Institutional structures were perceived as either unresponsive and out-
dated or too tied to politics and the federal government to represent them.
Most student personnel staff members did not enjoy the tenure status
that gave the majority of faculty the security to voice their disagreement.
Dialogue, controversy, and conflict was often bitter, not only among established scholars in the same field, but with students as well. Student
personnel staff found themselves walking a very narrow line. The progressive philosophy remained visible in the effort student personnel professionals extended to represent individual students in their right to protest
and the responsibility they felt to restrain student behavior to protect the
community.

Although by the end of the decade the student activism that dominated
student politics was beginning to change, it had had its impact and left its
scars on many college campuses. The Berkeley protests were credited by
many with helping elect Ronald Reagan governor in California in 1966,
and the Chicago demonstrators helped elect Richard Nixon as president
in 1968. During the Cambodian campaign in May 1970, students demonstrated their antagonism to the war with large strikes and other forms of
protest. A Gallup Poll taken in late May, however, revealed that the respondents, although overwhelmingly opposed to the war, thought the most
important problem facing the country was campus unrest (Gallup Political Index, July, 1970).

The viewpoint coming from the college campus is often different from
the one held by society at large. The college campus is frequently a more
closed community, and during this period a less diverse community. Many
students had been suddenly removed from the structure and restraint of
the parental family and placed in an environment where the peer group

pressures are especially intense and pervasive. For a period of time, they inhabit a world that is more homogeneous and less stratified than the general culture and in which the faculty, the dominant elite, is usually positioned somewhat to the left of most other groups in the larger society. Although the impact of this experience is by no means lost when students reenter the larger society after graduation, the intense pressure of career and family do seem to modify its affect considerably.

The decade of the 1960s closed with a heated debate underway between the campus community committed to vigorous dialogue over issues of national and world significance and the general public that was demanding restoration of order and civility. The academy had become for a time the arena in which demands for change, threats to existing lifestyles, angry protest and even violence, overrode order and reasoned debate. It generated anger that academic institutions were a long time, if ever, getting over. Many scholars felt the values on which their professional lives were built had been rejected. More significantly, forces outside the institutions of higher learning (i.e., legislatures, politicians, community leaders) felt the need to exert some influence and control to bring the campuses back to a state of acceptable order that these groups have not fully relinquished to this day. Institutions of higher learning were no longer in control of their own destiny.

Summary

During the Sixties the influence of progressivism continued to be a major factor in college student personnel. It was a turbulent time for the country and for higher education. It was a period in which college student personnel was tested beyond anything previously experienced in its history and survived. In the early years of the decade, civil rights, particularly for African Americans, became a major issue for the nation. The decade ended with the Vietnam War on center stage both as a moral and as a political issue. It was the decade in which John F. Kennedy, Martin Luther King, Jr., and Robert F. Kennedy were assassinated, creating an inestimable loss for the nation. It was also the decade in which a president of the United States chose not to run for re-election because of a war that could not be won.

During this decade student protesters took to the streets of city and campus and, because of the focus of television, influenced the direction of national politics in ways that were not possible before. It was a period when students began to redefine their relationship with institutions of higher learning and thereby affect their relationship with student personnel staff. The events of this decade forged reverberations that would be felt for years to come.

Chapter V

The Decade of the Seventies

The 1970s were years of significant changes and were greeted by avoidance and denial. It was somewhat like a person who does not feel well and is irritable, grouchy, cranky, but denies anything of significance is wrong. What was going wrong most in the 1970s was the economy. America's economy was slowly deteriorating marked by growing unemployment, increasing numbers of business failures, and declining productivity. At the same time, American politics was in disarray with narrow interest groups achieving victories and with weakened, broad-based political parties resulting in a succession of one-term presidents and a series of tax revolts.

All of the phenomena were related. Like water (H_20) the social order seemed made up of two parts business and economics and one part government and politics. They were inseparable and determined how people worked together to produce goods and services and pursue public goals. Economic growth, inflation, unemployment, investment, savings, and trade were problems in the realm of business and economics, whereas government and politics managed the issues of equal opportunity and civil rights, public education, transportation, crime, social security and welfare, the environment, and foreign affairs (Reich, 1983). Conservatives have traditionally been more focused on the former and liberals on the latter, but this distinction was breaking down in the 1970s and was becoming more stereotypical than real.

By the 1970s, with the assistance of the United States, Western Europe and Japan had fully recovered from World War II to become major competitors in the world market. The United States was no longer alone as the economic leader of the world but in serious competition with several mature industrial countries for a share of the world market. Other countries with more recently developed technology were actually in a better position to produce quality goods with lower worker wages. Although slow to admit its plight, America's new challenge would be to adapt to this changing world.

In the quarter century since World War II, Americans had developed a sense of economic invulnerability. But, by 1973 oil consumption in the United States exceeded its production and continued to grow. As a result Americans were rudely awakened by the 1973-74 Arab oil embargo. To discover that a small group of desert sheiks could force U.S. citizens to pay higher prices for gas to run the family car and, in addition, to wait in line at the gas pumps to receive it was not only humiliating but a bit frightening. The shutdown of a major oil exporter in 1979 again created long lines at the gas pumps and a sense of vulnerability that Americans had not felt before in the same way. Although the American economy had been generating the world's highest standard of living, it was now slipping down the scale, being surpassed in 1978 by Switzerland, Denmark, West Germany, and Sweden (International Monetary Fund, 1979, April, pp. 122, 156, 214, 352, 356, 390). Switzerland had a per capita GNP 45 percent larger than the United States. Kuwait had actually surpassed the United States standard of living in the early 1950s but was passed off as a simple case of being handed wealth for oil in the ground. Although it is generally easy to calculate per capita GNP, it is difficult to make precise standard-of-living comparisons among countries due to differing tastes, circumstances, traditions, and attitudes. For example, health care may be provided by the government in one country and obtained privately in another (see Thurow, 1980).

Regardless of the complexities involved, it was clear that other parts of the world were catching up to the United States. In the period from 1972 to 1978, industrial productivity in the U.S. rose one percent while it rose almost four percent in Germany and over five percent in Japan. Major American businesses were reduced to marketing products made in Japan (e.g., video recorders). Steel and other industries in the United States were forced to look to other countries for advanced technology. By 1973 U.S. oil consumption exceeded its production and continued to grow. By 1978 almost 50 percent of the oil consumed in the United States was imported. If the cheap Middle Eastern oil was withheld, world consumption significantly exceeded world production. By raising or lowering their production of oil the Middle East could control world oil prices. The Organization of Petroleum Exporting Countries (OPEC) was formed and tripled the price of oil in 1973-1974 (Thurow, 1980). Recognition that the United States was no longer self-sufficient was a difficult lesson for most Americans to accept.

Richard Nixon

A mild recession occurred in 1969 and 1970. It had not begun to recover by the summer of 1971, and unemployment stood at six percent. Fearing that it would effect his chances for reelection, President Nixon imposed price and wage controls to stop inflation and stimulate the economy to lower the rate of unemployment. When the controls were removed in 1973, the inflation that had been suppressed reappeared and was intensified. To raise the income of farmers and strengthen election efforts, the Nixon administration sold too much wheat to Russia, in 1972 leaving not enough to meet American demands and prices rose sharply. After 25 years of dealing with surpluses, the Agriculture Department found itself in the unfamiliar position of dealing with shortages, and it was slow to respond and did not remove controls on acres planted. Coupled with a corn blight in 1973, availability fell further behind with the result that farm prices rose 66 percent between 1971 and 1974. The combination of the rapid industrial growth, the farm economy, the OPEC price increase and the Arab oil boycott in 1973 produced the double digit inflation of 1973-1974. As a result of the Nixon administration's tight monetary and fiscal policies, real Gross National Product (GNP) stopped growing and gradually fell throughout the first three quarters of 1974. The rate of inflation did not respond, however, and monetary policies were further tightened creating the famous credit crunch of late 1974.

From 1972 to 1978, real per capita disposable income rose 16 percent. The average American was better off and his or her standard of growth was not slowing down. Although the real standard of living was rising slightly faster prior to 1972 than after 1972, the difference was small. From 1972 to 1978, real GNP grew by $228 billion, but there was essentially no change in the distribution of money income between the rich and the poor. The upper 40 percent of the population had 69.5 percent of total income in 1972 and 69.6 percent in 1977. The lower 40 percent of the population had 13.7 percent of the income in 1972 and 13.8 percent in

1977. Officially, unemployment ranged in 1978 from 8.4 percent for teenage black females to 2.6 percent for white males aged 55 to 65 (U.S. Department of Labor, Jan. 1979). Despite a 6 percent unemployment rate, many analysts were arguing at the beginning of 1979 that the economy was at full employment. Clearly there was a very uneven employment structure, however. Women, adult blacks, hispanics, elderly whites, and young whites ranged along a continuum between the extremes of black teenagers and prime-aged white males.

Elected in 1976, the Carter administration used an anti-inflationary strategy to fight inflation that had as a prime ingredient monetary and fiscal policies designed to create a substantial but moderate amount of idle capacity. Although everyone favors reducing inflation as long as it is done by lowering someone else's income, nearly everyone is also against anti-inflationary policy that lowers his or her income. The reality is, however, an effective anti-inflationary policy must lower someone's income below what it would otherwise be, which is not a matter of economic analysis but a simple mathematical fact. Deregulation of the airline industry was a program to achieve lower prices and to reduce the inflationary rate. The economic strategy was clear but the policies were not. No person wants their income reduced although it is part of an anti-inflationary strategy designed to benefit the larger number. Each industry protected by government policies to raise prices wants to keep these policies in place (e.g., truckers, farmers, etc.). In addition, issues between environmentalists and polluting industries that had economic implications were growing.

In the 50 years following World War I, the concept of scientific management was applied to almost every organization in the United States. It was predicated on three basic principles: (a) specialization of work through the simplification of individual tasks, (b) predetermined rules to coordinate the tasks, and (c) detailed monitoring of performance (see Reich, 1983). Organized labor supported this approach, too, and, as a result, American factories and businesses were operated with rigid job classifications and work rules that separated planners from workers. Planning was the responsibility of the executive, white collar supervisor, distinct from the blue collar worker who performed the mindless task. Prosperity had been created from the development of large organizations and high volume machinery patterned by "scientific management." "Specialization by simplification," "predetermined rules," and "feedback information" separated the manager (the thinker-planner) from the worker (the basic producer). Management and organized labor supported this system and endeavored to protect their economic status through its clearly defined roles and explicit work rules. The system that evolved was geared to high volume production and was maintained by the support of both labor and management long after the economic conditions that led to its creation and development had changed. It was not until about 1970 that business and industry began to recognize that this system no longer served their needs.

During the 1970s the American share of manufactured goods in total world sales declined by 23 percent, whereas every other industrialized nation, with the exception of Great Britain, maintained or expanded its share of the market. Japan's share rose from 6 percent to 10.5 percent, and developing countries with lower labor costs (e.g., Korea, Hong Kong, Taiwan, Singapore, Brazil, Spain) were taking advantage of their lower labor costs and production methods that could separate steps in the process to globally scattered operation centers to outcompete the United States. The growth of productivity in the United States went from a yearly increase of 3.2 percent between 1948 and 1965 to an average of 2.4 percent between 1965 and 1973. By the end of 1979, the average worker was only 98 percent as efficient as he or she was at the beginning of the year, and productivity continued to fall after 1980. It only began to move slowly upward again in the 1980s because fewer workers were employed. Regardless of what product is identified (e.g., steel, textiles, automobiles, rubber, electronics, etc.), production involving high-volume machinery and low trained workers could be achieved more economically in developing nations. By additionally reducing the need for unskilled workers in high volume production, automation accelerated the trend rather than reversing it.

Other industrial nations were faced with the same competitive threat. Europe and Japan moved to face this challenge by shifting to products and processes that required skilled labor (i.e., precision products, custom products produced by high technology), which required a flexible system that could adapt quickly with input of new information. This system depended upon the skills of employees who often worked in teams. The old, traditional method of separate functions (i.e., research, design, engineering, production, distribution, marketing, sales) were merged into a highly integrated system that could respond much more quickly to new opportunities (Reich, 1983).

Most organizations after World War II were developed on a hierarchial model with a major goal of its executive class to compete, dominate, and move up the managerial ladder. The new system demanded more than technology alone, but recognized that the economy is based on people and the relationship of people is a social relationship (Bowles, Gordon, &

Weisskopf, 1983). This new developing system of production required technically skilled workers that could work together and enhance the skill of one another. But, the educational system was not prepared to provide them. Public schools did not have the resources to prepare the scientifically educated person needed to work competently in this new flexible integrated system. The inability of public education to respond to this need undoubtedly was a major contributing factor to the unpreparedness of the United States to respond to the new economic demands.

Politics

As the 1970s began, Richard Nixon had been president for a full year. Nixon began his presidency by stating that the great objective of his administration would be to run an open administration and to bring the American people together (Schell, 1975). Nixon had mobilized a constituency of "silent" or "forgotten" Americans around social issues of patriotism, concern about crime, and traditional middle-class values. With advice from Attorney General John Mitchell, he pursued this "southern strategy." Using his opposition to civil rights, his anger at the Supreme Court's liberalism, and his contempt for student demonstrators, Nixon built a new base for the Republican Party in the "Sun Belt" (states of the Old Confederacy and the American West). At the same time, the political left was coming apart as a result of its failure to agree on a common agenda and "by the systematic harassment and sabotage of Nixon's counterintelligence agencies (Chafe, 1991, p. 381).

Vietnam

Nixon's much publicized "plan" to end the Vietnam War was more fiction than fact. Although declaring his intention to end the war in Indochina, in reality he widened it by secretly launching a bombing attack against Cambodia. In so doing he made the war his own. The principle of "credibility," plus the domino theory, worked to keep the United States locked into Vietnam. The government believed that if the United States lost its determination to prevail in Vietnam it would show it lacked sufficient will to confront conflict anywhere, and other nations would lose their confidence in the power of the United States. So strong was this belief by the government that when it lacked public support it created incidents to stir up public anger against the enemy and sustain the sentiment to continue the fight (Schell, 1975).

Richard Nixon and his Secretary of State, Henry Kissinger, thought much alike about foreign policy. They approached the world in classical balance-of-power strategies and were unwilling to give up U.S. influence in any part of the world. Nixon's basic policy was to wind down the war in Vietnam, encourage settlement in the Middle East between Israel and the Arab states, and reassure Europe of U.S. support and strengthen relationships there. In 1968, however, he was advised by Melvin Laird, his Secretary of Defense, and other advisors that a military victory in Vietnam was impossible. Laird tried to convince Nixon of the absolute necessity of moving out of Vietnam. The drain of a 10-year war, the loss of nuclear superiority in the world that had given Eisenhower the advantage in Korea and Kennedy in Cuba, made it very difficult to find a strategy that would explain a military withdrawal from Vietnam as prudent rather than as a defeat.

Increasingly defensive, Nixon attempted to rally the country in a nationwide speech by personalizing the issue. "We will not be intimidated" he declared (Chafe, 1991, p. 397). His decision to invade Cambodia with American troops in the spring of 1970 resulted in an immediate response of anger. Students all across the country took to the streets in protest, and the nation saw demonstrations larger than any they had seen since 1968. The antiwar movement focused on draft resistance and dissent within the armed forces. According to the Selective Service Center in Oakland, California, over half of those called to serve never responded and another 11 percent who did report refused to serve. Antiwar protestors burned their draft cards and conducted raids on Selective Service Offices across the country, destroying approximately a half million draft files. Within the Army desertions increased until by 1970 almost 70,000 American soldiers had fled from assigned duties. One entire battalion in Vietnam carried out a set-down strike refusing to go into battle. The new revolt was ignited at Columbia University in the spring of 1968 and reached its zenith at Kent State University in Ohio after Nixon's speech announcing the invasion of Cambodia in May of 1970.

Increasing numbers of college students identified with the New Left and believed that basic changes in the system were necessary to improve life in America. Nixon's own commission on campus unrest, a position created in the aftermath of the 1970 demonstrations, concluded that "A great majority of students . . . oppose the Indochina war" (Chafe, 1991, p. 405). If the war was wrong, students insisted, so were all policies that supported it from the draft to the military, from ROTC to recruiting for the defense industry.

Although advised from both within and without his administration to let university officials handle the antiwar movement on their campuses, Nixon seemed unable to let it alone. In March, 1969 he stated the federal government would not become involved, but on the other hand announced that the Secretary of Health, Education, and Welfare (H.E.W.) had, within a letter to college and university presidents, requested they advise their students of recently enacted statutes that denied government loans and scholarships to students convicted of crimes in campus disorders (Schell, 1975). Nixon became more occupied with the student antiwar movement during the spring of 1970. He raised the shadow of civil war in America but warned that if students and the government should go to war the government would clearly prevail. In a speech at General Beadle State College in Madison, South Dakota he stated:

> Our fundamental values [are] under bitter and violent attack. . . . We live in a deeply troubled and profoundly unsettled time. Drugs, crime, campus revolts, racial discord, draft resistance—on every hand we find old standards violated, old values discarded . . . the forces and threats of force that have reached our cities and now our colleges. . . . Force can be contained. We have the power to strike back if need be and to prevail. . . . It has not been a lack of civil power but the reluctance of a free people to employ it that has so often stayed the hand of authorities faced with confrontation. (Schell, 1975, p. 37)

Two days later, speaking at the graduation ceremony of the United States Air Force Academy in Colorado Springs, he broadened his attack on rebellious students to include "skeptics and isolationists," meaning members of Congress, mostly liberal Democrats, who were publicly asking when the war would be concluded.

Several weeks before these speeches, the Justice Department had begun wiretapping newsmen, cabinet aides, White House aides, and revealed later they had used electronic surveillance to monitor the conversations of several of the individuals indicted in the Chicago conspiracy trials. In 1968 Congress had passed a law permitting the Justice Department to wiretap American citizens in certain instances provided that a court warrant was first obtained in each case. Attorney General Ramsey Clark had declined its use because he considered it unconstitutional, but Richard Nixon had made clear during his campaign for president that he would make good use of this power. But, now the Justice Department was employing wiretaps without first obtaining a warrant. The attorney for the defendants in the Chicago conspiracy trial, in outrage stated, "For the first time in American history, a member of the president's cabinet [John Mitchell] has publicly—and proudly—stated that he has, in open violation of his oath of office, taken the law into his own hands" (Schell, 1975, p. 39).

Reversing the military build-up in Vietnam undoubtedly was one of the most difficult decisions of his presidency, but in June of 1969 Nixon made the announcement of the first troop withdrawals. He continued to talk a hard line, however, to avoid alienating the dominant conservative majority that had voted for him and Wallace in 1968. The result was that he created doubt in the minds of the intellectual and student peace bloc that he was serious about removing troops from Vietnam. He hoped the North Vietnamese would see it as an act of good faith and be persuaded to begin serious negotiating in the Paris peace talks taking place at the time, but that did not occur. The secrecy surrounding the bombing of Cambodia and the warrantless wiretaps were only the first steps in a broader separation of image and reality.

When Nixon announced to the world on April 30, 1970, that American troops were crossing over into Cambodia, he was aware that a large and strong public reaction was possible. But, with only about a month left in the spring term on college campuses there were few signs of unrest, and Nixon felt the campus response would subside as the initial impact of the Cambodia campaign faded. Further student reaction was less important than the attitude of the general public. The next morning, May 1, 1970, students across the country began marching, picketing, striking, and blocking entrances into classrooms. Approximately 2,300 students at Princeton agreed to strike, and students at the University of Maryland ransacked the ROTC office and a struggle with police resulted in an estimated $10,000 worth of damage and 50 injuries. Nixon, encouraged by good reports from the battle field, was in a fighting mood and verbally lashed out at the students. In a briefing on the same day at the Pentagon he referred to student demonstrators as ". . . these bums" who are "blowing up the campuses" and demonstrated no interest in understanding their position (Evans & Novak, 1972, p. 275).

Higher Education and Vietnam

In the face of a nationwide strike that was being organized on more than 100 college campuses, James M. Hester, president of New York University, wrote a letter to President Nixon that was signed by the presidents of 36 other colleges and universities asking him to consider the consequences of alienating American youth and to take immediate action to demonstrate his intention to end the war quickly. They requested an early meeting with the president, but were perceived by Moynihan and Ehrlichman as presumptuous and arrogant in their demand. Their request was denied (see Evans & Novak, 1972).

During a Saturday night riot on May 2, 1970, the ROTC building at Kent State University was burned down. Governor James Rhodes of Ohio declared martial law that same night and sent troops from the 145th Infantry, Ohio National Guard to the campus of 19,000 coeducational undergraduates. But, the demonstrations continued, and on Monday, May 4, 1970, apparently in an effort to clear an area of rock-throwing students, troops opened fire without warning, killing 4 students and wounding 11. Nixon continued to be unyielding, however. But, neither he, nor apparently the rest of the country, were prepared for the response immediately triggered by the Kent State tragedy on campuses all across the country. Fires did $100,000 damage on Long Island University's Brooklyn campus; Governor Ronald Reagan closed the University of California with its 280,000 students to prevent "radicals" from attempting to seize control of it; three students were stabbed in a demonstration at the University of New Mexico; nearly 40,000 students and faculty marched from the University of Minnesota to the state capitol; a $500,000 fire was set at Colorado State University; students at South Carolina occupied the first floor of the administration building and ransacked the treasurer's office. Many more incidences of a similar nature occurred across the country as moderates were radicalized and joined extremists. This student revolt confronted Richard Nixon and the nation with the most difficult, persistent, and unyielding social issue of the time. The student revolt reached its peak in the spring of 1970.

Although prominent members of his staff were faculty members from major institutions (Moynihan & Kissinger from Harvard; Anderson from Columbia), Nixon chose not to consult with them about the crisis, but, rather, turned to aides with less knowledge of higher education, such as John Ehrlichman who had a son at Stanford. Ehrlichman perceived the problem as one of communication and advised the president that it could be resolved by reassuring students of the president's goodwill. Nixon appeared to soften his stand. Although on the day of the Kent State tragedy, Nixon had refused the request of 36 college presidents to meet with him, Ehrlichman visited with six students from Kent State the day after the event and arranged for them to see the president the day following. At this time they told Nixon the problem on campus was being caused by the Vietnam war and the lack of communication between students and the federal government. On May 7 Nixon met with eight college presidents. Although a much smaller group than the 36 who had signed the letter, they presented to him a viewpoint not much different than the one delivered by the students from Kent State. In essence they told him the crisis was caused by the Vietnam War and the antistudent remarks emerging from his administration, particularly those of Vice President Spiro Agnew, but presumably referring to Nixon's own labeling of students as "bums" as well. Nixon gave everyone present the impression that there would be no more of this kind of talk in his administration.

Given the premise strongly voiced by the students that the main problem was communication, Nixon appointed G. Alexander Heard, Chancellor of Vanderbilt University and one the eight college chief executives he had conferred with, as Ambassador of the Campus to the president (Evans & Novak, 1972). Heard, like most college administrators in that period, was inclined toward the student dissent and reflected their complaints. He told the press that he believed Nixon was willing to listen and that he would do his best to help him hear.

Nixon had said on September 26, 1969, that under no circumstances would he be affected by student antiwar demonstrators. In May 1970, however, he was indicating a very different position. On May 8 Richard Nixon held a nationally televised press conference during which he seemed willing to be open to the thousands of nonviolent but potentially volatile students that were at that moment in Washington, with some surrounding the White House itself. Following the press conference, he was drained emotionally and could not sleep. After a number of phone calls to friends, at 4:55 a.m. he went by limousine from the White House to the Lincoln Memorial where a number of students were awake and preparing for the protest rally to be held the next day. Nixon attempted to establish in an hour long discussion with some of these students the communication that he and Ehrlichman believed was needed on a larger scale to resolve the problem with students. But even in this small more intimate circumstance, his difficulty making easy conversation again resulted in a failure to communicate. Students reportedly left the scene with recollections about Nixon's comments about football and surfing rather than the difficult issue that had brought them to Washington (for a more detailed description of this event see Evans & Novak, 1972, pp. 290-291).

Nixon's attempts at communication with students were unsuccessful;

and still another tragedy was to occur on May 15, 1970, on the campus of Jackson State College in Jackson, Mississippi. State highway patrolmen fired on students, killing 2 and wounding 11. On May 20, 1970, the president met with presidents of 15 predominantly black colleges at the White House. For more then two hours they discussed the tragedy at Jackson State and other problems confronting higher education. During the meeting a strong statement was read by Herman Branson, president of Central State University, Wilberforce, Ohio, in which the increasing alienation of black youth was attributed in no small part to "the policies and practices of your administration" (Evans & Novak, 1972, p. 291), and particularly the rhetoric of Spiro Agnew and John Mitchell. The president of Jackson State, John Peoples, Jr., showed Nixon a number of photographs of the killings at his college, but the president's response was to wonder what was needed to get more respect for the police from young people. This was an indication of the hard line and law-and-order policy that would soon return and dominate the gubernatorial and congressional election campaigns of 1970. Nixon had not entirely given up efforts at communicating with higher education and students, however. Much as had occurred during the prior meeting with white college presidents from which Heard's appointment had resulted, James E. Cheek, president of Howard University, attracted the president's attention. Two days later Cheek was made a consultant to Heard.

On May 22, 1970, James Allen, commissioner of education, read a prepared statement disagreeing with the administration over Cambodia. He did not immediately resign, however. Although Nixon knew as a result Allen could not remain in his position, he did not want to risk further antagonism with higher education and students. Rather than fire Allen, Nixon waited for him to resign; but when Allen did not, 20 days later on June 10, his resignation was announced for him.

A commission on campus unrest was formed headed by William Scranton, former governor of Pennsylvania and former presidential candidate, to investigate campus violence and explore ways of peacefully resolving campus unrest. It was a body with only one student member, although that was clearly progress for the time. On June 8 Nixon had sent eight young White House aides to college campuses to find out what was going on, what was being thought and said on campus. A week later they returned and reported that students blamed Nixon, Agnew, and the Vietnam war for their present situation. Memoranda began to flow in to the president from the "Ambassadors" Heard of Vanderbilt and Cheek of

Howard that defined an existing national crisis and indicated that the Cambodian operation had caused a sharp shift left among students. Heard wrote Nixon that his attempt at communicating with students was not working and that his famous trip to the Lincoln Memorial had backfired. Heard further wrote that talking about Syracuse football and California surfing "offended students who felt immersed in a national tragedy, like telling a joke at a funeral" (Evans & Novak, 1972, p. 299). On July 22 Cheek blamed the federal government for what was wrong with the nation's black colleges. Nixon was being told that the problem was his fault. At the same time, the Scranton Commission was taking testimony at Kent State, Jackson State, and Washington. The commission report released on September 26 blamed the president for not exerting moral leadership. Nixon was clearly making little or no progress toward persuading the majority in higher education to his purpose and, as the summer progressed, his position began to harden.

The shift in his position was indicated at a press conference held in the Century Plaza Hotel in Los Angeles on July 30. He declared that it was "very short sighted" for university presidents and professors and other leaders to blame the problem of the university on the government. He stated:

> But once all things are done, still the emptiness, the shallowness, the superficiality that many college students find in college curriculums will still be there. Still when that is done, the problem we have of dissent on campus. ... dissent becoming sometimes violent, sometimes illegal, sometimes shouting obscenities when visiting speakers come to campus, this is not a problem for government. We cannot solve it. It is a problem which college administrators and college faculties must face up to. We share part of the blame. I assume that responsibility. We'll try to do better. But they have to do better also. (Evans & Novak, 1972, p. 300)

Nixon understood the cultural politics of resentment, however, and following student demonstrations over the Cambodian invasion, he exploited popular anger to obscure the shortcomings of his administration. The White House blamed the victims at Kent State rather than the perpetrators, with Spiro Agnew calling the slayings "predictable and avoidable," a product of the "politics of violence and confrontation" (Chafe, 1991, p. 414). Spiro Agnew used his position as vice president as no one before him had to become the most controversial politician in the country with his hard divisive speeches. In the summer of 1970, he traveled throughout the country for the Republican party delivering frontal attacks on students and liberals. But Agnew became an issue himself that grew larger than the party or the election, and by election day was badly compromised as a public figure.

Getting Elected

The basic Nixon speech in 1970 began by defending his Vietnam policy (". . . after five years of men going into Vietnam, we have been bringing them home"), and followed this by pledging to continue fighting crime and inflation. He continued to attack protestors as a small minority who would not lead America in the future. Election results were mixed, perhaps, slightly in favor of the Democrats (Republicans lost nine seats in the House and a net loss of 11 governorships but gained a net two seats in the Senate).

In February, 1971 the Secret Service, acting at the request of President Nixon, installed microphones in the White House, which would record all conversations in the Oval Office and in the cabinet room. About two months later, the Secret Service installed microphones in the president's office in the Executive Office Building, and it also tapped the president's phones in the Oval Office and in the Lincoln Room. At the same time, it installed equipment to record phone calls in a cottage at Camp David, the president's Maryland retreat (see Schell, 1975, p. 147).

In the spring of 1971, issues resulting from the Vietnam War began being heard in the courts. The first was the case of First Lieutenant William Calley who had led a platoon that had massacred more than 300 people in the village of My Lai on March 16, 1968; and on March 29, 1971, he was found guilty of murder by a jury of his peers. The public split over the merits of the verdict, and on April 3, 1971, Nixon announced he would personally review Calley's final sentence, thereby opening the judicial system to the criticism that it was subject to political influence.

The second legal encounter occurred when a group of veterans calling themselves the Vietnam Veterans Against War came to Washington to demonstrate and voluntarily testify to war crimes they had committed. They camped on the Capitol Mall and, as a result of extensive television coverage, became the center of the country's attention. The Justice Department obtained an injunction against them sleeping on the Mall that was upheld by the Supreme Court; but for fear of political fallout that might result from sending police in to remove them forcibly (some were in wheelchairs), the Justice Department never issued the order, thereby declining to enforce the court order it had urgently requested.

The third legal encounter resulting from the war developed from another demonstration that led to a judicial scandal. A diverse group of young people gathered together on May 3, 1971, labeling themselves the "Mayday Tribe" with the publicly-stated intention of stopping the government if the government did not stop the war. Approximately 30,000 young people journeyed to Washington with a plan to sit down in Washington streets, stop traffic, and hopefully the government. The federal government stepped in once again. The CIA and the Washington police set up a joint command center, and the police incarcerated nearly 10,000 people taken from the streets of the Capital without charging them with any offense. Using a list of seven policemen, arrest forms were later falsified by rotating the name and badge number of a policeman in the space for "Arresting Officer." Later, judges had to decide what to do with the thousands of illegally jailed people, many of whom had been put in dangerous and unsanitary makeshift jails. As the cases were processed during the next several months, few were found guilty of anything. Although the government had not been stopped, the process of law had been severely violated.

The fourth incident arose on June 13, 1971, when the *New York Times* commenced printing excerpts from a top secret, multivolume study of the conduct of the Vietnam War that had been ordered by Defense Secretary Robert McNamara in 1967. The Pentagon Papers, as the study became known, showed how the American public had been misled about the Johnson administration's intentions in Vietnam and described a major breakdown of democratic government. Because of fear the study might reflect on its own policy, the Nixon administration again intervened and the Justice Department sought and received a temporary injunction in Federal District Court in New York ordering the *Times* to cease publication of the Pentagon Papers. Subsequently, newspapers in Washington, Boston, and St. Louis received copies of the Pentagon Papers and began publishing them but were also enjoined by the Federal Courts in their areas from continuing to do so. For the first time in the history of the U.S., the government had prevented the press from printing news for the public. On June 30, 1971, the Supreme Court ruled against the government by a margin of six to three.

Later the administration put together a group of people that included E. Howard Hunt, Security Coordinator for the Committee to Reelect the President; G. Gordon Liddy, a former CIA agent; Egil Krogh, on the staff of John Ehrlichman; and David Young, personal aide to Nixon, for the purpose of destroying the credibility of Daniel Ellsberg, a former aide to Secretary of State Henry Kissinger, who had provided the *Times* with the Pentagon Papers after becoming disillusioned with the war and, at the same time, attacking radicals in such a way that would seem to connect them with the liberal and moderate members of the Democratic Party. Ellsberg was indicted, but very few people understood the real goal was to discredit the Democratic Party and reelect Nixon president. During the last half of 1971 and the first part of 1972, the time when the Pentagon Papers were being published, clandestine preparation for the presidential campaign of 1972 was carried out. In August, 1971 to fight inflation, the president suddenly imposed wage and price controls and removed the dollar from the gold standard, which brought about an upturn of the economy.

On January 4, 1972, Senator Muskie announced his candidacy for the presidency, followed a week later by Senator Humphrey, both joining Senator George McGovern, who had announced his candidacy almost a year before. The campaign carried out by Nixon's staff planned not only to discredit and divide the Democratic Party but conducted an operation of sabotage supplemented by espionage that often involved racial, religious, or ethnic minorities in some way. Wiretapping and forgery were commonly used by this group. In late February, on the eve of the presidential primaries, President Nixon made his trip to China and the coverage was extensive. For the first time in history, a summit meeting was broadcast live, by satellite, back to the United States. By March Senator Muskie's campaign was losing strength, but at the end of March the North Vietnamese army invaded South Vietnam in force.

The American response to this politically embarrassing event was to expand the bombing, but on May 1, 1972, the northern defenses of South Vietnam broke and a complete collapse seemed possible. The next day the long-time director of the FBI, J. Edgar Hoover died, creating political complexity that would be a long time settling. On May 8, 1972, the president announced in a televised address to the nation that he was ordering the mining of the entrances to the ports of North Vietnam, and he would also order the bombing of railroad lines that connected North Vietnam and China, creating potential global crisis between nuclear powers. On May 15, while campaigning for the presidency, Governor George Wallace of Alabama was shot by an assassin and left paralyzed. On May 22 President Nixon arrived in Moscow where trade agreements and a limited strategic arms agreement were concluded. On May 28th Nixon addressed the Russian people and the American people simultaneously, using for the most part language of dtente (dtente stood for the efforts to reduce strained relations between the two nations; see Kissinger, 1979); but at the same time the heaviest bombing in the history of warfare was being carried out by American planes in Vietnam, and on the same night of the speech the White House burglary squad broke into the headquarters of the Democratic National Committee in the Watergate office building in Washington where they photographed documents and installed two wiretaps. On June 18, 1972, the *New York Times* reported that heavy American air strikes were continuing in North Vietnam; and on page 30 of the same issue was a story about five men arrested in the headquarters of the Democratic National Committee in the Watergate office building with burglary tools, cameras, and equipment for electronic surveillance.

For almost four years, Nixon had been "reorganizing" the executive branch of government with the goal of bringing the cabinet departments and agencies under his control. He then used some of these agencies to conceal crimes committed by his own people that included not only Watergate but four years of illegal activities by individuals in the White House. Among the nation's major newspapers, however, only one, the *Washington Post*, consistently placed the Watergate story on the front page. On September 15, 1972, the five men apprehended in the Democratic National Committee headquarters were indicted along with E. Howard Hunt and G. Gordon Liddy. At the end of September, the *Washington Post* reported John Mitchell had control of the secret funds for spying on Democrats. On October 26, 12 days before the election, Henry Kissinger told the nation that peace in Vietnam was "at hand" and that the bombing of North Vietnam had been halted. A few days later, Senator McGovern responded that this was not true, but Nixon led McGovern in the Gallup Poll by a margin of almost two to one and people found Nixon "more sincere and believable" than Senator McGovern by a margin of three to one. McGovern had declared that he was not a "centrist" candidate and then further hurt his chances when he dumped his first choice for running mate, Senator Thomas Eagleton, because Eagleton revealed that he had twice received electric shock for manic depression. After the election, which Nixon handily won, Kissinger announced on December 16, 1972, that negotiations with North Vietnam were 97 percent complete, but two days later Hanoi reported that "waves" of American planes were bombing the city and other parts of North Vietnam.

On February 7, 1973, by a vote of 77 to 0, the Senate established a Select Committee on Presidential Campaign Activities to investigate abuses in the presidential campaign of 1972, including the Watergate break-in.

The committee was to become known, with the appointment of Senator Sam Ervin of North Carolina as chairman, as the Ervin Committee. Although the president's popularity in the polls stood high (68 percent), the work of this committee began the process that would unravel the coverup. At the same time, Nixon was threatening to veto a number of bills and if they were overridden to impound the funds appropriated in the bills, creating fear of one man rule and loss of the constitutional system. Television began to cover the proceedings of the Ervin Committee and of the House Judiciary Committee when it began to consider impeachment of the president. Then the White House tapes were revealed and Vice President Spiro Agnew was forced out of office when his bribe-taking activities became known.

Nixon's foreign policy was intentionally directed away from confrontation and toward negotiations, and opening China was his most noticeable effort in foreign policy. Progress with the Soviet Union was slower than expected, however. Japan was concerned about trade barriers as a result of the overtures to China, and Nixon had backed Pakistan in a losing war with India whereas the Soviet Union had supported India. The goal of maintaining an even-handed policy in the Middle East between Israel and the Arabs went awry when pressure from the American Jewish community resulted in sending Phantom Jets to Israel. At home a deepening division was developing between Nixon and civil rights advocates. The Vietnam War and the antiwar movement with students at the center had become a battle of moral issues and for public opinion that was almost more significant than the actual combat in Vietnam. Nixon held a growing conviction that the courts, the news media, federal bureaucracy, and demonstrations in the public areas were restricting powers belonging to the president; and he chose to combat this with any means available, disregarding its legality.

The Watergate investigation led to impeachment proceedings in Congress and to Nixon's eventual resignation on August 8, 1974. Gerald Ford, vice president after Agnew's resignation, was sworn in as the country's new president. He declared "Our long nightmare is over." Although the crisis was resolved, the cost was enormous. Nixon's success in mobilizing a conservative majority, neutralizing his opponents, and destroying opposition from the left, culminating with the Watergate debacle, had diverted the country from the issues of equality, the economy, and social reform. There seemed little energy left after the major effort to insure survival of the American constitutional form of government (see Chafe, 1991). In a post-Watergate response, nearly 60 percent of the voters supported Democrats in the congressional elections of 1974. Republicans lost 48 seats in the House. Although Ford was successful during his time in office, reaching a new arms control agreement with the Soviet Union and with the Middle East shuttle diplomacy of Henry Kissinger, he also had to preside over the humiliating withdrawal of all Americans from Vietnam when the South Vietnamese were unable to stem the onrushing North Vietnamese in the spring of 1975. Americans at home were able with television to watch the desperate flight of the last Americans in Vietnam from the roof top of the American embassy and realized that the United States had lost a war for the first time.

Following Nixon. When Gerald Ford became president in August 1974, he brought with him a large reservoir of political currency and the hopes of the nation to finally put things right and get back on the road again, but, within weeks of taking office, he gave away most of this favor in one single action. Ford pardoned Nixon for all wrongdoing, freeing him forever from answering for his crimes while his aides were serving jail terms for carrying out orders to obstruct justice. Ford reduced his popularity further by being the most conservative president since Herbert Hoover. He vetoed 39 bills in one year, including federal aid to education and health care legislation. Interest rates reached an all-time high as the country entered its worst recession since the 1930s, but Ford vetoed a tax cut bill designed to increase consumer spending.

Jimmy Carter

In many ways Democratic presidential candidate governor of Georgia Jimmy Carter was ideally suited to fill America's post Watergate political needs. He was a deeply moral "born again" Christian who prayed daily and sincerely cared about his beliefs. There had rarely been such a candidate on the American scene. He tirelessly campaigned across the country, telling people that they deserved a government as good, as competent, as moral, and "as filled with love as are the American people" (Chafe, 1991, p. 451). His concern for the basic values and his personality helped create a new hope for the future, and he narrowly won the presidency with 51 percent of the vote. He won 75 percent of the vote of Americans whose primary concern was jobs, however. Democrats won more than two-thirds of all seats in Congress.

During his administration Carter continued to appeal to the average American. He walked down Pennsylvania Avenue on election day in a business suit rather than a cutaway; he wore a cardigan sweater for a televised "fireside" chat; he frequently held town meetings in small communities and would stay with "average" families; and he nominated a record number of women and blacks to administrative posts. But, he came to Washington as an "outsider" and never achieved a good working relationship with the other institutions of government. As a result he was prevented from solving the economic problems that were the major concern for blacks, women, and white blue-collar workers.

The energy crisis that occurred during the Carter years is a good illustration of the strength and weaknesses of his administration. President Carter confronted the problem directly. He pointed out that Americans used 40 percent more energy than they produced and that, by importing oil, they were also affecting inflation and unemployment. Congress would not respond to his legislative request, however, and when he tried to go over their heads to the American people, the result was he blamed America's "malaise" less on the energy crisis than on the "crisis of confidence [in the American people] . . . a crisis that strikes at the very heart and soul and spirit of our national will" (Chafe, 1991, p. 453). With unusual shrewdness Carter perceived the nature of the problem—a narrow concern with self over community and a loss of faith in institutions because of political assassination, Vietnam, and the shame of Watergate. Despite his courage and forthrightness, he was unable to create solutions and failed to break the political impasse that existed.

The American people had lost faith during the 1970s in the political process as a way to achieve change. Perhaps the most significant factor about the large margin of victory Ronald Reagan received in the 1980 presidential election was that he was chosen by only 28 percent of the potential electorate. Nearly 47 percent of the people who could have voted did not go to the polls. The mass of nonvoters would become the single most dominant political group in the country. In Sweden, West Germany, Italy, and France, more than 85 percent of those eligible to vote during the 1970s took part in the national elections contrasted with only 53 percent in the United States during the 1980 election. Nonparticipation had not always been the case in American politics. In the late 1880s, approximately 90 percent of the potential electorate had gone to the polls, and as late as 1960 almost two-thirds of the potential voters in this country had voted. If the same proportion of eligible voters had cast ballots in 1980 as had voted in 1888, more than 40 million additional voters would have gone to the polls. If the 1940 voting percentage had resulted, more than 19 million additional votes would have been cast. Compared with only 18 years before, the decline in voting was nearly 30 percent, a tremendous drop out of American people participating in the political process (see Chafe, 1991).

The Changing Social Attitude

American society changed more during this decade than during any previous period. It witnessed the American defeat in Vietnam, the constitutional crisis of Watergate, the OPEC oil embargo, and 53 Americans seized and held in the American Embassy in Tehran for more than 400 days by Iranian revolutionaries. Coupled with an increasingly difficult economy, the Carter administration was unable to effectively respond and allowed Ronald Reagan to ride in out of the sunset to save the nation. As Yankelovich (1974) pointed out, there was a vast change in the complexion and outlook of an entire generation of young people from one generation to the next.

In the post-Vietnam era, campus rebellion ceased almost entirely and criticism of America as a "sick society" faded. A new sexual morality had ascended among most youth, including both those attending college and those not attending college. Criticism of the college or university and the military decreased markedly and concern for minorities decreased, too. The New Left almost disappeared from the campus, and "law and order" became more accepted by students. The college campus was probably the "trendsetter" or leader in setting the new value structure and the new morality. Although students in the early 1970s indicated that less emphasis should be placed on money, they also expressed their belief that career and making money were very important to their well-being and the well-being of their families. Just working hard to obtain a good living with economic security, and money to buy possessions, a new home, and a good education for the kids was no longer sufficient. Career in itself was becoming a means of self-fulfillment and although money, security, and possessions were a part of its overall structure and a standard of success within it, there was increasing need for work and career to be psychologically fulfilling as well (Yankelovich, 1981).

Changing Meaning of Sexuality and Family Structure

According to D'Emilio and Freedman (1988), from the middle of the 1960s to the 1980s, the nation experienced what was perhaps the greatest transformation in the meaning of sexuality it had ever experienced. A number of observations bolstered this position. The important shifts in attitudes, the changes in the life cycle of Americans, and the marketing of sex were creating change in the patterns of sexual behavior. They argued that the focus on sex in the culture was seen in television, in the "Dear Abby" and Ann Landers columns in newspapers, and in magazines and newspapers that began offering space for personal advertisements where a "DWM" (divorced white male) could seek "SF" (single female) for walks, talks, and an afternoon affair (p. 328). By the 1970s books giving marital advice were being replaced in sales by sex manuals such as Comfort's (1972) *The Joy of Sex.*

As sexuality was being promoted by entrepreneurs, there were changes in the population patterns occurring. The baby-boom of the 1950s and 1960s changed dramatically. Between 1960 and 1980, marriages declined by 25 percent and by 1985, the median age of marriage for men had increased to 25.5 years and for women to 23.2 years of age. Along with later marriages came a decline in fertility. From a peak reached in the late 1950s, the fertility of American women declined to about the replacement level by the middle of the 1970s. The availability of legal abortions, the more reliance on sterilization, and easily obtainable and reliable contraceptives placed nearly complete control of having children within the hands of the married couple. Particularly within the middle class, to not bear children was emerging as a serious choice. By the end of the 1970s, more than 25 percent of married women in their late twenties were childless.

Not only were Americans marrying later in life and producing fewer children, but marriages were much less likely to survive. Aided by liberalized state laws, the divorce rate began to climb dramatically in the 1960s. Between 1960 and 1980, the number of divorced men and women increased by almost 200 percent; the divorce rate increased 90 percent; and the divorce rate among blacks was even higher. By 1980, over 25 percent of black men and women between the ages of 25 and 54 were divorced as compared with less than 10 percent for whites. Although many of the divorced would eventually remarry, second marriages were even less likely to survive (Blumstein & Schwartz, 1983, p. 34). Although the divorce rate had slowed somewhat by 1980, marriages taking place in the late 1970s had only a one-in-two chance of remaining intact (Blumstein & Schwartz, 1983).

One result was American households were growing smaller and more diversified. Over one-half of the new households created in the 1970s were nonfamily ones. By 1980 only three-fifths of all living arrangements were the traditional two-parent family with children, and many of these families would dissolve in divorce or separation. By 1980 most Americans could expect to be in "nontraditional" situations for at least a part of their childhood and adult years.

Cohabitation among men and women was on the rise during the 1970s and was becoming a visible and increasingly acceptable practice. Although cohabiting couples constituted only three percent of American households at a point in time, the probability of an individual participating in this arrangement was much higher. One study found that almost one-in-five American men had lived for at least six months with a woman other than their wife (Blumstein & Schwartz, 1983). At the same time, the number of working mothers was increasing. Among married couples in 1980, families with incomes between $25,000 and $50,000 were most likely to have both spouses working. By 1980 almost half of black households were headed by a female. A majority of black infants were born to unmarried women, and a minority of black children were being raised in two-parent households. Auletta (1982) found "There is a direct correlation between poverty and whether a family is maintained by one wage earner or two" (p. 256). By 1980 the majority of poor lived in families maintained by women, a rise of 25 percent in a decade.

Poverty was rapidly becoming feminized with the number of families being maintained by women increasing by 62 percent in the 1970s and by the end of the decade, 3.1 million poor families were supported by women. In 1980 about one-half of all poor families were maintained by women. Whether family dissolution was a cause or an effect of poverty, it clearly was a factor.

Survey data from several sources confirmed a definite shift in sexual values in the direction of approval of nonmarital sex. Particularly among younger heterosexuals, the sexual life of unmarried youth, as well as married couples, experienced significant modifications (e.g., sexual experience was beginning at a younger age, acts previously considered deviant were now practiced, the differences between the sex lives of men and women were reduced). The availability of effective contraception in the 1960s that was more widely used in the 1970s gave a major sense of freedom to sexually-active adults, particularly among females. Health services on college campuses were beginning to routinely distribute contraceptive information and devices to students (D'Emilio & Freedman, 1988). By the middle of the decade, three out of four married couples used the pill, the IUD, or sterilization, and the legalization of first-trimester abortions provided a means of last resort for women when contraception failed. As they became sexually active earlier in life, as the age of marriage rose, and as their participation in the labor force provided the possibility of more autonomy, women were developing different expectations for the sexual experience. In the midst of the growing trend toward more sexual freedom, two factors emerged, however, that created some concern. With the discovery of penicillin, the threat of venereal disease had diminished to a large degree; but Herpes, a new venereal disease, appeared. Although it posed far less physical threat than syphilis, it did cause restraint in some people and, for others, represented the ethical and moral concerns in sexual permissiveness. By the end of the 1970s, an older and more conservative approach to sexual behavior had reappeared and this effort would be reinforced a few years later with the epidemic of AIDS/HIV infection.

Secondly, a movement to curtail the practice of abortion was developing. The Supreme Court's decision in 1973 that gave women the right to choose, *Roe v. Wade*, surprised many, but a number of local antiabortion groups formed quickly. In 1976 Representative Henry Hyde of Illinois succeeded in attaching a rider to an appropriations bill that prohibited the use of federal dollars to fund abortions, and the following year the Supreme Court ruled that government had the authority to bar financial support of abortion with tax dollars. As a result both the federal and state governments cut back considerably on their funding of abortion; and by the summer of 1979 only nine states continued to pay for abortions.

In the 1950s gay men and women were regarded by the majority as moral perverts and national security risks, and the FBI conducted surveillance of the gay community. It used the information collected to prevent homosexuals and lesbians from obtaining federal jobs. A number of events would occur in the next two decades that seemed to put a different light on this issue. In the case of *Roth v. United States* (1957), the forces favoring censorship of sexual content in written and artistic work gained a limited victory. During the following 10 years, a number of cases involving pornographic classics, erotic films, contemporary fiction, nude photography, and pulp novels were before the Supreme Court. The justices on the Warren Court seldom reached unanimity. Although denying obscenity under the protection of the First Amendment, their decisions broadened considerably the content of material available to most Americans.

During the same period, the Kinsey (1948, 1953) reports related that many Americans engaged in erotic acts for reasons other than reproduction and that increasingly larger numbers of women were having sex outside of marriage. In 1960 the Food and Drug Administration gave approval to the marketing of oral contraceptives and within a few short years millions of women would use the pill. Five years later in the case of *Griswald v. Connecticut* (1965), the Supreme Court overturned Connecticut's anticontraception law, thereby eliminating restrictions on the sale and distribution of contraceptives that dated from the nineteenth century (see D'Emilio, 1983). There was clearly a shift in attitude toward sexual activity occurring among the American people, and although perhaps less visible at the time, important changes in the perceptions and lifestyle of gay men and women. By 1965 there were clear signs of a growing militancy among gay people. It was a period when young radicals in different movements (i.e., "Black Power," "New Left," the counterculture, women's liberation, gay activists) spoke to each other in at least a limited way and refused to accept the ways of the past or moderation in reform politics.

By 1970 the gay movement was seeking the extension of the civil rights statutes to include provisions that prohibited discrimination on the basis of sexual orientation. Activists in the movement worked hard to secure passage of municipal and county ordinances that would later lead to the same goals at the state and national levels. By 1977 they were successful in a number of instances including one in Dade County, Florida, which aroused the anger of Anita Bryant, a singer with national recognition. Bryant successfully led a crusade for repeal, a pattern that would repeat itself on numerous occasions in other places in the country.

With roots in traditional conservatism that had been largely built on anticommunism, a "New Right" revolt was gaining strength, fueled largely from anger and fear of changes that had recently taken place on the national level (e.g. busing, feminism, abolition of prayer in the schools, sexual freedom and permissiveness). For conservatives America's most important and cherished values were at stake and they rallied Americans to single-issue campaigns opposed to the Equal Rights Amendment, to defend the "right to life" of unborn fetuses, or to ban homosexuals from teaching in schools (see Chafe, 1991). Groups such as the Conservative Caucus, the Committee for the Survival of a Free Congress, and the National Conservative Political Action Committee saw the opportunity to advance their causes; and their leaders in 1979 persuaded Jerry Falwell, whose television program *The Old Time Gospel Hour* reached 18 million viewers weekly, to organize the "Moral majority" as a means to mobilize the fundamentalist population. They also organized the Religious Roundtable that brought together conservative politicians and television preachers such as Falwell,

Pat Robertson, Jim Bakker, James Robinson, and others. Ronald Reagan actively sought the fundamentalist vote during the 1980 presidential campaign and was openly supportive of the New Right's position on abortion, school prayer, and pornography.

Women's rights. Of all the efforts that gained momentum during the 1960s, the struggle for women's rights achieved the most strength and maintained it on into the 1970s. In the 1950s most women in the labor force were over the age of 35 years and had children who were in high school or out of the home. During the 1960s the largest employment increase was among women between the ages of 25 and 35 years but generally after their children had entered school. By 1970 over 50 percent of mothers whose children were ages 6 to 17 years were employed. Women's jobs, however, continued to be seen, for the most part, as helping the family rather than as a means to an independent or autonomous life. But, the numbers of working women 20 to 24 years of age increased from 50 percent in 1964 to 61 percent in 1973. Eighty-six percent of college women in that age group were employed. By 1980 more than 50 percent of mothers with children under age six were in the labor force. Within a period of 35 years, the relationship between most women and work was redefined as a lifelong obligation with time out for childbearing, and almost all women expected to work most of their lives. This was a radical change in the economic structure of the nation.

All across the country, women began to participate in consciousness-raising sessions aimed to unite and support each other in demanding an end to unequal status (e.g., lower pay for the same work, household duties, child care, career priorities, taking minutes at meetings). By the early 1970s, the movement was front page news. Women picketed professional meetings to demand equal employment opportunities. Women boycotted the Miss America Pageant to protest the treatment of women as sex objects, and they demonstrated before state legislatures for repeal of antiabortion laws.

But, the road to change would not be easy. The movement would generate resentment and resistance from without and spawn internal conflicts from within. Lesbian women expected "straight" women to support their cause, but many feminists like Betty Frieden perceived gay activists as a threat to the movement. Both men and women outside the movement were frequently appalled and angered, and men often felt threatened and attacked.

Although many women in the early 1970s felt the movement was going too far, they actively supported feminist positions on day-care centers, repeal of abortion laws, equal job and career opportunities for women, and more equal sharing of household duties. A Gallup Poll in 1962 asked American women if they felt themselves victims of discrimination, and two out of three said no. Eight years later, in response to the same question, half of the women indicated that they were victims of discrimination; and four years after this, when asked the question again, American women declared by a margin of two-to-one they were treated unequally and that they supported efforts to improve their status. This changing attitude correlated with the accelerated movement of women into the paid labor force.

The movement, perhaps, had its greatest influence on college students. Near the close of the 1960s, Yankelovich (1981) reported that the women's movement had made virtually "no impact on youth values and attitudes," but by the early 1970s he noted a "wide and deep" acceptance of women's liberation arguments. In the short span of only two years, the number of students who viewed women as oppressed had doubled. Over two-thirds of college women surveyed agreed "the idea that a woman's place is in the home is nonsense." In 1970 a survey of college freshmen indicated half of the men and more than one-third of the women supported the statement that "the activities of married women are best confined to the home and the family." Five years later only one-third of the men and less than one-fifth of the women supported the same position (see Yankelovich, 1981; Yankelovich, Zetterberg, Strumpel, & Shanks, 1985).

The next phase was for college women to begin moving into careers historically restricted to males. By 1975 women were showing increased interest in entering fields traditionally reserved for men (e.g., business, engineering, medicine, law). During the same period women entering the traditionally feminine fields of elementary and secondary school education dropped from 31 percent to 10 percent. During the 1970s the proportion of women entering law school grew dramatically by 500 percent, and an increasing number of medical schools experienced entering classes that were 40 percent women as compared with well under 10 percent during the 1940s, 1950s, and 1960s. During the 1950s more than 70 percent of all American families were made up of a father who worked and a mother who stayed at home to care for the children, but by 1980 only 15 percent of all families fit that description. During the same period, the birth rate was dropping radically from more than three children in the average family at the height of the "baby boom" to less than 1.6 children per family by 1980. The dramatic change in attitude was demonstrated in two Gallup polls conducted in 1967 and 1971. The 1967 survey showed that 34 percent of women in the prime childbearing years expected to have four or more children, but by 1971 the figure dropped to 15 percent. Women continued to face an uphill battle, however, in receiving equal salaries, promotions, and rewards compared with men.

Student culture. In the fall of 1969, 7,976,834 students were enrolled in American colleges and universities. Ten years later the number had risen to 11,669,429. During this same period, the number of students attending part-time increased 10 percent, and students attended more than one college with greater frequency than before, 24 percent in 1969 compared with 34 percent in 1976 (see Carnegie Survey, 1975, 1980). Diversity was increasing with the enrollment of African-American students increasing from 7 percent in 1969 to 11 percent in 1976; women from 28 percent in 1969 to 51 percent in 1979; and adults 25 years or older from 28 percent in 1972 to 35 percent in 1977.

The majority of students resided off campus, with only approximately one-third living on campus, and a little over 27 percent living with parents or members of their family. As a result, by 1976 nearly 7 out of every 10 students were commuting to campus in some way, and over half held jobs, up from 45 percent in 1969. College was no longer the central focus for many of these students. Older students in many instances were balancing college with family and work, and college was not the first priority for many of them. Students residing off campus were far less involved with campus activities, and the problems with parking increased. For some students the cost of transportation to and from campus become a factor and determined the frequency with which they made the trip and whether they might return for special events. Work also cut deeply into their time for such activities. Drinking became the "fun" activity chosen most often by students. Although used less frequently than alcohol by students, drug usage was on the increase, and marijuana was already an experience many students brought with them to college. Sexual relations were far more open, and sleeping together in residence halls occurred more frequently and was even prevalent in many places. Hard studying and hard partying characterized the life of many students.

Periods of change have followed every war, and each period has witnessed a search for meaningful values and has been affected by the economic conditions of the period. In the aftermath of the Vietnam War, the

1970s produced what was labeled as the "me" generation. "Meism" was called "the third great awakening" by Tom Wolfe (1977), "the new narcissism" by Peter Marin (1975), and "psychic self-help" by Christopher Lasch (1979). Campuses saw the revival of novels by Ayn Rand (1943, 1957) and best sellers included *Your Erroneous Zones* (Dyer, 1976), *Pulling Your Own Strings* (Dyer, 1978), *My Mother/Myself* (Friday, 1977), and *Passages* (Sheehy, 1976). There was less sense of identity among students, however. As Levine (1981) pointed out, what students wanted and needed and did not find in the curriculum, they soon found as a part of the "extra curriculum."

Although student attitudes were by no means consistent, the effects of Vietnam and Watergate were negative and student interest in political affairs dropped significantly (Astin, 1977). Student interest and commitment to radical politics had decreased dramatically and there was a strong movement to the "middle of the road" or even the "Right." Students had already become one of the larger consumer groups in America. With the October 25, 1971 passage of the twenty-sixth amendment to the Constitution that gave voting rights to 18- to 20-year-olds, college students became a voting block to which politicians, particularly at the local level, had to pay attention. It did not, however, radically alter the pattern of politics in the nation as many had feared. Although often somewhat more active and a little more liberal, college students generally reflected the attitudes of the general public. Ideological politics among students declined and SDS, the most visible group on college campuses during the 1960s, disappeared by the end of that decade as a result of splits and dissention within its leadership. SDS and other ideological groups were supplanted by self-interest groups concerned with the interests and welfare of specific types of people (e.g., blacks, women, gays, religion). These types of groups were more fragile and less stable, however, often appearing and disappearing within a semester or two (Levine, 1981). Student protests decreased significantly, and when they did occur, were quite often focused on local issues (e.g., student fees, curricular changes, use of facilities).

Students began using litigation and lawsuits to achieve their goals and, perhaps as a result of receiving the vote, lobbying through Public Interest Research Groups (PIRGs) and state student associations. In 1971 a national student lobby, later called the United States Student Association, became active in Washington, D.C., and, like any lobby group, it worked for legislation favorable to its constituency. Student participation in institutional government increased during the 1970s. Students were appointed to important committees in a majority of institutions. Budget and personnel committees were often an exception, but even appointment to these types of committees has become acceptable in more recent years. Although the large majority of students seldom actively participated in student governance and, like the public-at-large, often did not vote, they were through the payment of student activity fees, supporting on the one hand services the college or university could not afford to provide and on the other hand opposing the same institutions in the courts, legislatures, and media on specific issues (usually aimed at egalitarian issues and reducing the control of institutions over their lives). The power of the purse or checkbook was becoming a factor. Student buying power was not only a power in the community as local business had long recognized but was beginning to influence the institutions of higher learning in many ways. As the strength of budgets and financial resources gradually began to weaken, what students were willing to pay for strengthened. Even the curriculum would feel the influence of the student's checkbook.

An increased emphasis on career preparation by students was taking place during the 1970s. In 1969 undergraduates ranked "learning to get along with people" as the most important thing to get out of college, but by 1976 this had changed to getting a "Detailed grasp of a special field" (Levine, 1981, p. 61). The Carnegie Surveys indicated that the majority of students (85 percent) were going to college with a specific career in mind. This trend was reflected in more time spent in studying, but it was also leading to increased specialization and decreased interest in general education. After a decade of rising inflation and three recessions, students found they were no longer guaranteed employment upon graduation. Competition for jobs and for slots in graduate or professional schools increased dramatically. Although it had always existed to some degree, cheating and academic dishonesty began to rise (e.g., cheating on exams, cutting material from library holdings, stealing books from libraries, paying someone else to write a paper, etc.). Grades were the primary credential to a better world and were fiercely sought by some in almost any way necessary. Grade inflation that had begun in the late 1950s continued to grow, and the relationship between grades and what a person knew was becoming much less certain. College students increasingly expressed their belief that grades were not good evidence of what they knew, but they pursued them relentlessly because grades were so heavily weighted by those who held the keys to the future.

The trend toward seeing students as consumers began in this decade. Increasing numbers of older students attending college who were paying their own way was a major factor in creating this trend. This direction had begun in 1944 with the G. I. Bill that brought veterans to the campus who could not be responded to as "kids." Another factor was a series of court cases beginning with *Dixon v. Alabama State Board of Education* in 1961 and culminating with *Goldberg v. Regents of the University of California* in 1967 striking down the doctrine of *in loco parentis* that had been practiced by colleges and universities for years. The Higher Education Act of 1965 emphasized financial aid to students, particularly with loans, and in 1972 amendments to the act expanded the role of federally supported financial aid to students attending college. After 1980 emphasis in student financial aid would be shifted to the Guaranteed Student Loan Program. Loans to be repaid after college were usually assumed to be the responsibility of the student, and students were learning to expect to be treated accordingly.

Although political conservatism would grow during this decade and appear full blown during the Reagan years of the 1980s, this was a socially liberal generation. The majority of students supported expanded roles for women, legalized abortion, and eliminating prohibitions on homosexual relations and living together before marriage. Drinking was what most students chose first to do for fun (they started earlier and drank more), and drug usage was on the increase. Marijuana was not a new experience for many college students having already experimented with it in high school. Sexual activity was more open. Sleeping over in residence halls was much more prevalent. The proportion of students living on campus in residence halls or in Greek houses dropped by a third between 1969 and 1976, and the proportion of students living off campus in apartments or homes nearly tripled. By 1976 nearly 70 percent of all students were commuting to campus and 54 percent of all students held jobs. More students were finding less time for campus activities and the traditional college life. For a growing number of students, college was no longer the only focus or even the most important part of their lives. There were indications that students were identifying less with the campus and of a growing philosophy "Study hard, party hard."

The decade of the 1970s had commenced on a violent note. Although only 28 percent of the college students in 1969 had participated in demonstrations of any type (Gallup International, 1969) and during the week of the most widespread unrest in the history of American higher education following the Kent State and Jackson State shootings, 43 percent of the nation's colleges and universities had been "unaffected" (Lipset, 1993) this experience did have a huge impact on students everywhere. Young people had become television's largest audience; and most college students learned about Vietnam, Watergate, and the world through this media. Whether or not a student participated personally in demonstrations, it was very easy to witness the protest activities of fellow students on their own campus or on other campuses across the nation via the tube.

The world had grown more complex for students as it had for everyone else. Entering college as part of a much more liberal generation, college students were faced with making every day choices that for previous generations were determined for them by rule or law. Drugs were available on most campuses and alcohol usage was increasing. The growing practice of premarital sexual intercourse was often limited more by the presence of roommates than any other force. There were increased numbers on the campus, increasing diversity, growing pressure to succeed with a career, more desire to earn money, less sense of identity, increasing individualism, and increasing isolationism. Although polls indicated that expectations for the country had dropped dramatically by 1979, personal expectations had dropped only slightly. By 1976 students thought it was more important to acquire "training and skills for an occupation" and get a "detailed grasp of a special field" than to get along with people or formulate life goals, which had been their strongest preference in 1969 (Astin, 1984). Competition for grades was growing, and students were becoming increasingly grade conscious as more students were applying for medical school, law school, and other professional schools (e.g., the number of students applying to medical school from 1965 to 1975 more than doubled with 45,000 applicants competing for 16,000 slots). The drive to succeed in this more complex world was generating higher levels of frustration and anxiety in students. Horowitz (1987) saw the hostility in many undergraduates growing from a sense of entitlement that came from paying big money for college tuition and living expenses and standing in line for a book on reserve.

The University of Michigan's Survey Research Center conducted in the late 1950s a survey of the nation's mental health, and they repeated the same questions of a comparable cross section of participants again in the late 1970s. They found a dramatic increase in worrying during this period, especially among young Americans. In the late 1950s, only a minority of younger Americans (32 percent) held anxious attitudes about their lives, but by the late 1970s worriers had increased to a majority of all young Americans (52 percent). The data showed a steep rise in behavioral symptoms of increased anxiety (greater frequency of headaches; loss of appetite; trouble sleeping; upset stomachs; and higher levels of feeling nervous, fidgety, and tense). The suicide rate among white adolescents increased an amazing 171 percent between 1950 and 1975, from 2.8 per 100,000 to 7.6 per 100,000 (see Yankelovich, 1981, pp. 178-191). Accompanied by a significant erosion in a trust of government and other social institutions and a high concern for the economic condition of the nation, personal security was often threatened, and college counseling centers began receiving increased traffic. There were reports of despair, depression, emotional crisis, and increased suicide among college students (Horowitz, 1987).

The attitude toward "extra curricular" was changing among college students. There was an increased tendency to consider how an activity would help prepare participants for their chosen careers, the beginning of greater efforts toward developing service learning experiences. The numbers of organizations began to grow that provided professional development, personal growth, religious experience, physical fitness, and recreational opportunities; at the same time, participation in student government dwindled and student government elections produced low voting numbers. Although major college athletic events (i.e., football and men's basketball) were still a strong attraction for many students, more students were choosing other interests. There was less formal dating and more informal group partying. The practice of swallowing goldfish popular 50 years earlier was never revived, but its more modern version, streaking (dashing naked across campus and through public places) was more sensational and seemed to capture the imagination of a number of undergraduates. As Moffatt (1989) pointed out, despite the popularity of the movie *Animal House*, social life on campus seemed to be declining and college students in the early 1970s seemed not to be having very much fun. Each new organization seemed more and more career-oriented.

College Student Affairs in the 1970s

Student Affairs was entering a new stage in the progression of its symbiotic relationship with higher education. Although often criticized and sometimes scapegoated, it had survived the turbulent period of antiwar demonstrations and antiestablishment protests. It would soon face, however, even greater challenges to its continuation and development. As a result of this experience, and affected by a changing culture and a changing economy, it too was beginning to rethink its position. As the "me" generation developed, student affairs professionals were confronted with cultivating a different relationship with students. In large part students were not satisfied with society in general and with what they were receiving from their educational institutions in particular. Faculties in research centered institutions were beginning to question the relationship of their institutions to the federal government, and the public was growing disenchanted with higher education. Students wanted greater personal freedom and control over their private lives. They were demanding the free exercise of their civil and political rights, which included the right to plan on-campus political activity that would be acted on somewhere off-campus, and the right to hear speakers of every persuasion. In the face of great moral dilemmas in society, they were beginning to question the resolve and ability of their institutions of higher learning to help them do anything about these great issues. The Cold War was still being waged and the threat of atomic warfare was a continuous concern.

A "Joint Statement on Rights and Freedom of Students" (1968) was drafted by members of the American Association of University Professors (AAUP), the Association of American Colleges (AAC), the United States National Student Association (USNSA), the National Association of Student Personnel Administrators (NASPA), and the National Association of Women Deans and Counselors (NAWDC) that centered on "provisions for student freedom to learn" (p. 258). The document dealt with in-class and out-of-class activity both on and off campus and included an effort to establish disciplinary standards. It was endorsed by the Jesuit Education Association on Colleges and Universities January 14, 1968; the National Catholic Education Association, January 15, 1968; the American Association of Junior Colleges, February 27, 1968; the American Association for Higher Education, March 6, 1968; NASPA on April 2, 1968; and ACPA on April 8, 1968. The field of College Student Personnel entered the decade searching for its proper niche within higher education. As *in loco parentis* was being dropped, relationships with students were becoming defined more and more in legal terms. There was a search for a new framework within which to work in the institutions of higher learning and for new models within which to work with students and faculty. At one moment issues would center on the legal requirements of due process and, at the next moment concern would focus on teaching and learning.

Clearly the insulating boundaries between the campus and the community were dissolving, both at the political and the social levels. The influx of veterans on the campus had not ceased with the education of World War II veterans but was followed by Korean and Vietnam veterans. The G.I. Bill was a major factor in converting most institutions of higher learning from being rather elitist to more egalitarian. In 1940 the majority of young people graduating from secondary schools did not expect to go on to college. Colleges and universities stood apart from general society. But, following World War II in the later 1940s and the 1950s an expectation was created that all people should develop their abilities to the fullest extent, and the college campus was the primary place to accomplish this goal.

A second factor in this process of dissolving boundaries and changing the relationship between higher education and the federal government began with the major role played by universities in the creation of the atomic bomb. Early in World War II, Franklin Roosevelt's decision to use the talent and laboratories of the universities rather than build separate facilities for war research changed the future of higher education more dramatically than anything that had occurred since the Morrill Act. On the one hand, it vastly expanded the universities' resources and capabilities in science; but, on the other hand, the university-government partnership resulted in a relationship that thrust higher education into the everyday political and economic world (e.g., the National Science Foundation). The Russian success with the launch of Sputnik in October 1957 reinforced this relationship; and, in 1958 with the National Defense Education Act, Congress gave direct aid through loans to students who were not veterans, provided large numbers of fellowships for graduate study, and added significantly to funds available for research. But, the aid was made available only in areas of study targeted as central to the nation's defense (i.e., science, mathematics, foreign languages, health science).

John F. Kennedy continued the trend when in 1963 he called for direct federal help to colleges themselves, and in the next two years a number of laws followed affecting almost every facet of higher education. New buildings were authorized, student loans expanded, support for fields of study broadened, libraries enlarged, and graduate study and research further encouraged. Under Lyndon B. Johnson, the Higher Education Act first broke the barrier to providing direct government grants to undergraduate students, and Johnson was the first president to demand a "long-term strategy of federal aid to higher education, a comprehensive set of goals, and a precise plan of action." Between 1960 and 1970, five million new students crowded onto campuses, 500 new campuses were constructed, and by 1970 more than 1,000 community colleges, most of them public, were in exist-ence. Faculty salaries nearly doubled, and 250,000 faculty jobs were added. States increased their appropriations for higher education from $1.37 bil-lion to $5.79 billion, and by 1970 the federal government accounted for four billion dollars or 16 percent of all funds spent by colleges and univer-sities. Higher education became accustomed to the income it was receiv-ing from various sources outside of itself, including the federal government, and became increasingly dependent upon it. Even private institutions with large enrollments were not immune.

A number of students and some faculty would point to this close tie during the late 1960s and early 1970s as unmoral and subverting colleges and universities to the will of the government. They declared it an unholy alliance and often protested this connection, for example, when recruiters for the CIA or companies with large military contracts appeared on cam-pus. But, with the end of the Vietnam War and the felt impact of a troubled economy, higher education was to experience growing stress resulting from the gradual reduction of federal support. Student protests also began to diminish, and what became known as the "meism" generation would soon appear.

Literature

There were no great texts written for the field during this period, but the literature was not void of significant contributions. One of the most influential publications was Feldman and Newcomb's (1969) *The Impact of College on Students*. It brought together and assessed the available evidence about the outcomes resulting from college impact on students. In one sense it was a continuation of Jacob's (1957) *Changing Values in College* that elicited so much attention several years before. Although this volume ar-rived at only a slightly different conclusion, it was somewhat more opti-mistic than had been Jacob's conclusions. Feldman and Newcomb concluded that, despite limitations of available data, "it seems altogether likely that some students in some colleges experience some changes that are attributable to the fact of being in college" (p. 327). They made a plea for "educational distinctiveness" resulting from new ideas that would re-quire new organizational structures. The significance of this work was that it relied heavily upon empirical data to demonstrate that colleges have some impact upon student values albeit not always intentional.

In 1970 the American College Personnel Association (ACPA) under the editorship of John Whiteley produced a document titled *Students In*

The University And In Society that included papers from notables such as Harold Taylor, Joseph Shoben, Jr., Lewis Mayhew, and Gilbert Wrenn. It also included papers from three students. The message from students was that they felt higher education was not providing what they needed and was not responding to the real needs of students. This document reflected the struggles that educators and students were experiencing in this significant period when the war in Vietnam was still being waged full force by the Nixon administration with the invasion into Cambodia, with greater numbers of minorities seeking attendance at colleges and universities, and with the institutions generally increasing their size. With ideas not always well formed, several of the writers in this document were beginning to note the changing nature of institutions of higher learning as a result of the demand being made by the technological society, its students, and its faculties. Perhaps the most thoughtful concern was expressed by Shoben (1970a, 1970b) in his article "Student Unrest and Cultural Criticism: Protest in The American College," reprinted from *Daedalus*, in which he noted that it was not wrong for academic institutions to serve government or industry, but there was a real inherent danger in the influence this may have on its capacity to criticize the values it is being paid to practice. He made an eloquent and moral plea for colleges to preserve the capacity to "behave critically," and not lose their most essential role of cultural critic.

This was becoming increasingly difficult. Institutions, particularly public institutions, continued to reflect the conflicts within society, and conflict within American society had never been greater since the Civil War than it was at that moment. As the decade transpired and the economy slipped, less support would be forthcoming from the government and private sources. The pangs of withdrawal made what was available seem all the more precious, however, and it was not received well to "bite the hand that feeds you."

It was Brown's (1972) monograph "Student Development in Tomorrow's Higher Education—A Return To The Academy," that became a major focal point in the literature and the field for the next 20 years. Written as the culmination of the first phase of the American College Personnel Association's project, Tomorrow's Higher Education (T.H.E.), it was aimed at reconceptualizing college student personnel's "specific roles, functions, methods, and procedures" (p. 4). An ACPA task force that included Paul Bloland, Russell Brown, W. Harold Grant, Donald Hoyt, Jane Matson, Albert Miles, and Philip Tripp, commissioned Brown to write this monograph for the purpose of focusing dialogue as a precursor to subsequent model-building and implementation phases of the project that were to follow. The monograph succeeded admirably in achieving its purpose, although the subsequent model-building and implementation phases would prove less successful.

The monograph focused on "student development" and declared that "it has been and must remain one of the primary goals of higher education" (p. 7). Defining Student Development as the "whole student" or the "liberally educated" person, the monograph identified "Key Student Development Concepts," that, although derived from the research literature, could more appropriately be called assumptive. It continued by proposing "Alternative Roles" for student personnel workers that would direct the profession toward closer involvement with the academic world and becoming attitudinally more scientific. Brown argued for giving greater attention to basic skills such as "the ability to learn and solve problems" (p. 15) and equated intellectual learning with "critical thinking" or "reflective thinking" (p. 38). He believed that these skills were not being adequately cared for in the classroom and that something must be done about it if students were to be prepared to live in the real world. He called for joining with faculty to revolutionize higher education by revitalizing the curriculum and eliminating the extracurricular, but he placed the fault for lack of progress primarily with the faculty. It is the faculty who must change, "it is their behavior that is central if higher education is to be different" (p. 26). He seemed to imply that the curriculum should move toward impacting the "affective life of students" as outlined by the student development concept. If a goal of the monograph was to open "honest dialogue between the academy and student personnel" (p. 11) about this issue, there is no evidence to indicate it succeeded. It would become something of a benchmark in the profession of college student affairs, however.

In June 1974 Harold Grant, then president of ACPA, called "an invitational student development model-building conference" held at the University of Georgia that was followed by a second conference held in February 1976 at Overland Park, Kansas to explore "organizational issues." This phase of the T.H.E. project culminated in 1976 with the publication of a book, *The Future of Student Affairs*, written by Theodore Miller and Judith Prince. The book was primarily a guide for implementing principles identified in the T.H.E. project.

At the same time as Brown's monograph was published, the Council of Student Personnel Associations in Higher Education (COSPA) published a shorter monograph "Student Development Services in Higher Education" that emphasized the developmental goals in educating students. Many of the same student development principles were highlighted by the Council in this document as were emphasized in the T.H.E. publications. Although Penney (1969) had concluded that student personnel work would never be recognized as a vital aspect of the academic world, student personnel was emphasizing more and more its role directly in educating students and, thereby, attempting to place itself side-by-side with the faculty as equal partners in the educational process. The faculty played an increasing and critical role in determining what would be taught and how it would be taught (Cremin, 1988, p. 564). As can be seen from these documents, "student development" was the model or paradigm that most professionals would accept as their philosophy or rationale. The problem was that in practice the partnership with faculty was not always achieved and competition for existing resources within institutions of higher learning was often the result.

Although Mayhew's (1972) prediction did not come to pass that the system of student personnel services such as student activities, counseling services, testing services, student housing, and health services would probably become obsolete, certainly the nature of student personnel work in each of these areas and in all areas of student personnel was changing. The professional journals, although always a delayed reflection, were publishing articles in the early 1970s dealing with drug abuse and student protests. Interest in the use of peer helpers was beginning to appear in the literature, and ACPA published in the *Journal of College Student Personnel* (1972, pp. 90-96) one of the first statements directed toward the use of group experiences on the college campus. ACPA and the American Psychological Association (APA), although working separately, were leaders in this concern for the proper use of group work. APA (1973) issued a similar statement in its journal. ACPA (1974) continued its work in this area with an addendum statement establishing ethical guidelines for group facilitators, although the Association intentionally avoided use of the word "ethical." This was followed in 1975 (American College Personnel Association, 1975) with a statement of guidelines for the preparation of group facilitators. In 1976 ACPA published the entire document (American College Personnel Association, 1976, pp. 161-168), producing one of the most comprehensive statements about group work on the college campus. One of the first articles in the gay movement appeared in the *Journal of College Student Personnel* in 1974 (Gibbs & McFarland, 1974), and concerns with substance abuse continued.

Following Brown's monograph, articles on student development began to appear in the journals, particularly the *Journal of College Student Personnel*. A debate or dialogue was initiated in the January, 1973, issue of the *Journal of College Student Personnel* with short statements by Cross and Vermilye and a response by Brown (Kubit, Cross, Vermilye, & Brown, 1973). Parker and Morrill (1974) believed that student development was made synonymous with humanism and this was a "shortsighted and limited view" (p. 163). Parker (1974) continued to be critical of the student development concept. In 1970 and again in 1977 he proposed that what was needed in "student personnel services" was a comprehensive review of the college student. In 1978 Blaesser lamented a lack of solid theories of human development and also of a mature science of organizational psychology. It is interesting to note, too, in an article that set out to identify a "a core literature of general concern to all professionals in the field" how few of the authors of the material presented were from the main stream of student affairs itself (Reilly & Cauthen, 1976).

Sincere efforts to present human development theory that would relate to student development were underway, however. Following Erikson (1963, 1968), Chickering (1969) was one of the earlier writers to promote the student development concept with his psychosocial theory that included seven vectors of development: (a) developing competence, (b) managing emotions, (c) developing autonomy, (d) establishing identity, (e) freeing interpersonal relationships, (f) developing purpose, and (g) developing integrity. This paralleled cognitive development theory such as Perry's (1970).

Of particular note in the literature was the Bakke case (*Bakke v. Regents of the University of California*, 1976) in which reverse discrimination was charged. It asserted that racial classification was unconstitutional and created a shift from protecting racial or ethnic groups to more concern for the rights of the individual under the 14th Amendment to the U.S. Constitution. Given the efforts to encourage enrollment and attendance of minorities, this case required a rethinking of how this should be best accomplished.

The Nature of Practice

In a COSPA document (Straub & Vermilye, 1968), a shift can be noted in emphasis to "learning" rather than "teaching." This document suggested that "student personnel workers" take positions on emerging issues in higher education rather than simply keeping the store. There is some indication during the decade of the 1970s that this was slowly beginning to happen. A few years later Young (1975) in a short document, again for COSPA, discussed the implications that lowering the age of majority were having. Citizens 18 years old had been able to vote in some states and 18-year-old males for some time had been required to serve in the Armed Services. It is the prerogative of each state to determine what the age of majority will be, and by 1975 legal status as an adult was accorded to individuals 18 years of age in a plurality of states. This change meant that instead of the majority of students in institutions of higher learning being minors, colleges and universities were suddenly being filled with nearly all adult students, creating a very different relationship. In addition to reducing further *in loco parentis* applications, other ramifications included residency for out-of-state tuition, residence hall residency requirements, student records, student financial support, and tort liability. The nature of student affairs work was, perhaps, required to change the most. For example, the responsibility was placed on the institution to show that a requirement to live in college housing units was related to the institution's educational process and not just to create revenue for the housing system; it would change the right of parents to know about grades, whether a student was involved in disciplinary or legal action, and parents' right to know about counseling or health information. It would also place more responsibility on the individual student for his or her own behavior, however.

The Family Education Rights and Privacy Act of 1974 (20 U.S.C. 1232g), more commonly known as the "Buckley Amendment," regulated for the first time the data-handling practice of federal agencies. Under its provisions, individuals can learn which agencies have information about them, see their files, correct errors, and consent to "non-routine" use of data. Most students were not motivated to view their records as a result, but some parents voiced a concern when they did not automatically continue to receive their off-spring's grades.

There was a high turnover rate among chief student affairs officers. These individuals began showing signs of wanting to move away from control responsibilities and grant students more freedom in conducting their own lives. The title "Dean of Students" would largely disappear during this decade as had the titles "Dean of Women" and "Dean of Men" before it. It was also the decade in which the term "College Student Affairs" would replace former labels "College Student Personnel" or "College Student Services."

It was Crookston (1976) that marked the change in terminology taking place to refer to the field as "student affairs" rather than "student personnel." Equally important, he saw the field firmly established as a "major administrative subdivision in American higher education" (p. 28), and that the dualistic nature of its practice would only be resolved as members of the profession became truly educators. Defining the field as administrative, however, did little to resolve the conflict that student affairs professionals felt caught between in their advocacy of students and their relationship with the faculty. Student affairs professionals still showed signs of feeling neither fully administrative, on the one hand, nor fully educative on the other hand. It was difficult to identify the value of being in between. The rewards were perceived as few and far between and seldom high.

Professional organizations. In mid-September of 1970, ACPA, NASPA, and NAWDC jointly held a meeting in Denver to consider the need for a single professional association to serve their members in higher education whose primary concern was the broad field of student personnel work. There was a realization that the three associations performed similar functions for overlapping memberships (i.e., placement, publications, conventions, resolutions, etc.). The three associations represented approximately 12,000 members. A report of "The Feasibility Task Force" was issued in March, 1971 by representatives of all three organizations. Although the intent of the report was clearly to move the three toward much closer working relationships and embodied the hope that at some point in the future their combined strength could be realized in a single organization, it was also clear that little urgency to do so was felt within the separate organizations. ACPA's commitment to APGA was of concern to some. NASPA's focus on the chief administrative officer in student personnel worried others, and women were not playing as yet much of a role in NASPA. ACPA, by far the largest of the three associations with membership on April 6, 1971, of 7,135, seemed to threaten others. The organizational structures were different. What this might mean for members who had already achieved some status in the separate associations was not clear.

During its Atlantic City convention in 1971, the ACPA Executive Council endorsed "in principle" plans to develop a single national association of student personnel professionals that would join together ACPA, NASPA, and NAWDC, but it was not to be. Executive officers of the three associations meeting jointly in 1973 passed a motion moved by Merril C. "Jack"

Beyerl that a single national association made up of the three associations was not feasible at the time. In February 1974 the ACPA membership voted to continue affiliation with APGA and on March 1974, its membership reached 8,336. Membership in ACPA reached 9,166 in 1975, going over the 9,000 mark for the first time. (See Appendix for presidents of the four professional organizations serving in this decade.)

The forty-sixth annual convention of ACPA was held jointly with NAWDC in Cleveland in 1972, at which time a decision to poll ACPA membership on its continued affiliation with APGA was made. During this period, national higher education organizations were appointing committees and commissions to study student unrest, but as Charles Lewis, then president of ACPA, observed in the March 1970 issue of the *Journal of College Student Personnel,* most were not including student personnel workers in their membership. During Bloland's term as president of ACPA, a position paper was commissioned on student unrest and delivered to the Scranton Commission, and Bloland wrote to President Nixon and Governor Scranton in February 1971 conveying ACPA's endorsement of the Scranton Commission's report (Sheeley, 1991).

On April 5, 1973, NAWDC changed its name to the National Association for Women Deans, Administrators, and Counselors (NAWDAC). In resolutions passed at its Fifty-Fourth Conference in 1974, NASPA indicated support for women by urging that funds be budgeted by individual institutions for the attendance of women at a professional meeting of their choice and for a Tripartite Task Force on Women.

Organizations were also beginning efforts to achieve meaningful involvement of students. ACPA was perhaps the leader in this effort when the ACPA Executive Council on November 9, 1969, voted that student membership status should not deny opportunity for students to participate fully in all phases of the association. Specialization was receiving more recognition. The work of 14 separate commissions in ACPA, each representing a specialty or interest area within the field of college student affairs is an indication of this trend. A Coordinator of Commissions was appointed as a voting member of the ACPA Executive Council in 1972, and in 1973 the association created the office of Vice President for Commissions and Vice President for State Divisions as voting members on the executive council of the organization. The ACPA Commission V for Financial Aids was a viable part of ACPA at this time, although the Association of Financial Aids Administrators had been organized and published a quarterly journal, the *Journal of Financial Aid.* Within a few years, Commission V was deactivated but is still an open slot among the commissions of ACPA.

Professional journals. Publishing was becoming more important as a part of a professional's contribution to the field of college student affairs, particularly if a person had aspirations for a faculty appointment. As is the case with most scholarly journals, the three major journals in the field during this period were supported by the three student affairs professional associations, ACPA, NASPA, and NAWDAC. Albert B. Hood became editor of the *Journal of College Student Personnel* with the January 1971 issue (vol. 12), replacing Robert Callis. After two terms of three years each, he was succeeded by Laurine E. Fitzgerald. The *NASPA Journal* entered the decade with Robert H. Schaffer as its editor. In 1972 Martin J. Meade succeeded Schaffer, followed by David C. Tilley in 1975. Tilley was succeeded by R. Mikell O'Donnell in 1978. The *Journal of the National Association of Women Deans and Counselors* had been established in June 1938 with Ruth Strang as its first editor. She served in this role for 22 years until October 1960 when Kate Hevner Mueller succeeded her. Mueller was followed as editor by Betty Soldwedel in 1970, and Margaret C. Berry took over in 1972. After NAWDC changed its name in 1973 to the National Association for Women Deans, Administrators, and Counselors (NAWDAC), the journal's name, of course, followed suit.

Although these journals clearly represented the field of college student affairs, they were also dedicated to serving their respective associations. Each of them did this in a way that reflected the nature and bias of the supporting organization. The *Journal of the National Association of Women Deans, Administrators, and Counselors* was clearly committed to serving the role of women and furthering their development in the field. In 1976 NAWDAC made a change in its constitution that opened membership to deans, administrators, and counselors of both sexes. This change, however, seemed little noted and did not visibly affect the direction of the organization or the nature of its journal. Males did publish in it, but clearly on topics with specific content for women professionals in the field.

On becoming Editor of the *NASPA Journal* in 1978, O'Donnell declared that it was not primarily a research journal, although research articles for the "generalist" were welcomed. This journal had previously followed this dictum and continued to do so. Position papers and reasoned opinions were much more evident in the two organs representing NASPA and NAWDAC.

On the other hand, the *Journal of College Student Personnel* was evolving toward a more scholarly and research oriented representative of the field. Throughout the decade in its guidelines to authors it declared its purpose was to publish "manuscripts directed to the common interests of college student personnel, particularly articles dealing with research, professional issues, and new approaches to improve student services . . ." Its content clearly supported the interest in publishing research. The combined efforts of all three journals produced a very respectable literature, not only of college student affairs, but of a large segment of higher education. A reader of their contents cannot help but be aware of the major issues confronting all of higher education during this period.

During the early years of this decade, the professional journals were carrying articles that predominantly dealt with career development, residence halls, mental health, academic adjustment and advisement, use of groups, study methods, administration of student affairs, drug usage, women's issues, campus environment, community colleges, and paraprofessionals. By 1975 attention was being given to the impact of coed living in residence halls on both males and females. By 1976 noticeable attention was being given to the problems being experienced by minority students. The work of the counseling center on campus received attention. On one hand, an article was published in the *Journal of College Student Personnel* (Schroeder, 1976) dealing with adventure training and on the other hand articles concerned with student consumption of alcohol were beginning to appear. As the decade wore on, increased attention was given to mental health problems interfering with college success. More distinction was made between students with educational and vocational concerns and students with personal problems (e.g., Lacy, Franks, & Kirk, 1976). By 1977 more attention was given to gender issues and attitude towards rape. By 1978 and 1979, the use of computers as well as the use of alcohol appeared and adult development issues were receiving attention (e.g., Schlossberg, 1978); and concern for the relationship between faculty and student affairs, veterans, student characteristics, and study or learner skills continued. But focus on counseling, career development and planning, minority and women's issues, and residence halls predominated. New behavioral problems such as eating disorders began to emerge as attention to student activism declined.

As the decade commenced and progressed, articles were published about legal issues (as *in loco parentis* was being dropped, relationships with students were becoming defined more and more in legal terms), women and minority students, race relations and civil rights, milieu management, teaching and what is taught, married students and commuter students, sexuality, and student development. Toward the end of the decade, articles began to appear dealing with "attrition" or as it would later be reframed "retention," and on "accountability." Concentration on student activities was still high and concern with the consumption of alcohol by students was growing. There was some indication that writers were becoming aware of the affect of the lower age of majority and the increased intrusion of the federal government into nearly every phase of higher education.

Perhaps most significant, however, was the clear indication throughout the decade in the journal literature of the effort by student affairs professionals to find their niche and define their role in the educational process and the organizational structure of their institutions. The search for a new relationship with students as *in loco parentis* faded seemed only to complicate this problem. Concerns with due process and discipline procedures were evident, and the effort to create or adopt models that saw students as "customers" was appearing for the first time. The desire to lead was as evident as in the decades before World War II and immediately following, but the direction was no longer as clear.

In 1971 the Editor of the *Journal of College Student Personnel* noted in one of his editorials a trend toward violation of policy followed by most professional journals (Hood, 1971). This violation was submitting the same study for publication in different journals under a slightly revised title and including only very minor changes. At about the same time, COSPA was working on questions of ethics and the confidentiality of both professional and student records. The issues of ethical practice would receive growing attention in the future.

Professional education and training. Given the uncertainty about the future projected at the time for the field of college student affairs, it is not surprising that this would also be reflected in attitudes toward professional education and training for entering the field. In a survey of chief student personnel administrators, they indicated no agreement about what was the best training for their position (they did agree that ". . . the chief student personnel administrator should be male, married with children, and between 40-49 years of age") (Upcraft, 1971, p. 135). In the same survey, respondents indicated that student personnel administrators should avoid being publicly critical of major institutional policies, seek close ties with the faculty, conduct research, and hold faculty rank. A survey of NAWDAC members (Berry, 1976) found that only 14 percent of the respondents held doctoral degrees. The more scholarly expectations of the chief student personnel administrator role would increase the demand for the earned doctorate.

Although one association, ACPA, maintained a commission devoted to "Professional Preparation" and there were indications that the number of preparation programs were growing (Ferrari, 1972), there was surprisingly little in the literature about training programs. There were occasional calls to improve the curriculum of preparation programs and to define standards of performance of students within the programs. Accrediting standards and an accreditation body with a national accreditation program were suggested (Penn, 1974), and an effort to determine competencies that preparation programs should require of students was made (Newton & Richardson, 1976). There were also occasional efforts to outline models for professional preparation (e.g., Arner, Peterson, Arner, Hawkins, & Spooner, 1976; Connors & Pruitt, 1978; Rentz, 1976), or to study the characteristics and research interests of students in preparation programs (Kuh, Greenlee, & Lardy, 1978; Kuh, Lardy, & Greenlee, 1979), but no one was exerting great leadership in graduate preparation for entry into college student affairs. The COSPA (1972) publication devoted a short section to "Professional Preparation." By the middle of the decade, the anchor points in discussions of preparation programs in the literature were clearly the Brown monograph (1972) and the monograph "Commission on Professional Development" (1972) report for COSPA. There is little evidence that ACPA's T.H.E. gave consideration to this area in the final two stages of its project.

Summary

The 1970s was an important decade in higher education. It was a watershed for student affairs and all of higher education. College student affairs entered a new stage in its symbiotic relationship with higher education. Much happened during this decade that would have strong bearing on the shape of the field for years to come. Student affairs was searching for its place in the grand scheme of higher education, but with a changing culture and a changing economy the whole of higher education was being confronted with a different world. The field entered the decade referring to itself as "college student personnel" and would leave the decade titling itself as "college student affairs."

This was the decade in which one president of the United States resigned his office under pressure and two served only one term, indicating the uncertainty that reigned in politics. The nature of higher education's relationship to society was changing. The boundaries between campus and community were dissolving. The nature of the relationship with students was altering as the attitude of students toward higher learning and the institution was also changing. At the same time, in most institutions student affairs had become a well established administrative area if not a major administrative division.

It was one of the most turbulent decades in the nation's history. It began when student involvement was high in the quest for civil rights and was fueled further by the protests against the war in Vietnam. Students were seeing a connection between their own every day activities and the policies of the government, between their own institutions and the government, and were motivated to act. The violence peaked in May 1970 at Kent State University in Ohio and Jackson State in Mississippi. For many students a new set of values evolved that would set them apart from the generation in power and helped propel student affairs into a new phase in its own development.

Student affairs was changing from the old style dean who had a tendency to manage largely in self-styled ways to keep order on campus to a new effort to relate to students in more developmental ways. *In loco parentis* was fading. Dissatisfaction with the classroom experience by both students and teachers was growing, and a battle was being waged in the courts to redefine the relationship between students and the institutions. The issue of student rights was a matter of conflict and debate throughout this decade, and student affairs people were very much involved in this process. It was clearly a factor influencing the change in student affairs practice, and student affairs people behind the scenes were in turn influencing much of its outcome.

Although leadership in the field continued to be fractured among several professional organizations and muted as a result, there were evidences of growing maturity in the profession as a whole as illustrated in its journals and other literature, the growing number and quality of training programs, and its growing opportunity to be genuine mediators of the educational experience on individual campuses.

Epilogue

Looking back, a person always, it seems, tries to make sense of what has taken place, to find connection, pattern, and meaning. How did we get to where we are now? What does it mean for where we are going? It is hard to envision the significant changes that have taken place in the nation, in the world, and in education during the past 50 or more years. The world has experienced a half-century of nuclear capability; women and minorities have experienced control of their lives profoundly change as a result of legal and economic modifications; political polarization within the nation has increased even as the cold war came to a close; and complexity is begetting complexity at almost all levels of living. Changes that would seem so small in their beginning would have such enormous results. No one could guess what would happen when Rosa Parks refused to move to the back of the bus. No one could have predicted in 1989, as television and radio commentators reminded us at the time, what was happening to the Soviet Union and the Berlin wall. The world was not quite sure how to catch its balance after a half century of the cold war, which had affected both international and domestic policy in the U.S. The way ahead can never be quite the same and new ideas must be tried and tested.

The 1980s and early 1990s have been largely covered politically by the Reagan-Bush years. Because of their proximity, it is hard to envision the significance of this period with any certainty. Reagan is best understood, perhaps, in the sense of purpose or mission he portrayed. Seemingly help-

189

less without a script, he was able to play a role that communicated what many people wanted to hear. He seemed almost devoid of curiosity or reflection and would block any data that conflicted with his chosen beliefs. Although there seems little in Reagan of what might be sought in a truly educated person, he did believe strongly in a very few simple ideas that he communicated with strength and passion, and when on stage he could create a vision that despite facts to the contrary seemed realistic and attainable. But, in the meantime the economy was not improving and government was running up increasing deficits that would affect the nation and higher education. In 1940 the average tax payer spent $75 for national defense, but in the early 1990s the average tax payer would spend nearly $900 for defense, which is almost double allowing for inflation. The sense of possibility for many people was weakening as problems of substance addiction, homelessness, poverty, crime, and mental health were on the rise.

In some ways the decades of the 1980s and the 1990s have seemed to provide for American higher education greater opportunity than ever before. So much had been accomplished since World War II. Discrimination had been reduced, a larger percentage of young people were seeking higher education than ever before (only 15 percent of young people in 1940 sought a higher education whereas nearly 50 percent were doing so by the early 1990s), and although the economy was still struggling, support received from outside resources for higher education was greater than ever before. A recent and major work to assess the efforts of higher education (Pascarella & Terenzini, 1991) focused on "the outcomes of college for individual students" (p. 6). Their review of the research over the previous 20 years indicated that students do seem to learn significant amounts of subject matter and academic skills; communication skills do improve; and socially relevant psychosocial development does occur in students. In contrast to Jacob's charge in 1956 that college had little impact on student values, they presented evidence that college does affect change in student values and attitudinal positions as a consequence of attending college and not as a simple response to maturation or historical, social, and political trends; that attending college does influence increases in principled moral reasoning; and the benefits of obtaining a college degree are passed on from one generation to the next and do have important implications for a person's lifetime earnings. The story is often told of a person wondering how he or she got to where he or she was because the person never really went to school but mother or father insisted that she or he learn to read. But, for most people going to school and getting a bachelor's degree has made a difference.

It is, perhaps, this very success that has created the greatest problem for higher education. Expectations for what higher education will do for both the individual and for society as a whole have become high. Higher education, both public and private, has tended to promise all things to all people with the result that it is impossible to meet all that is expected of it. Higher education has had its failures and successes, but even its successes seem like failures if they do not meet the public's expectations. There are signs that it may be recognizing the reality of this problem as institutions much more frequently are defining their mission and establishing specific goals to work toward, although these mission statements are seldom communicated to students. There is evidence of more activity that is seeking a better balance between learning (teaching) and research. Educational attainment has a strong pivotal influence on a person's ultimate occupational and economic status. What is expected of education beyond high school? What percentage of the population will seek it? Is something more expected from the more educated individual? A problem with stressing increased income and status as the primary educational outcome is that for so many people education has become viewed almost totally as an economic investment. This expected benefit from higher education may be like light from a star received from a distance after the star has died. The nature of the relationship of higher education with society may be changing as a result. Higher education has historically reflected rather well the nature of society, but interesting stressors are occurring in a society that is becoming increasingly diverse and complex.

In most institutions, Student Personnel, now more commonly called Student Affairs, has become a well-established administrative unit or division. It has achieved this status during the past 100 years by successfully carrying out the difficult and often unrewarding tasks of keeping the institution in touch with its students and supporting the agendas of other administrative and academic units. It came into existence because someone else found the need for assistance in carrying out the day-to-day tasks required in educating students, and, therefore, student affairs has usually been viewed as a means to a more important objective, instruction in the classroom or laboratory. The major concern in this work has, therefore, not been about "what" so much as about "how." On the one hand its members have led toward truly progressive educational goals while on the other hand practicing diplomacy in skillful ways as mediators in a war of wills between educators and students. Mediation requires that all parties involved are willing to make modifications in either conditions over which they have control, or their behavior, or both. If one party enters mediation unwilling to make modification, then the process is at best negotiation toward a given end. The act of diplomacy is influencing both parties to be willing to see a different perspective. Often when student affairs professionals have wanted and expected to mediate between students and other governing units of institutions they have been given the task of negotiating specific decisions. With amazing diplomacy they have usually succeeded in these tasks.

The promise of the Reagan administration to lead the country back to its former self would not happen and could not happen. It would not happen for higher education either because the leadership within was not there. In the years that would follow, institutions of higher learning were compelled to ration their resources. Sometimes this has led to competition within institutions that has produced internal divisiveness. Faculty would complain that there were too many administrators, that other disciplines were obsolete, or that the teaching loads were too heavy. More recently, however, limited resources have produced efforts to better define the purposes of higher education, and each institution has looked more critically at its own individual mission. Is the university or college better defined as a teaching institution than as a more narrowly defined research institution? Is an integration of academic pursuits more easily achieved within a framework of community service? The problem is not finding the changes that are needed but of finding ways to put them into effect. The need toshare resources within institutions is bringing about greater emphasis on the need for faculty, student affairs professionals, and students to collaborate and work together to support the central mission of the institution.

It may be at this point student affairs professionals began to realize that no one else, including the faculty, had the necessary answers about the future direction of higher education. It may be that student affairs is now better positioned and more willing to exert leadership to achieve new educational directions much within the spirit of the progressive educational philosophy upon which it has developed. Words written well before the present time by Phenix (1958) are appropriate. "Human development goes beyond growth in basic human competencies, and it is in relation to these further elaborations that other claims are advanced and other values affirmed" (p. 62). Perhaps, there is better understanding now that learning outside the classroom is not much different than learning inside it, only more complex, and that the two areas can and should be joined more fully in mind and in reality. If so, the opportunity to lead in this direction may well be upon the profession of student affairs. Whether there is the will to do so is still in doubt.

Notes

1. Freedom Riders were student protestors that Ella Baker had gathered together at her alma mater, Shaw University, in Raleigh, North Carolina, on Easter weekend in 1960. James Lawson gave this group a moral voice and under the leadership of Baker and Lawson the group tested the freedom of interstate bus facilities for people of both races when in 1961 they set out to ride a bus from Washington DC to New Orleans. Along the way they were brutally beaten, but others quickly took their places.

2. In 1954 Dwight Eisenhower articulated the key reason for trying to contain communism in Asia. He used the analogy of dominoes set up in a row. When the first one is knocked over, it is very quickly followed by the last one in the row.

3. A "hawk" in politics is a person who advocates an aggressive or warlike policy; whereas a "dove" is an advocate of peace or peaceful policies.

4. On January 30, 1968, the first day of the Vietnam New Year, a small squadron of Vietcong fighters entered the compound surrounding the U.S. Embassy in Saigon. For six hours the attackers held the courtyard of the Embassy until in a bloody battle all of them were killed. Within 24 hours the Vietcong mounted attacks on virtually every target within South Vietnam. It required three weeks and 11,000 U.S. and South Vietnamese troops to dislodge 1,000 Vietcong from the Cholon district of Saigon alone. During the three weeks the offensive lasted, an estimated 33,000 enemy troops were killed, but 3,400 allied soldiers also died, including 1,600 Americans, with an additional 8,000 American soldiers wounded. With nearly total surprise, the

Vietcong had waged a massive attack that cast doubt on almost any reason for American involvement in Vietnam.

5. Freedom Summer in Mississippi was the activity that resulted from 700 college students who received two weeks training at Oxford, Ohio to go into Mississippi and hold Freedom Schools to promote voter registration. Three members of the project, Michael Schwerner, James Chaney, and Andrew Goodman, were murdered. Although both black and white project workers stuck out the full summer, there were tensions between the two groups.

References

A dialogue on discipline. (1963). *NASPA Journal, 1,* 7-10.

Aceto, T. D. (1962). Students in pre-professional staff roles. *Journal of College Student Development, 4,* 23-27.

American College Personnel Association. (1964). Summary, luncheon, and business meeting minutes, American College Personnel Association, San Francisco, CA, March 23, 1964. *Journal of College Student Personnel, 6*(1), 51-53.

American College Personnel Association. (1972). A proposed statement for ACPA regarding the use of group experiences in higher education. *Journal of College Student Personnel, 13,* 90-96.

American College Personnel Association. (1974). Addendum I: Guidelines for group facilitators in higher education. *Journal of College Student Personnel, 15,* 157-159.

American College Personnel Association. (1975). Addendum II: Guidelines for the preparation of professional group facilitators. *Journal of College Student Personnel, 16,* 342.

American College Personnel Association. (1976). ACPA statement regarding the use of group experiences in higher education. *Journal of College Student Personnel, 17,* 161-168.

American Council on Education. (1937). *The student personnel point of view* (Revised in 1949, p. 66).

Anderson, J. D. (1989). Training the apostles of liberal culture: Black higher education, 1900-1935. In L. F. Goodchild & H. S. Wechsler (Eds.), *ASHE reader on the history of higher education* (pp. 455-477). Needham Heights, MA: Simon & Schuster.

Appleby, J., Hunt, L., & Jacob, M. (1994). *Telling the truth about history*. New York: Norton.

Arbuckle, D. S. (1953). *Student personnel services in higher education*. New York: McGraw-Hill.

Arendt, H. (1951). *The origins of totalitarianism*. New York: Harcourt, Brace.

Arner, T. D., Peterson, W. D., Arner, C. A., Hawkins, L. T., & Spooner, S. E. (1976). Student personnel education: A process-outcome model. *Journal of College Student Personnel, 17*, 334-341.

Association Exchange. (1960). Commission on the education of women of the American Council on Education. *Journal of College Student Personnel, 2*, 25-27.

Association Exchange. (1962). Executive Council minutes. *Journal of College Student Personnel, 3*, 195-202.

Association News. (1963). *Journal of College Student Personnel, 4*, 251.

Astin, A. W. (1977). *Four critical years*. San Francisco: Jossey-Bass.

Astin, A. W. (1984). *The American freshman: National norms for fall 1984*. Washington, DC: Cooperative Institutional Research Program of the American Council on Education and the University of California at Los Angeles.

Atlantic (Eds.). (1966). *The troubled campus*. Boston: Little, Brown.

Auletta, K. (1982). *The underclass*. New York: Random.

Bakke v. Regents of the University of California, 18 Cal. 3rd 34, 132 Cal. Reports, 680 (1976).

Baldwin, J. (1952). *Go tell it on the mountain*. New York: Signet.

Baldwin, J. (1963). *Nobody knows my name*. New York: Dell.

Barry, R., & Wolf, B. (1957). *Modern issues in guidance and personnel work*. New York: Teachers College, Columbia University.

Baumgart, N. K., & Martinson, W. D. (1961). A descriptive profile method for predicting academic achievement. *Journal of College Student Development, 2*, 9-12.

Beck, C. E. (1963). *Philosophical foundations of guidance*. Englewood Cliffs, NJ: Prentice-Hall.

Becker, H. S. (1970). *Campus power struggle*. New York: Aldine.

Bell, D. (1960). *The end of ideology*. Glencoe, IL: Free Press.

Bellamy, D. C. (1984). "Social Darwinism" revisited. In B. Bailyn, D. Fleming, & S. Thermstrom (Eds.), *Perspectives in American history* (pp. 1-129). New York: Cambridge University Press.

Bellamy, E. (1887). *Looking backward, 2000-1887*. New York: Houghton Mifflin.

Bellows, S. (1953). *The adventures of Augie March, a novel*. New York: Viking Press.

Berry, M. (1976). The state of student affairs: A review of the literature. *NASPA Journal, 13(3),* 2-4.

Binet, A., & Simon, T. (1985). *The development of intelligence in children* (E. S. Kite, Trans.). Nashville, TN: Williams.

Blaesser, W. W. (1978). Organizational change and student development. *Journal of College Student Personnel, 19,* 109-118.

Blaesser, W. W., & Committee. (1945). Student personnel work in the postwar college. *Series VI. Personnel Work in Colleges and Universities, (6),* American Council on Education.

Blegen, T. C., & Committee. (1950). Counseling foreign students. *Series VI. Personnel Work in Colleges and Universities, (15),* American Council on Education.

Bloland, H. (1969). Politicization of higher education organizations. In G. K. Smith (Ed.), *Agony and promise* (pp. 10-27). San Francisco: Jossey-Bass.

Blumstein, P., & Schwartz, P. (1983). *American couples: Money, work, sex.* New York: Morrow.

Boorstin, D. J. (1953). *The genius of American politics.* Chicago: University of Chicago Press.

Boruch, R. F. (1969). *The faculty role in campus unrest.* Washington, DC: American Council on Education.

Bowles, S., Gordon, D. M., & Weisskopf, T. E. (1983). *Beyond the waste land: A democratic alternative to economic decline.* Garden City, NJ: Anchor/Doubleday.

Bragdon, H. D., Brumbaugh, A. J., Pillard, B. H., & Williamson, E. G. (1939). Educational counseling of college students. *Series VI. Personnel Work in Colleges and Universities, (1),* American Council on Education.

Brown v. Board of Education of Topeka, 347 U.S. 495 (1954).

Brown, R. D. (1972). *Student development in tomorrow's higher education: A return to the academy.* Washington, DC: American College Personnel Association.

Brubacher, J. S., & Rudy, W. (1976). *Higher education in transition: An American history, 1636-1956* (3rd ed.). New York: Harper.

Brumbaugh, A. J., & Berdie, R. (1952). Student personnel programs in transition. *Series VI. Personnel Work in Colleges and Universities, (16),* American Council on Education.

Brunner, K. (Ed.). (1981). *The great depression revisited.* Boston: Martinus Nijhoff.

Buckley, W. F. (1954). *National review.* New York: National Review.

Bultmann, R. K. (1960). *Existence and faith: Shorter writings of Rudolf Bultmann.* New York: Meridian Books.

Bureau of Census. (1957). Washington, DC: U.S. Government Printing Office.

Burroughs, W. S. (1959). *Naked lunch.* New York: Grove Press.

Butler, W. R. (1965). Forces at work in the development of fraternities. *Journal of College Student Personnel, 6,* 240-243.

Butts, R. F. (1955). *A cultural history of Western education: Its social and intellectual foundations* (2nd ed.). New York: McGraw-Hill.

Byrne, J. C. (1966). The Byrne report. *NASPA Journal, 3(3),* 15-23.

Callis, R. (1969). The colleges and the courts: 1968. *Journal of College Student Personnel, 10,* 75-86.

Camus, A. (1956). *The Fall.* New York: Knopf.

Capote, T. (1948). *Other voices, other rooms.* New York: Vintage Books.

Carlisle, J. C. (1962). How much is enough? *Journal of College Student Personnel, 3,* 206-208.

Carnegie Foundation for the Advancement of Teaching. (1975). *Sponsored research of the Carnegie Commission on Higher Education.* New York: McGraw-Hill.

Carnegie Foundation for the Advancement of Teaching. (1980). *The Carnegie Council on Policy Studies in Higher Education: A summary of reports and recommendations.* San Francisco: Jossey-Bass.

Caro, R. A. (1990). *The years of Lyndon Johnson: Means of ascent.* New York: Knopf.

Cartwright, D., & Zander, A. (1953). *Group dynamics: Research and theory.* Evanston, IL: Row, Peterson.

Chafe, W. H. (1986). *The unfinished journey.* New York: Oxford University Press.

Chafe, W. H. (1991). *The unfinished journey* (2nd ed.). New York: Oxford University Press.

Chickering, A. W. (1969). *Education and identity.* San Francisco: Jossey-Bass.

Childs, J. L. (1956). *American pragmatism and education, an interpretation and criticism.* New York: Holt.

Cohen, M., & Hale, D. (Eds.). (1967). *The new student left* (rev. ed.). Boston: Beacon.

Comfort, A. (1972). *The joy of sex.* New York: Simon & Schuster.

Commager, R. (1949). *Documents of American history* (5th ed.). New York: Appleton-Century-Crofts.

Commission on Professional Development. (1972). *Student development services in higher education.* Unpublished report, Council of Student Personnel Associations in Higher Education.

Committee on the College Student, Group for the Advancement of Psychiatry. (1966). *Sex and the college student.* New York: Athenaeum.

Committee on the Preparation of Ethical Standards. (1959). A proposed code of ethics for A.P.G.A. *Personnel and Guidance Journal, 38,* 168-170.

Committee on the Preparation of Ethical Standards. (1961). Ethical standards: American Personnel and Guidance Association. *Personnel and Guidance Journal, 40,* 206-209.

Committee on Student Personnel Work. (1949). The student personnel point of view. *Series VI. Personnel Work in Colleges and Universities, (13)*, American Council on Education.

Comte, A. (1853). *The positive philosophy* (Vols. I-II; H. Martineau, Trans.). Paris: Bachelier. (Original work published 1830-1842)

Connors, M. R., & Pruitt, A. S. (1978). Teaching goal-setting in the preparation of student development specialists. *Journal of College Student Personnel, 19,* 527-531.

COSPA proposal for college student personnel professional preparation. (1965). *NASPA Journal, 3*(1), 45-47.

Cottle, W. C. (1955). APGA Committee Report on professional training, licensing, and certification. *Personnel and Guidance Journal, 33,* 356-357.

Cowley, W. H., and Committee. (1939). Occupational orientation of students. *Series VI. Personnel Work in Colleges and Universities, (2),* American Council on Education.

Cox, A. (1968). *Crisis at Columbia: Report of the fact-finding commission appointed to investigate the disturbances at Columbia University in April and May 1968.* New York: Vintage.

Cremin, L. A. (1961). *The transformation of the school: Progressivism in American education, 1876-1957.* New York: Knopf.

Cremin, L. A. (1970). *American education: The colonial experience 1607-1783.* New York: Harper & Row.

Cremin, L. A. (1988). *American education: The metropolitan experience 1876-1980.* New York: Harper & Row.

Crookston, B. (1976). Student personnel—All hail and farewell! *Personnel and Guidance Journal, 55*(1), 26-29.

Curti, M. (1989). The setting and the problems. In L. F. Goodchild & H. S. Wechsler (Eds.), *ASHE reader on the history of higher education* (pp. 294-308). Needham Heights, MA: Simon & Schuster.

Darley, J. G., & Committee. (1947). The use of tests in counseling. *Series VI. Personnel Work in Colleges and Universities, (9),* American Council on Education.

D'Emilio, J. (1983). *Sexual politics, sexual communities: The making of a homosexual minority in the United States, 1940-1970.* Chicago: University of Chicago Press.

D'Emelio, J., & Freedman, E. B. (1988). *Intimate matters: A history of sexuality in America.* New York: Harper & Row.

Dennett, D. C. (1995). *Darwin's dangerous idea.* New York: Simon & Schuster.

Dewey, J. (1899). *The school and society.* Chicago: University of Chicago Press.

Dewey, J. (1916). *Democracy and education: An introduction to the philosophy of education.* New York: Macmillan.

Dickstein, M. (1977). *Gates of Eden: American culture in the Sixties.* New York: Basic Books.

Diggins, J. P. (1988). *The proud decades: America in war and peace, 1941-1960.* New York: Norton.

Dinklage, K. T., Gould, N. B., & Blaine, G. B., Jr. (1992). Evolution of the mental health services of Harvard's University Health Services. *Journal of College Student Psychotherapy, 7*(2), 5-33.

Dixon v. Alabama State Board of Education, 494 F. 2d 150 (5th Cir. 1961), *Cert. denied,* 368 U.S. 930.

Dyer, W. (1976). *Your erroneous zones.* New York: Funk & Wagnalls.

Dyer, W. (1978). *Pulling your own strings.* New York: Funk & Wagnalls.

Ellison, R. (1952). *Invisible man.* New York: Random House.

Ely, R. T. (1894-1895). Fundamental belief in my social philosophy. *The Forum,* 173-183.

Emmet, T. A. (1963). Editorial. *NASPA Journal, 1,* 5-6.

English, J. W., & Williams, R. (1984). *When men were boys.* Lakemont, GA: Copple House.

Erikson, E. H. (1950). *Childhood and society.* New York: Norton.

Erikson, E. H. (1963). *Childhood and society* (2nd ed.). New York: Norton.

Erikson, E. H. (1968). *Identity: Youth and crisis.* New York: Norton.

Evans, R., Jr., & Novak, R. D. (1972). *Nixon in the White House: The frustration of power.* New York: Vintage.

Faber, D. (Ed.). (1994). *The Sixties.* Chapel Hill: University of North Carolina Press.

Family Education Rights and Privacy Act of 1974 (20 U.S.C. 1232g).

Farnsworth, D. L. (1957). *Mental health in college and university.* Cambridge: Harvard University Press.

Faulkner, H. U. (1948). *American political and social history.* New York: Appleton-Century-Crofts.

Faulkner, H. U. (1954). *American economic history* (7th ed.). New York: Harper.

Faulkner, H. U. (1957). *American political and social history.* New York: Appleton-Century-Crofts.

Feder, D. D., Bishop, J. F., Dysinger, D. S., & Jones, L. W. (1958). The administration of student personnel programs in American colleges and universities. *Series VI. Personnel Work in Colleges and Universities, (19),* American Council on Education.

Feldman, K. A., & Newcomb, T. M. (1969). *The impact of college students.* San Francisco: Jossey-Bass.

Fenske, R. H. (1980). Historical foundations of student services. In U. Delworth, G. R. Hanson, & Associates, *Student services: A handbook for the profession* (pp. 5-24). San Francisco: Jossey-Bass.

Ferrari, M. R. (1972). National study of student personnel manpower planning--1972. *NASPA Journal, 10*(2), 91-100.

Festinger, L. (1957). *A theory of cognitive dissonance.* Evanston, IL: Row, Peterson.

Fley, J. A. (1966). An honorable tradition. *Journal of the National Association of Women Deans and Counselors, 29,* 106-110.

Fowler, G. A. (1984). The legal relationship between the American college student and the college: A historical perspective and a renewal proposal. *Journal of Law and Education, 13*(3), 401-416.

Frankl, V. E. (1963). *Man's search for meaning.* New York: Washington Square.

Friday, N. (1977). *My mother/myself.* New York: Delacorte.

Friedan, B. (1963). *The feminine mystique.* New York: Dell.

Friedland, W. H., & Edwards, H. (1970). Confrontation at Cornell. In H. S. Becker (Ed.), *Campus power struggle* (pp. 79-99). New York: Aldine.

Galbraith, J. K. (1958). *The affluent society.* Boston: Houghton Mifflin.

Galbraith, J. K. (1967). *The new industrial state.* Boston: Houghton Mifflin.

Gallup International. (1969). Princeton, NJ: Gallup International.

Gallup Political Index. (1970). Princeton, NJ: Gallup International.

George, H. (1879). *Progress and poverty: An inquiry into the cause of industrial depressions and of increase of want with increase of wealth: The remedy.* New York: Appleton.

Gibbs, A., & McFarland, A. C. (1974). Recognition of gay liberation on the state-supported campus. *Journal of College Student Personnel, 15,* 5-7.

Ginzberg, E. (1952). Toward a theory of occupational choice. *Personnel and Guidance Journal, 30,* 491-494.

Ginzberg, E., Ginzberg, Axelrod, & Herma, J. L. (1951). *Occupational choice: An approach to a general theory.* New York: Columbia University Press.

Gladstein, G. A. (1968). Doctoral research in college student personnel work. *Journal of College Student Personnel, 9,* 24-31.

Goldberg v. Regents of University of California. 57 Cal. Repts. 463 (1967).

Golding, W. (1955). *Lord of the flies.* New York: Coward-McCann.

Goldman, E. F. (1955). *Rendezvous with destiny.* New York: Random.

Goldworn, W. J. (1965). Student violations of criminal statutes or ordinances. *NASPA Journal, 2*(4), 33-35.

Goodchild, L. F. (1989). Introduction. In L. F. Goodchild & H. S. Wechsler (Eds.), *ASHE reader on the history of higher education.* Needham Heights, MA: Simon & Schuster.

Goodspeed, T. W. (1916). *A history of the University of Chicago founded by John D. Rockefeller: The first quarter century.* Chicago: University of Chicago.

Griswald v. Connecticut, 381 U.S. 479 (1965).

Gross, S. J. (1968). Student sexual expression. *Journal of College Student Personnel, 9,* 9-16.

Gruber, C. S. (1989). Backdrop. In L. F. Goodchild & H. S. Wechsler (Eds.), *ASHE reader on the history of higher education* (pp. 181-196). Needham Heights, MA: Simon & Schuster.

Habein, M. (1959). American Council on Education. Problems and Policies Committee. Washington: American Council on Education.

Hacker, L. M., & Zahler, H. (1952). *The United States in the 20th century.* New York: Appleton-Century-Crofts.

Halbertstam, D. (1993). *The Fifties.* New York: Villard.

Hall, C. S., & Lindzey, G. (1957). *Theories of personality.* New York: Wiley.

Handlin, O., & Handlin, M. F. (1970). *The American college and American culture: Socialization as a function of higher education.* New York: McGraw-Hill.

Hardee, M. D. (1959). *The faculty in college counseling.* New York: McGraw-Hill.

Harper, F. D. (1969). Black student revolt on white campuses. *Journal of College Student Personnel, 10,* 291-295.

Hartz, L. (1955). *The liberal tradition in America: An interpretation of American political thought since the revolution.* New York: Harcourt, Brace.

Havighurst, R. J. (1960). *American higher education in the 1960s.* Columbia: Ohio State University Press.

Heller, J. (1961). *Catch-22.* New York: Simon & Schuster.

Hemingway, E. (1952). *The old man and the sea.* London: Cape.

Higher Education Act of 1965 (HR 9567—PL 89-329).

Hilgard, E. R., & Bower, G. H. (1956). *Theories of learning.* New York: Appleton-Century-Crofts.

Hill, G. E. (1961). The selection of student personnel workers. *Journal of College Student Personnel, 2*(3), 2-8.

Hodgkinson, H. L. (1969). Who decides who decides. In G. K. Smith (Ed.), *Agony and promise* (pp. 139-144). San Francisco: Jossey-Bass.

Hofstadter, R. (1962). *Anti-intellectualism in American life.* New York: Vintage.

Hofstadter, R. (1965). *The paranoid style in American politics, and other essays.* New York: Knopf.

Hofstadter, R., & Hofstadter, B. K. (Eds.). (1982). *Great issues in American history: From reconstruction to the present day, 1864-1981.* New York: Vintage Books.

Hood, A. B. (1971). Editor's page. *Journal of College Student Personnel, 12,* 402.

Hook, S. (1946). *Education for modern man.* New York: Dial.

Hopwood, K. L. (1961). Who's for the ark? *Journal of College Student Personnel, 2*(4), 2-8.

Horney, K. (1950). *Neurosis and human growth.* New York: Norton.

Horowitz, H. L. (1987). *Campus life: Undergraduate cultures from the end of the eighteenth century to the present.* New York: Knopf.

Howe, I. (1954). *Dissent.* New York: Foundation for the Study of Independent Social Issues.

Hoyt, D. P. (1968). Report to members. *Journal of College Student Personnel, 9,* 290.

Hutchins, R. M. (1936a). *The higher learning in America.* New Haven: Yale University Press.

Hutchins, R.M. (1936b). *No friendly voice.* Chicago: University of Chicago Press.

International Monetary Fund. (1979, April). *International Financial Statistics, 32,* 47, 122, 156, 214, 352, 356, 390.

Jacob, P. E. (1957). *Changing values in college.* New Haven, CT: Edward W. Hazen Foundation.

James, H. (1907). *The American.* Boston: Houghton Mifflin.

James, W. (1890). *The principles of psychology.* New York: Holt.

James, W. (1899). *Talks to teachers on psychology: And to students on some of life's ideals.* New York: Norton.

Jarrell, R. (1954). *Pictures from an institution.* New York: Knopf.

Joint statement on rights and freedom of students. (1968, Summer). *A.A.U.P. Bulletin, 2,* 258.

Jones, T. J. (1917). *Negro education: A study of the private and higher schools for colored people in the United States* (2 vols.; Bureau of Education Bulletin, 1916, No. 36). Washington, DC: U.S. Government Printing Office.

Kamm, R. B. (1954). ACPA Professional Standards Committee studies graduate student selection and admission. *Personnel and Guidance Journal, 32,* 362-366.

Kaufmann, W. A. (1956). *Existentialism from Dostoevsky to Sartre.* Cleveland: World.

Kerr, C. (1963). *The uses of the university.* Cambridge, MA: Harvard University Press.

Kerr, J. C. (1989). From Truman to Johnson: Ad hoc policy formulation in higher education. In L. F. Goodchild & H. S. Wechsler (Eds.), *ASHE reader on the history of higher education* (pp. 498-528). Needham Heights, MA: Simon & Schuster.

Kindleberger, C. P. (1986). *The world in depression* (rev. ed.). Berkeley: University of California Press.

Kinsey, A. C. (1948). *Sexual behavior in the human male.* Philadelphia: Saunders.

Kinsey, A. C. (1953). *Sexual behavior in the human female.* Philadelphia: Saunders.

Kirkpatrick, F. H., & Committee. (1949). Helping students find employment. *Series VI. Personnel Work in Colleges and Universities, (12),* American Council on Education.

Kissinger, H. (1979). *White House years.* Boston: Little Brown.

Klein, M. (Ed.). (1969). *The American novel since World War II.* Greenwich, CN: Fawcett.

Knowles, L. L., & Prewitt, K. (Eds.). (1970). *Institutional racism in America.* Englewood Cliffs, NJ: Prentice-Hall.

Koile, E. A. (1966). Student affairs: Forever the bridesmaid. *NASPA Journal, 4*(2), 65-72.

Kubit, D. E., Cross, K. P., Vermilye, D. W., & Brown, R. D. (1973). Student development in tomorrow's higher education: The beginning of a dialogue. *Journal of College Student Personnel, 14,* 77-86.

Kuh, G. D., & Arnold, J. C. (1993). Liquid bonding: A cultural analysis of the role of alcohol in fraternity pledgeship. *Journal of College Student Development, 34,* 327-334.

Kuh, G. D., Greenlee, F. E., & Lardy, B. A. (1978). A profile of graduate students in college student personnel. *Journal of College Student Personnel, 19,* 531-537.

Kuh, G. D., Lardy, B. A., & Greenlee, F. E. (1979). Research orientation of graduate students in college student personnel. *Journal of College Student Personnel, 20,* 99-104.

LaBarre, C., & Committee. (1948). Graduate training for educational personnel work. *Series VI. Personnel Work in Colleges and Universities, (11),* American Council on Education.

Lacy, O. W., Franks, A. C., & Kirk, B. A. (1976). Number of counseling sessions, client personality, and reason for seeking counseling. *Journal of College Student Personnel, 17,* 405-409.

Lasch, C. (1979). *The culture of narcissism.* New York: Norton.

Lee, W. S. (1959). *God bless our queer old dean.* New York: Putnam.

Leonard, E. A. (1956). *Origins of personnel services in higher education.* Minneapolis: University of Minnesota Press.

Levine, A. (1981). *When dreams and heroes died.* San Francisco: Jossey-Bass.

Lewin, K. (1951). *Field theory in social science.* New York: Harper.

Lewis, C. L. (1970). Report to members. *Journal of College Student Personnel, 11,* 82.

Lipset, S. M. (1993). *Rebellion in the university.* New Brunswick, NJ: Transaction.

Lipset, S. M., & Wolin, S. S. (Eds.). (1965). *The Berkeley student revolt.* Garden City, NJ: Anchor.

Lloyd, H. D. (1894). *Wealth against commonwealth.* Englewood Cliffs, NJ: Prentice-Hall.

Lloyd-Jones, E., & Committee (1940). Social competence and college students. *Series VI. Personnel Work in Colleges and Universities, (3),* American Council on Education.

Lloyd-Jones, E., & Smith, M. R. (1954). *Student personnel work as deeper teaching.* New York: Harper.

Loucks, D. (1961). A triad of race riots. *Journal of College Student Personnel, 2,* 13-18.

Lucas, C. (1985). Out at the edge; notes on a paradigm shift. *Journal of Counseling and Development, 64,* 165-172.

Malamud, B. (1957). *The assistant.* New York: Farrar, Straus, & Cudahy.

Malamud, B. (1961). *A new life.* New York: Farrar, Straus, & Cudahy.

Malone, D. (1970). *Jefferson the president: First term, 1801-1805* (vol. IV of *Jefferson and his time*). Boston: Little Brown.

Marcuse, H. (1964). *One dimensional man.* Boston: Beacon.

Marin, P. (1975). The new narcissism. *Harpers Magazine, 251*(1505), 45-46.

Matusow, A. J. (1984). *The unraveling of America.* New York: Harper.

May, R. (1939). *The art of counseling.* Nashville, Cokesbury Press.

May, R., Angel, E., & Ellenberger, H. F. (Eds.). (1958). *Existence.* New York: Simon & Schuster.

Mayhew, L. B. (1969). *Colleges today and tomorrow.* San Francisco: Jossey-Bass.

Mayhew, L. B. (1972, Summer). Higher education—toward 1984. *Educational Record,* 215-221.

McCarthy, M. (1952). *The groves of academe.* New York: Harcourt Brace.

McCullough, D. (1992). *Truman.* New York: Simon & Schuster.

McEvoy, J., & Miller, A. (1970). The crisis at San Francisco State. In H. S. Becker (Ed.), *Campus power struggle* (pp. 57-77). New York: Aldine.

Merriam, T. W., & Committee. (1943). Religious counseling of college students. *Series VI. Personnel Work in Colleges and Universities, (4),* American Council on Education.

Mill, J. S. (1852). *A system of logic, ratiocinative and inductive: Being a connected view of principles of evidence and method of scientific investigation.* New York: Harper.

Miller, A. (1954). *The crucible.* New York: Dramatists Play Service.

Miller, T. K., & Prince, J. S. (1976). *The future of student affairs.* San Francisco: Jossey-Bass.

Miller, W. (1958). *A new history of the United States.* New York: Braziller.

Minter, W. J. (Ed.). (1967). *The individual and the system: Personalizing higher education.* Boulder, CO: Western Interstate Commission for Higher Education.

Moffatt, M. (1989). *Coming of age in New Jersey.* New Brunswick: Rutgers University Press.

Morgenthau, H. J. (1951). *In defense of the national interest: A critical examination of American foreign policy.* New York: Knopf.

Mueller, K. H. (1961). *Student personnel work in higher education.* Boston: Houghton-Mifflin.

Mueller, K. H., & Committee. (1947). Counseling for mental health. *Series VI. Personnel Work in Colleges and Universities, (8),* American Council on Education.

Muskie, E. S. (1969). Open the door to participation. In G. K. Smith (Ed.), *Agony and promise: Current issues in higher education* (pp. 245-250). San Francisco: Jossey-Bass.

Nabokov, V. (1955). *Lolita*. New York: Vintage Books.

National Supervisory Board. (1967). The NSA position in the CIA. *NASPA Journal, 4*, 187-190.

Neubeck, G. (1960). Marriage counseling at the University of Minnesota. *Journal of College Student Development, 2*, 30-32.

Newton, F. B., & Richardson, R. L. (1976). Expected entry-level competencies of student personnel workers. *Journal of College Student Personnel, 17*, 426-430.

Nickerson, D. L., & Harrington, J. T. (1968). *The college student as counselor: Guide to residence hall counseling*. Moravia, IL: Chronicle Guidance.

Niebuhr, R. (1947). *Faith and history*. New York: Harper.

Nietzsche, F. (1967). *Thus spoke Zarathustra* (T. Common, Trans.). New York: Heritage.

Norris, F. (1901). *The octopus: A story of California*. New York: Doubleday, Page.

Norris, F. (1903). *The pit: A story of Chicago*. New York: Doubleday, Page.

The Oxford dictionary of quotations (3rd ed.). (1979). Oxford: Oxford University Press.

Parker, C. A. (1970, March). *Ashes, ashes, . . .* Paper presented at the American College Personnel Association Convention, St. Louis.

Parker, C. A. (1974). Student development: What does it mean? *Journal of College Student Personnel, 15*, 248-256.

Parker, C. A. (1977). On modeling reality. *Journal of College Student Personnel, 18*, 419-425.

Parker, C., & Morrill, W. (1974). Student development alternatives. *Journal of College Student Personnel, 15*, 163-167.

Parker, F. W. (1894). *Talks on pedagogics*. Chicago: Kellogg.

Pascarella, E. T., & Terenzini, P. T. (1991). *How college affects students: Findings and insights from twenty years of research*. San Francisco: Jossey-Bass.

Penn, J. R. (1974). Professional accreditation: A key to excellence. *Journal of College Student Personnel, 15*, 257-259.

Penney, J. F. (1961). The student personnel worker views accreditation. *Journal of College Student Personnel, 3*, 2-5.

Penney, J. F. (1969). Student personnel work: A profession stillborn. *Personnel and Guidance Journal, 47*, 958-962.

Pepinsky, H. B., Hill-Frederick, K., & Epperson, D. L. (1978). The *Journal of Counseling Psychology* as a matter of policies. *Journal of Counseling Psychology, 25*, 483-498.

Pepinsky, H. B., & Pepinsky, P. N. (1954). *Counseling: Theory and practice.* New York: Ronald Press.

Perry, W., Jr. (1970). *Forms of intellectual and ethical development in the college years: A scheme.* New York: Holt, Rinehart & Winston.

Phenix, P. H. (1958). *Philosophy of education.* New York: Holt.

Phenix, P. H. (Ed.). (1961). *Philosophies of education.* New York: John Wiley & Sons.

Plessy v. Ferguson, 163, 537 (N.Y. 1895).

Polkinghorne, D. (1983). *Methodology for the human sciences: Systems of inquiry.* Albany: State University of New York Press.

President's Commission on Higher Education. (1947). *Higher education for American democracy, a report, I.* Washington, DC: Author.

Problems and Policies Committee. (1960). *The price of excellence: A report to decision makers in American higher education.* Washington, DC: American Council on Education.

Rand, A. (1943). *The fountainhead.* New York: Signet.

Rand, A. (1957). *Atlas shrugged.* New York: Signet.

Ratterman, P. H. (1964). Campus activity problems. *NASPA Journal, 1*(2), 21-25.

Ray, W. S. (1964). *The science of psychology: An introduction.* New York: Macmillan.

Reich, C. (1970). *The greening of America.* New York: Random House.

Reich, R. B. (1983). *The next American frontier.* New York: Times Books.

Reilly, R. R., & Cauthen, I. A. (1976). The literature of college student personnel. *Journal of College Student Personnel, 17,* 363-367.

Rentz, A. L. (1976). A triadic model masters program in student development. *Journal of College Student Personnel, 17,* 453-458.

Rhatigan, J. J. (1968). Professional preparation of student personnel administrators as perceived by practitioners and faculty. *Journal of College Student Personnel, 9,* 17-23.

Rhatigan, J. J. (1991). NASPA history. In NASPA, *1991-1992 member handbook* (pp. 5-6). Washington, DC: National Association of Student Personnel Administrators.

Rhutman, & Committee. (1953). Personnel principles in the chapter house. *Series VI. Personnel Work in Colleges and Universities, (17),* American Council on Education.

Riesman, D. (1969). The collision course of higher education. *Journal of College Student Personnel, 11,* 363-369.

Riesman, D., Glazer, N., & Denney, R. (1956). *The lonely crowd.* New York: Doubleday Anchor.

Robertson, R. M. (1955). *History of the American economy.* New York: Harcourt, Brace.

Robinson, D. W. (1966). Analysis of three statements relative to the preparation of college student personnel workers. *Journal of College Student Personnel, 7,* 254-256.

Roe, A. (1956). *The psychology of occupations.* New York: Wiley.

Roe v. Wade, 410 U.S. 113 (1973).

Rogers, C. R. (1942). *Counseling and psychotherapy.* Boston: Houghton-Mifflin.

Rogers, C. R. (1951). *Client-centered therapy.* Boston: Houghton-Mifflin.

Rosenberg, M. (1957). *Occupation and values.* Glencoe, IL: Free Press.

Ross, D. (1972). *G. Stanley Hall: The psychologist as prophet.* Chicago: University of Chicago Press.

Rostow, W. W. (1990). *The stages of economic growth: A non-communist manifesto* (3rd ed.). New York: Cambridge.

Roszak, T. (1969). *The making of a counter culture: Reflections on the technocratic society and its youthful opposition.* Garden City, NY: Doubleday.

Roth v. United States, 354 U.S. 476 (1957).

Rovere, R. H. (1959). *Senator Joe McCarthy.* New York: Harcourt, Brace.

Rudolph, F. (1962). *The American college and university, a history.* New York: Knopf.

Rudolph, F. (Ed.). (1965). *Essays on education in the early republic.* Cambridge: Belknap Press of Harvard University Press.

Salinger, J. D. (1951). *The catcher in the rye.* Boston: Little, Brown.

Sartre, J. (1947). *The age of reason.* New York: Knopf.

Schell, J. (1975). *The time of illusion.* New York: Vintage.

Schlesinger, A. M., Jr. (1945). *The age of Jackson.* Boston: Little, Brown.

Schlesinger, A. M., Jr. (1948). *The vital center: The politics of freedom.* Boston: Houghton Mifflin.

Schlesinger, A. M., Jr. (1959). *The age of Roosevelt: The coming of the New Deal.* Boston: Houghton Mifflin.

Schlesinger, A. M., Jr. (1978). *Robert Kennedy and his times.* New York: Ballantine.

Schlossberg, N. K. (1967). An ombudsman for students. *NASPA Journal, 5*(1), 31-33.

Schlossberg, N. K. (1978). Five propositions about adult development. *Journal of College Student Personnel, 19,* 418-422.

Schroeder, C. C. (1976). New strategies for structuring residential environments. *Journal of College Student Personnel, 17,* 386-390.

Shaffer, R. H. (1966). Letters to the editor. *Journal of College Student Personnel, 7,* 258-259.

Shank, D. J., & Committee. (1948). The teacher as counselor. *Series VI. Personnel Work in Colleges and Universities, (10),* American Council on Education.

Sharpe, R. T., & Committee. (1946). Financial assistance for college students. *Series VI. Personnel Work in Colleges and Universities, (7),* American Council on Education.

Sheehy, G. (1976). *Passages.* New York: Dutton.

Sheeley, V. L. (1991). *Fulfilling visions: Emerging leaders of ACPA.* Washington, DC: American College Personnel Association.

Shoben, E. J., Jr. (1958). A rationale for modern student personnel work. *Personnel-O-Gram, 12*(3), 9-11.

Shoben, E. J., Jr. (1970, Summer). Student unrest and cultural criticism: Protest in American colleges. *Daedalus, 99,* 676-699.

Shoben, E. J., Jr. (1970). Student unrest and cultural criticism: Protest in American colleges. In J. M. Whitely (Ed.), *Students in the university and in society* (pp. 69-83). Washington, DC: American College Personnel Association.

Shute, N. (1957). *On the beach.*

Sinclair, U. (1906). *The jungle.* New York: Doubleday, Page.

Slosson, P. W. (1930). *The great crusade and after: 1914-1928.* New York: Macmillan.

Snyder, T. D. (1987). *Digest of educational statistics.* Washington, DC: Government Printing Office.

Snygg, D., & Combs, A. W. (1949). *Individual behavior.* New York: Harper.

Sorensen, T. C. (1965). *Kennedy.* New York: Harper & Row.

Spencer, H. (1864). *First principles.* New York: Appleton.

Spencer, H. (1876-1897). *The principles of sociology* (3 vols.). New York: Appleton.

Standards for the preparation of school counselors. (1961). *The Personnel and Guidance Journal, 40,* 402-407.

Strang, R. (1941). *Group activities in college and secondary school.* New York: Harper.

Straub, J. S., & Vermilye, D. W. (1968). Current and developing issues in student life. *Journal of College Student Personnel, 9,* 363-370.

Strozier, R. N., & Committee. (1950). Housing of students. *Series VI. Personnel Work in Colleges and Universities, (14),* American Council on Education.

Students for a Democratic Society. (1962/1990). *The Port Huron Statement.* Chicago: C. H. Kerr.

Super, D. E. (1949). *Appraising vocational fitness by means of psychological tests.* New York: Harper.

Super, D. E. (1955). Transition: From vocational guidance to counseling psychology. *Journal of Counseling Psychology, 2,* 3-9.

Super, D. E. (1957). *The psychology of careers.* New York: Harper.

Super, D. E., & Associates. (1957). *Vocational development: A framework for research.* New York: Teachers College, Columbia University.

Sutherland, & Committee. (1953). Students and staff in a social context. *Series VI. Personnel Work in Colleges and Universities, (18),* American Council on Education.

Thelen, H. A. (1954). *Dynamics of groups at work.* Chicago: University of Chicago Press.

Thorndike, R. L. (1898). *Animal intelligence.* New York: Macmillan.

Thorndike, E. L. (1913-1914). *Educational psychology* (vols. 1-3). New York: Teachers College.

Thorndike, R. L., & Hagen, E. (1955). *Measurement and evaluation in psychology and education.* New York: Wiley.

Thurow, L. C. (1980). *The zero-sum society.* New York: Basic.

Tillich, P. (1957). *Dynamics of faith.* New York: Harper.

Trent, J. W. (1966). Encouragement of student development. *NASPA Journal,* 4(1), 35-45.

Trimberger, E. K. (1970). Columbia: The dynamics of a student revolution. In H. S. Becker (Ed.), *Campus power struggle* (pp. 27-55). New York: Aldine.

Trueblood, D. L. (1960). The counseling role in a group activity advisory context. *Journal of College Student Personnel, 3,* 13-17.

Trueblood, D. L. (1961). The universities responsibility for racial and religious discriminatory practices in fraternities. *Journal of College Student Personnel, 2,* 23-31.

Upcraft, M. L. (1971). Does training make a difference? *NASPA Journal, 9,* 134-137.

U.S. Department of Labor. (1979, January). *Employment earnings, 26*(1), 160.

Vahanian, G. (1957). *The death of God.* New York: Braziller.

Vatter, H. G. (1963). *The U.S. economy in the 1950s: An economic history.* New York: Norton.

Veblen, T. (1899). *The theory of the leisure class.* New York: Macmillan.

Watkins, T. H. (1993). *The great depression.* Boston: Little Brown.

Wechsler, H. S. (1989). An academic Gresham's Law: Group repulsion as a theme in American higher education. In L. F. Goodchild & H. S. Wechsler (Eds.), *ASHE reader on the history of higher education* (pp. 389-400). Needham Heights, MA: Simon & Schuster.

Whitehead, A. N. (1933). *Adventures of ideas.* New York: Macmillan.

Whiteley, J. M. (Ed.). (1970). Students in the university and in society. *Monographs in the Student Personnel Series,* American College Personnel Association, No. 13.

Whiteley, J. M. (1984). Counseling psychology: A historical perspective [special issue]. *The Counseling Psychologist, 12.*

Whyte, W. H. (1956). *The organization man.* New York: Simon & Schuster.

Williamson, E. G. (1967) Some unsolved problems in student personnel work. *NASPA Journal, 5*(2), 91-96.

Williamson, E. G., & Cowan, J. L. (1965). The role of the president in the desirable enactment of academic freedom for students. *The Educational Record, 46,* 351-372.

Williamson, E. G., & Cowan, J. L. (1966). *The American student's freedom of expression: A research appraisal.* Minneapolis, MN: University of Minnesota Press.

Wise, W. M. (1958). *They come for the best of reasons: College students today.* Washington: American Council on Education.

Wise, W. M. (1965). The meaning of Berkeley. *NASPA Journal, 3,* 17-24.

Wolf, T. H. (1973). *Alfred Binet.* Chicago: University of Chicago Press.

Wolfe, T. (1977). *Mauve gloves and madmen, clutter and vine.* New York: Bantam.

Wrenn, C. G. (1951). *Student personnel work in colleges and universities.* New York: Kenald.

Wrenn, C. G. (1967). In W. J. Minter (Ed.), *The individual and the system: Personalizing higher education.* Boulder, CO: Westin Interstate Commission for Higher Education.

Wright, R. (1940). *Native son.* New York: Harper.

Yamamoto, K. (1968). *The college student and his culture: An analysis.* Boston: Houghton Mifflin.

Yanitelli, V. R. (1963). Procedural due process. *NASPA Journal, 1,* 9-10.

Yankelovich, D. (1974). *The new morality.* New York: McGraw-Hill.

Yankelovich, D. (1981). *New rules, searching for self-fulfillment in a world turned upside down.* New York: Random House.

Yankelovich, D., Zetterberg, H., Strumpel, B., & Shanks, M. (1985). *The world of work: An international report on jobs, productivity, and human values.* New York: Octagon.

Young, D. P. (1975). *Ramifications of the age of majority* (prepared for the Council of Student Personnel Associations in Higher Education). Athens, GA: University of Georgia.

Appendix

NAWDC Past Presidents

1916–1920	Ellis L. Phillips
1920–1922	Mina Kerr
1922–1923	Mary Ross Porter
1923–1925	Agnes E. Wells
1925–1926	Florence Perry
1926–1931	Thyrsa W. Amos
1931–1932	Florenco Kelso
1932–1935	Agnes Ellen Harris
1935–1937	Irma E. Voigt
1937–1939	Harriett M. Allyn
1939–1941	Sarah A. Blandling
1941–1943	Alice C. Lloyd
1943–1945	Elsie May Smithies
1945–1947	Helen Threlkeld
1947–1949	Dorthy Gebauer
1949–1951	Anne L. Rose Hawkes
1951–1953	Ruth O. McCarn
1953–1955	Lucile Allen
1955–1957	M. Eunice Hilton
1957–1959	Katherine A. Towle
1959–1961	Margaret Habein
1961–1963	Lillian M. Johnson

1963–1965	Helen B. Schleman
1965–1967	Martha Peterson
1967–1969	Miriam A. Sheldon
1969–1970	Ruth H. Weimer
1970–1971	Catherine M. Northrup
1971–1972	Elizabeth A. Greenleaf
1972–1973	Patricia A. Thrash
1973–1974	Dorthy Truex
1974–1975	Ann Bromley
1975–1976	Barbara I. Cook
1976–1977	Marjorie M. Christiansen
1977–1978	Jane E. McCormick
1978–1979	Betty J. Soldwedel
1979–1980	Joan S. King

NASPA Past Presidents

1919–1920	Scott H. Goodnight
1920–1921	Thomas A. Clark
1921–1922	Edward E. Nicholson
1922–1923	Stanley Coulter
1923–1924	J. A. Bursley
1924–1925	Robert Rienow
1925–1926	C. R. Melcher
1926–1927	Floyd Field
1927–1928	Scott H. Goodnight
1928–1929	G. B. Culver
1929–1930	J. W. Armstrong
1930–1931	W. L. Sanders
1931–1932	W. I. Moore
1932–1933	C. E. Edmonson
1933–1934	H. E. Lobdell
1934–1935	B. A. Tolbert
1935–1936	William E. Alderman
1936–1937	Dabney S. Lancaster
1937–1939	D. H. Gardner
1939–1940	J. F. Findlay
1940–1941	J. J. Thompson
1941–1942	L. S. Corbett
1942–1943	Joseph A. Park
1943–1944	J. H. Julian
1944–1946	Earl J. Miller

1946–1947	Arno Nowotny
1947–1948	E. L. Cloyd
1948–1949	J. H. Newman
1949–1950	L. K. Neidinger
1950–1951	Wesley P. Lloyd
1951–1952	A. Blair Knapp
1952–1953	Victor F. Spathelf
1953–1954	Robert M. Strozier
1954–1955	John H. Stibbs
1955–1956	John H. Hocutt
1956–1957	Frank C. Baldwin
1957–1958	Donald M. Dushane
1958–1959	Fred H. Turner
1959–1960	H. Donald Winbigler
1960–1961	William S. Guthrie
1961–1962	Fred J. Weaver
1962–1963	J. C. Clevenger
1963–1964	James McLeod
1964–1965	Victor R. Yanitelli
1965–1966	Glen T. Nygreen
1966–1967	Edmund G. Williamson
1967–1968	Carl W. Knox
1968–1969	O. D. Roberts
1969–1970	Mark W. Smith
1970–1971	Earl W. Clifford
1971–1972	Chester E. Peters
1972–1973	Thomas B. Dutton
1973–1974	John L. Blackburn
1974–1975	James R. Appleton
1975–1976	James J. Rhatigan
1976–1977	Alice R. Manicur
1977–1978	Arthur Sandeen
1978–1979	Donald V. Adams
1979–1980	George W. Young

ACPA Past Presidents

1924–1925	May L. Cheney
1925–1927	Margaret Cameron
1927–1928	Robert K. Speer
1928–1930	Francis F. Bradshaw
1930–1933	Jack E. Walters

1933–1935	Karl M. Cowdery
1935–1937	Esther Lloyd–Jones
1937–1939	A. J. Brumbaugh
1939–1941	Helen Voorhees
1941–1945	E. G. Williamson
1945–1947	Daniel D. Feder
1947–1949	C. Gilbert Wrenn
1949–1950	Thelma Mills
1950–1953	Everett H. Hopkins
1953–1955	Gordon V. Anderson
1955–1956	Harold B. Pepinsky
1957–1958	Willard W. Blaesser
1957–1958	Robert Kamm
1958–1959	Catherine N. Northrup
1959–1960	Robert Callis
1960–1961	Kathryn Hopwood
1961–1962	William Craig
1962–1963	Melvene D. Hardee
1963–1964	Dennis L. Trueblood
1964–1965	Barbara A. Kirk
1965–1966	Ralph F. Berdie
1966–1967	Bernard M. Black
1967–1968	Elizabeth A. Greenleaf
1968–1969	Donald P. Hoyt
1969–1970	Charles L. Lewis
1970–1971	Paul A. Bloland
1971–1972	William R. Butler
1972–1973	G. Robert Ross
1973–1974	Merril C. Beyerl
1974–1975	W. Harold Grant
1975–1976	Theodore K. Miller
1976–1977	Anne S. Pruitt
1977–1978	Mary T. Howard
1978–1979	Don C. Creamer
1979–1980	Phyllis Mable

Division 17, Counseling Psychology, Past Presidents

1947	E. G. Williamson
1948	G. F. Kuder
1949	Hugh Bell
1950	John Darley

1951	C. Gilbert Wrenn
1952	Donald Super
1953	Mitchell Dreese
1954	Milton Hahn
1955	Francis Robinson
1956	Edward Bordin
1957	Harold Pepinsky
1958	Ralph Berdie
1959	E. Joseph Shoben
1960	Leona Tyler
1961	Harold Seashore
1962	Robert Waldrop
1963	Albert Thompson
1964	Irwin Berg
1965	Frank Fletcher
1966	David Tiedeman
1967	William Cottle
1968	Dorothy M. Clendenen
1969	John F. McGowan
1970	John L. Holland
1971	Arthur Brayfield
1972	C. H. Patterson
1973	John O. Crites
1974	Barbara A. Kirk
1975	John D. Krumboltz
1976	Roger A. Myers
1977	Norman I. Kagan
1978	Samuel H. Osipow
1979	Carl E. Thoreson
1980	Allen E. Ivy

Index

About the Author

Richard B. Caple's graduate training and professional career has been in the field of college student affairs and counseling psychology. He received an Ed.D. from Teachers College, Columbia University. Mr. Caple has been a full-time counselor (New Mexico State University); chief student affairs officer (Northwestern State College); professor, Housing Office associate director, and is currently director of the Counseling Center at the University of Missouri-Columbia.

Mr. Caple is a licensed psychologist and health service provider in Missouri. He has been involved in professional activities on the national level primarily with the American College Personnel Association. He has published and served as the editor of the *Journal of College Student Development*. Mr. Caple has served on a national accreditation board (CACREP) and has had the opportunity to evaluate a number of counseling preparation programs. He is presently director of the Core Council for the Generation and Dissemination of Knowledge for the American College Personnel Association. He has been a life-long equestrian.